Prussian Apocalypse

Prussian Apocalypse
The Fall of Danzig 1945

By
Egbert Kieser

Translated by
Tony Le Tissier

Pen & Sword
MILITARY

First published in Great Britain in 2011 by
Pen & Sword Military
an imprint of
Pen & Sword Books Ltd
47 Church Street
Barnsley
South Yorkshire
S70 2AS

German text 1978 by Bechtle at F.A. Herbig Verlagsbuchhandlung GmbH,
München (Original title: Danziger Bucht 1945. Dokumentation einer
Katastrophe) www.herbig.net

English text © Tony Le Tissier, 2011

ISBN 978-1-84884-674-6

A CIP catalogue record for this book is available from the British Library.

Typeset in 11/13 Ehrhardt by Concept, Huddersfield, West Yorkshire
Printed and bound in England by the MPG Books Group

Pen & Sword Books Ltd incorporates the Imprints of Pen & Sword
Aviation, Pen & Sword Family History, Pen & Sword Maritime, Pen &
Sword Military, Pen & Sword Discovery, Wharncliffe Local History,
Wharncliffe True Crime, Wharncliffe Transport, Pen & Sword Select,
Pen & Sword Military Classics, Leo Cooper, The Praetorian Press,
Remember When, Seaforth Publishing and Frontline Publishing.

For a complete list of Pen & Sword titles please contact
PEN & SWORD BOOKS LIMITED
47 Church Street, Barnsley, South Yorkshire, S70 2AS, England
E-mail: enquiries@pen-and-sword.co.uk
Website: www.pen-and-sword.co.uk

Contents

Introduction
by Tony Le Tissier

Egbert Kieser's book tells the horrific tale of how the eastern provinces of Germany, once the central core of national unity, came to an abrupt end with the Soviet invasion of 1945. The population fled and those that contrived to remain behind were soon rounded up and deported. Part of East Prussia was annexed to the Soviet Union, the remainder being incorporated into today's Poland.

Grand Admiral Alfred Dönitz, who was to succeed Hitler as the leader of Nazi Germany, ordered a massive evacuation by sea which, despite the intervention of Soviet submarines, succeeded in transporting an estimated 1,950,000 refugees and wounded soldiers westwards across the Baltic to Germany and Denmark. A further 1,900,000 managed to make their way overland from Prussia and Pomerania to the other side of the Oder River, the eastern boundary of post-war Germany.

Preface
by Egbert Kieser

The initiative for this documentation is a thank-you from the refugees to the Navy, who made me aware of my predecessors in the Danzig Bight during the last months of the war in 1945. After further research I became convinced that the flight of the East Prussians, West Prussians and Danzigers across the Danzig Bight to the west had no parallel in European history. The drama of these predecessors began to fascinate me, but soon the first long interviews with those involved opened up other dimensions and uncovered the tragedy of events and the extent of human victims. The whole cruelty and senselessness of the Second World War provoked by Hitler exploded within a few weeks on a shrewd population completely unprepared by the Nazi Party in its false security. Surprised by the fighting, they had to take to flight in utterly chaotic conditions and the deepest winter to the sea, from where the majority of the refugees could be brought to safety to the west in an unparalleled rescue operation – a safety that nevertheless for many involved a year of deprivation in Danish internment camps.

An extremely extensive collection of factual information enables an objective presentation of these events. Help and support has come to me from many sides. I must therefore express my gratitude to all those who took part. Above all my thanks go to every East Prussian, West Prussian and Danziger who provided me with such detailed, living – and also patient – accounts. Many names are not to be found in this book, but nearly all accounts can be traced in one form or other, thus contributing to the presentation as a whole.

Individual thanks go to the selfless assistance of the Federal Executive of Landmannschaft Westpreussen, Hans-Jürgen Schuch, Münster, and Professor Dr Werner Schienemann, Tuttlingen, who honoured me with their support. For much valuable advice I thank Professor Dr Jürgen Rohwer, Stuttgart, Dr Hümmelchen, Stuttgart, retired General of Tank Troops Gerhard Graf von Schwerin and retired General of Tank Troops Walther Nehring.

Especial thanks go to Dr Joseph Henke, Dr Hofmann and Frau Ina von Theim of the Koblenz Federal Archives, who enabled my wife and I to evaluate the extensive documentation on the East for so many months. This also applies to Dr Maierhöfer of the Federal Archives – Military Archives in Freiburg, who made the naval records available to me.

Here I must also express my thanks to my wife, who bore the largest part of the archival work and prepared the final copy of the manuscript. During the whole time of this work, Dr Hans Josef Mundt has provided me with his valuable advice.

Maps

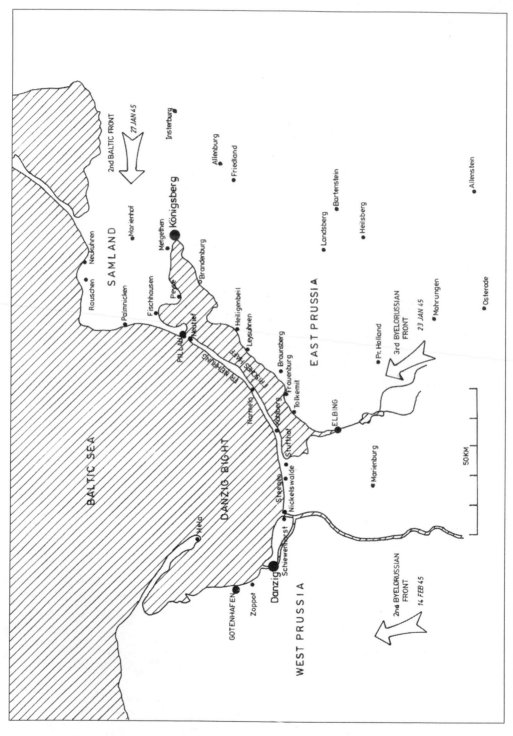

Map 1. The Danzig Bight, 1945

Chapter 1

The Eastern Front

On Monday, 1st January 1945, Hitler released his 'New Year Appeal to the German People' from his headquarters in Ziegenberg, near Bad Nauheim.

> Millions of Germans of all professions and positions in life, men and women, boys and girls, even children, have taken up spade and shovel. Thousands of Volkssturm battalions have been raised or arc in the process of doing so. Divisions have been newly raised. Volks Artillery Corps, mortar and assault gun brigades, as well as armoured units have been stamped out of the ground, fighter squadrons freshened up and equipped with new machines, and above all, in the German factories the German male and female workers have achieved amazing things. In this way, whatever our enemies have smashed will be rebuilt with superhuman industry and courage, and this will happen until our enemies find an end one day. That, my comrades, will be entered in history as the wonder of the 20th Century! A people that in the front line and at home suffer so immeasurably, cndure and bear so much, cannot therefore ever be defeated. It will emerge stronger and more firmly uplifted out of this melting pot than ever before in its history.

But the people were at the end of their strength. The war was long since lost; on all fronts the German armies were having to give ground to their enemies. Defeat was only a matter of months, but soldiers and civilians still believed in the imminent release of wonder weapons that would avert disaster at the last minute, and the armed forces fought on determinedly. The chiefs of staff squabbled over the few available divisions: Colonel-General Guderian, chief of the general staff of the Army High Command, wanted to reinforce the eastern front at whatever cost, while Colonel-General Jodl, his counterpart in the Armed Forces High Command, did not want to release any men from the western front following the collapse of the Ardennes offensive. Hitler had chosen the west for his last heroic battle.

The east was no longer important to Hitler. When Colonel-General Guderian announced the latest figures about the colossal Russian advance between Memel and Budapest, Hitler exploded in anger, shouting at Guderian: 'That is the biggest bluff since the time of Jenghis Kahn!'

On New Year's Day he hosted his henchmen at a reception. The atmosphere was strained. They talked about the New Year offensive in Alsace and of a third blow that the greatest field marshal of all time would soon lead. Guderian stood silently by. He was waiting for the ceremony in which Luftwaffe Lieutenant-Colonel Rudel would receive the newly conceived Golden Oak Leaves with Swords and Diamonds to the Knights' Cross of the Iron Cross together with his promotion to Colonel.

Once the award ceremony was over, Guderian drove back to his headquarters in Zossen. On the 4th January he started a several-day inspection journey of the eastern front. At Army Group *South* he established that the situation on the Hungarian front was far from stable. The superiority of the Russians was so great that General Wöhler could only supply a single division for the threatened northern or central sectors. SS-General Gille shrugged his shoulders: 'We no longer have the equipment we had in 1940. I need three men where formerly I managed with two or even one.'

Guderian then drove to Krakau to see General Harpe, the commander in chief of Army Group *A*. Here, or at neighbouring Army Group *North*, the Russians would start their big winter offensive.

Harpe suggested saving troops by withdrawing 20 kilometres from the banks of the Vistula. Guderian said that he would pass it on to Hitler. 'But I must warn you, Harpe. This could have the worst personal consequences for you.' 'If he sacks me,' Harpe said quietly, 'I am only doing my duty.'

That same evening Guderian telephoned the commander-in-chief of Army Group *Mitte*, Colonel-General Reinhardt, in his headquarters in Wartenburg near Allenstein. Guderian, the west Prussian, was so confident in the situation in East Prussia that he could save himself the journey. The 3rd Panzer Army was holding the area between the Memel and Gumbinnen, the 4th Army lay in eastern East Prussia in a protruding bow to the east that stretched from Gumbinnen via Fillipow to the Narev, from where its positions connected with those of the 2nd Army, covering the northern part of Poland.

Army Group *Mitte* with 35 divisions stood opposite over 100 rested Soviet divisions. Colonel-General Reinhardt was also aware of the great danger. He therefore requested permission to withdraw his exposed right flank from the Narev to the East Prussian border. Guderian promised to do everything possible, but here it was not just avoiding a great military risk, for over two million Germans lived in the army group's area. If the front broke here, they would be at the mercy of the Russians – and what that entailed everyone knew from the massacre at Nemmersdorf the previous autumn when the Russians had encroached on German territory for the first time. Before reducing the front, the armed forces wanted to evacuate the German civil population, but Gauleiter Koch had sworn to defend every square metre of East Prussia to the last drop of blood. No civilian could leave East Prussia without the Party's permission, and Koch had Hitler's full support. Guderian was powerless, and his fears were very quickly realised. While Guderian had been in Hungary, the dice had been thrown in Moscow.

Churchill had already requested Stalin in December to bring forward the Soviet offensive in order to relieve the heavily pressed troops in the Ardennes. Nevertheless, Stalin needed a strong frost, not wanting his tanks to sink in the east Polish swamps or the Masurian Lakes. On Thursday, the 4th January, the meteorologists at last gave hope. A high pressure area had developed over Finland that was moving slowly southwards bringing polar air with it. The thermometers in Leningrad were already at minus 15 degrees. At the latest it would reach the Black Sea within a week. Heavy frost reigned. Stalin had named the 12th January, a Friday, as the first day of the attack.

The Soviets had never been so well prepared for an offensive, not least because of American arms deliveries arriving at Murmansk, Vladivostock and Odessa; freighter after freighter with tanks, artillery, aircraft parts and boundless ammunition. Soviet industry was working flat out. Officers and men of the five army groups committed to the great offensive against Hitler's Germany from the Baltic to the Carpathians had never seen so many weapons. Since the autumn offensive of 1944 the Soviet units had been restocked and reinforced with fresh Mongolian and Caucasian formations. To deceive the Germans, some of the troops had been assigned to digging trenches, especially the supply units brought forward, giving the appearance of being happy with their progress so far and now building a strong defensive position. For months there had been a strong ban on leave. After the daily arms drill, selected political commissars showed the men films about the atrocities of the fascist imperialists, the destruction of Russian towns and villages, the corpses of the women and children of Leningrad, Charkov and Stalingrad. Down to the last gunner, revenge for Tannenberg 1914 was driven into them and, for the first time, they would be thrusting deep into German territory and acquiring booty.

Marshal K.K. Rokossovski had been nominated commander-in-chief of the 2nd Byelorussian Front a few days earlier. He would thrust through the northern part of Poland and through East Prussia to Pomerania, while the 3rd Byelorussian Front under Marshal Tscherniakovski would be occupied with the difficult Baltic coast. To the south were Marshals Zhukov and Koniev with the 1st Byelorussian and 1st Ukrainian Fronts ready to thrust on Berlin from Silesia. Over 200 Russian divisions were facing about 70 German divisions along a 600 kilometre front.

As the last commander-in-chief to reach the front, Rokossovski made himself familiar with his new troops. Less than three weeks later he drove past the house in Kulm on the Vistula where the German Chief of Staff Guderian had been born.

By the 8th January Colonel-General Guderian had completed his inspection tour and was back in his office in Zossen, situated in the bunker complex close to Potsdam and about 30 kilometres south of Berlin. Meanwhile General Gehlen's *Enemy Armies East* department had completed the latest Soviet strength assessment. Now, under the impression of the weakness of his army groups, he was confronted with this report. For the whole of the length of the East Front the enemy held at least a three-fold superiority. As the attackers, the Soviets could concentrate their forces any way they liked, so that the relative strengths at the endangered places were even more unfavourable to the German troops: for the infantry 1:11, armour 1:7, artillery 1:20. Against the growing armada of Russian bombers and ground-attack aircraft the 6th German Air Fleet had almost nothing to deploy. Their commander, Colonel-General Ritter von Greim, could only promise to keep the main roads and railways open.

On Tuesday the 9th January Guderian packed his paperwork and flew to the Führer's Headquarters at Ziegenberg. At the evening conference he informed Hitler of the newest figures and suggested a strategic withdrawal from Italy, Norway and the Balkans and the evacuation of the enclosed Kurland Army from Lithuania in order to reinforce the front with the troops thus released. Hitler swept the paper angrily from the table and turned his back on his Chief of the General Staff.

Unflustered, Guderian continued: 'In view of the thin manning and the scanty reserves, the East Front will collapse like a house of cards to a single Russian penetration.' Hardly had Guderian left the room when Hitler began to rage: 'The East Front has never been as strong as it is now. It will not be reinforced and we will not yield a foot of German soil. It goes badly with me whenever I hear of strategic withdrawal – I have now been hearing it for two years – and every time the result was a catastrophe.' Three days later the storm broke in which the German East and with it the Third Reich would go under. On the 12th January the 1st Byelorussian Front broke out of its bridgeheads west of the Vistula after a heavy artillery preparation on Army Group *A*, Army Group *Mitte*'s southern neighbour, tearing the front apart to a width of 150 kilometres. On the 13th January the 3rd Byelorussian Front opened fire with 350 heavy batteries and Stalin-Organs on the 3rd Panzer and 4th Armies that were holding the northern flank from the Masurian

Lakes to the Kurischen Lagoon. The two-hour long drumfire concentrated north of the Ebenrode-Gumbinnen road, about 120 kilometres in a straight line east of Königsberg. The subsequent Russian attack hit the forward troops with an eight- to ten-fold superiority. Next day, Sunday the 14th January, the Soviets also attacked the 2nd Army's central sector. The German troops defended themselves bitterly and the Russian superiority was only able to penetrate a few kilometres until the 17th January.

Meanwhile winter had arrived everywhere. On the 16th January it was already down to minus 10 degrees. The bright weather now enabled the enemy to bring his overwhelming air force into action. Squadrons of bombers and ground-attack aircraft flew in uninterrupted flights against the German front and deep into the hinterland. Only a few German aircraft could be seen in the sky. The enemy crushed every resistance with artillery and Stalin-Organs, and those that survived were torn apart by the tanks shooting up points of resistance and crushing the foxholes. The German divisions wasted away. The gaps could no longer be filled with alarm units formed from the survivors. The front broke up into individual defensive groups, each fighting where it already stood.

All attempts to form a line of resistance were foiled by the Russian tanks pressing forward, often carrying infantry. The enemy superiority in fire power, mobility and manpower condemned the German troops to defeat and doubt. The Russian steamroller was rolling forward and could no longer be stopped.

The civilian population behind the German front had no idea of the danger hanging over them. Life went on even in these days almost as if in peacetime. Cattle markets were held in the towns, the cinemas were sold out, the streets populated with horse-drawn carts and pedestrians. In the villages and farms they were occupied with threshing and brewing schnaps. In the big sugar factories half of the latest turnip crops had been processed.

One felt safe behind the 'East Wall'. Since the previous harvest ten thousand anti-tank ditches had been dug between Insterburg and Danzig. Kilometre after kilometre these six metre deep, seven metre wide ditches went around Königsberg, through the Masurian Plain, around Neidenburg, from the Frisches Haff lagoon past Elbing to Marienburg and over the heights before Danzig and Gotenhafen.

Gauleiter Forster had declared Elbing the safest town in the whole of East Prussia. No one could imagine that within a few days this county town would be like East Prussia's coffin lid.

Permanently there were 4–5,000 men, and at weekends about 20,000 men of all kinds in the city with spades, shovels and wheelbarrows building traps for the Russians. From the Frisches Haff lagoon in the northeast to the

Drausensee lake in the south, the anti-tank ditch extended across the heights in front of the town for 20 kilometres to where the Marienburg fortifications began. Most of the 100,000 inhabitants were convinced that the Führer would never let the Russians get so close to the old Hansa town.

The Elbingers had never made much fuss about the discreet beauty of their town. Peace and calm exuded from the Biedermeier-like market place, as from the beautiful facades of the old Hansa buildings and villas hidden in the gardens dating back to the town's foundation. The Elbingers prided themselves in the fact that Germans had lived here long before Columbus discovered America. But, without direct access to the Baltic, Elbing had never had the importance of Danzig or Königsberg. Nevertheless, Germany's first iron ship had been built here and later the first torpedo boat for Kaiser Wilhelm. Later yet came the mini submarines, locomotives and anti-aircraft guns.

The Elbingers were particularly proud of their environment. The nearby Frisches Haff lagoon and especially the bathing place of Kahlberg on the lagoon had formerly been a centre of attraction for weekenders and summer holidaymakers. To the east was the wooded hill of Vogelsang and to the south the Drausensee lake, which even had a world sensation to offer. Ships coming from the Oberländer Canal further to the south and wanting to enter the deeper Drausensee were taken overland instead of coming through locks. To the west was the flat landscape of the rich Vistula marshes.

During the first two weeks of January Elbing was as busy as ever. The dockyard and the supply industries were working overtime, and the ration coupon issuing stations were very busy, the hostelries crammed. The smell of fresh mash from the Englischer Brunnen brewery hung over the town. In the town theatre, which had been converted into a cinema, the film *Opfergang* from a novel by Rudolf G. Binding was showing. The Armed Forces Reports of the 13th, 14th and 15th January, with the news of the beginning of the big Russian winter offensive, were received calmly. Finally the Russians had been thrown out of Goldap again in the autumn. The officials continued ticking off their forms, the riveting hammers banged away in the dockyard, and the housewives sat in the market café with their coffees while outside the town the columns of diggers continued their work.

The picture changed on the 19th January. The news of a breakthrough by the Russians increased. Warsaw had fallen, Ziechenau was in Russian hands and Neidenburg 125 kilometres to the south no longer reported. Without waiting for the official order to evacuate, the Elbingers packed their bags. Many of the better socially placed left the town on a pretext. Those who did not have an officially authorised vehicle, with the obligatory red stripe, used the railway via Dirschau and Danzig back to the Reich. Finally thousands of people crowded the railway station. Many had to wait a day or longer before they could squeeze into an overfilled train. The offices still functioned, the shops remained open and the shifts at the factories continued normally at full strength.

At about 1700 hours on Tuesday the 23rd January Mayor Fritz Leser was sitting in his office at the town hall and was once more going through a list of food wholesalers and food stores with a colleague. That morning they had had a conference with the deputy head of the county economic office and concluded that Elbing's stocks would suffice for at least two months. Only salt was in short supply and the two officials were racking their brains for where they could acquire some, when there was an explosion outside. The grinding and clattering of tank tracks could clearly be heard. Dr Leser and his assistant rushed to the window. Firing tanks were rolling across Friedrich-Wilhelm-Platz. Dr Leser rushed down to the cellar, where the command post was located. People were standing around white with shock, having come in from the street. Russian tanks – where had they come from?

Chapter 2

Precipitate Flight

The debacle of the German 2nd Army was complete. Marshal Rokossovski's shock armies streamed through northern Poland, parallel to the southern boundary of East Prussia, without encountering any earnest resistance. On the 18th January, four days after the beginning of the offensive, they occupied the headquarters of the 2nd Army that had just been abandoned by Colonel-General Weiss and his staff. That same day they took the Milau training area, whose commandant, Major General Sauvant, had left only hours before with five tanks and a field bakery, heading towards Marienburg.

Elements of the Soviet 2nd Guards and 48th Armies now wheeled to the north to reach the Frische Lagoon in the rear of the German 4th Army and thus cut off East Prussia from the west.

Before the start of the 19th January the Russian elite troops had crossed the German border jubilantly. They sat on tanks, self-propelled guns and fully packed trucks, wearing grey-brown uniforms, padded jackets and grey fur caps on top with a small red star, not much bigger than a Party badge. They crossed the snow-covered fields in their ranks by the thousands and broke into the villages and towns, shooting at everything that moved.

At the 2,300 acre Seythen Farm in the Osterode District, about 20 kilometres north of the border with Poland, this Thursday, the 18th January, ended like all other previous working days, the 35 Russian and 14 French prisoners of war being shut up for the night in old barred stables. A chaff cutter rumbled away in the barn at the rear and the dairymen rattled the milk cans in the cow stalls as Chief Inspector Romalm made his rounds. The wife of the owner, who had been called up into the armed forces, had already gone to bed. Romalm had heard about the partisans and wanted to ensure that everything was locked up. Before going to bed he sat in his office for an hour making out the work details for the coming day.

About 0200 hours a thickly wrapped, snow-encrusted motorcyclist made his way up the hill to the farm. He stopped at the Inspector's house and hammered on the door with his fist. Not taking time to remove the blackout from his window, Romalm pulled an overcoat over his pyjamas and went across the cold floor and down the staircase.

'The District Group Leader sent me,' reported the motorcyclist. 'Your Volkssturm unit is to occupy the positions at Osterschau immediately!'

'Immediately?' asked Romalm unbelievingly. 'Why, what's up?'

'I don't know either. You have to get out there in any case. The Russians are not far off.' The man accelerated and slipped away over the icy road.

Back in his room, Romalm first smoked a cigarette. This could not be serious, for the front was somewhere far off to the southeast. Two days ago the Armed Forces Report had mentioned fighting on the Narev. Apparently the Party only wanted to show that it too could play at war and the whole thing was an exercise. He would complain, for the people had to work hard all day. He got the night watchman to round up the old men and the boys. Half an hour later the platoon of twenty men, sullen and half asleep, were on their way to the positions five kilometres away that they themselves had dug a few weeks earlier.

The inspector remained behind. He could not leave the night watchman alone with the prisoners of war. Restlessly, he went round the buildings again. The wind had died down since the evening and he believed he could hear thunder quite faintly to the south. He climbed up to the tower room with his telescope slung around his neck and checked the horizon. No question, there was a broad strip of red fire.

Romalm was still not unduly concerned. Perhaps it was only partisan bands. It was difficult to judge the distance but, however far it was, the Hohenstein Line and the Tannenberg still lay between.

At about 0300 hours the messenger was back again. The people on the farmstead were to get ready for the trek. 'Pack up orders' it was called, but no one was to leave until the District Group Leader gave the order to evacuate. Romalm waited until dawn before assembling the trek. A cart was allocated to every two families with either two heavy or three light horses. The lady of the manor and her two children had a rubber-tyred wagon, while the inspector had a small one-horse wagon with a very young horse. His riding horse was saddled and fastened to the wagon so that he could be more mobile if necessary.

The Russian prisoners of war were sent off with two escorts to an Armed Services collecting point, the Frenchmen allocated to the wagons as drivers. The Volkssturm men returned in the early morning. There were no weapons available for them and they had been sent home.

There had been some ugly scenes during the packing, the people arguing about what they should take and who should go with whom. There were tears and swearing and still nobody knew exactly why they had to leave so suddenly. In the middle of this excitement six Russian low-flying aircraft appeared. In two approaches they fired several rounds of machine-gun fire at the buildings. No one was hurt. Half the people had dived into the cellars and would not come out again.

The six Soviet aircraft flew off to the northeast.

About ten kilometres away, farmer's wife Christa Dux was already feeding the pigs, as the sound of engines and the tacking of the machine guns was heard. Shocked, she ran out into the yard and saw how the machines were banking over the village and shooting towards Waplitz, where the Schwirgsteiners had shovelled the snow out of the anti-tank ditches only a few days earlier. However, also in this direction was the school where her two children were already attending class.

Christa Dux ran as fast as she could. Other women ran after her. Several times she fell on the icy village street. Running past the village pond through the big school playground, she found her children unharmed in a corner of the classroom, crouched against the wall. The young school mistress was sitting crying among the children, not knowing what to do.

The uproar had hardly died down when two trucks with German soldiers stopped in the village. Some of them were wounded and all looked the worse for wear. They asked for food and told the villagers that the Russians were after them. The whole of Neidenburg Border District was fleeing towards Allenstein and Osterode. The roads were all completely blocked.

Nobody wanted to believe these stories. The soldiers did not look very confidence-inspiring. The deputy mayor called the district farmers' union in Osterode, but no one there knew anything about an evacuation order, so they too, like the people of Seythen, were waiting until Saturday.

It snowed again during the night, hiding the ice under a 20cm thick blanket of snow. The temperature read minus 18 degrees. The cloud cover was torn away during the morning and the sun shone over a peaceful winter landscape. The Steffenswalde Farm had also received the order to pack. The lady of the manor, Ella Brümmer, was on her way to Osterode that morning to purchase items for the trek: boots for the drivers, calks for the horses' hooves, and minor items from a long list that seemed essential for such an unusual journey. Ella Brümmer was driving a one-horse carriage without a coachman. The road was very busy. She overtook several refugee treks and was herself overtaken by military trucks that were in obvious haste. Beyond Döhringen Russian aircraft appeared over the road, firing for all they were worth. Horses bolted, shafts broke, women screamed – but no one was hurt. Frau Brümmer was undecided for a moment. Should she simply turn back? But then she drove on.

She had trouble getting through to Osterode. In the town itself all the streets were blocked with farm carts and military vehicles. The shops were hung with signs inscribed 'Closed by order of the Police'. She went to the

District Senior Administrator and heard the chief doctor of the hospital tell him: 'You must arrange things so that the people no longer take flight. The Russians have been beaten back near Gilgenburg [about 40 kilometres to the south] and one can now quietly wait out the next few days. If the people go on fleeing like this, my sick will never be able to get to the station. The situation there is indescribable.'

Frau Brümmer inserted herself between them and asked the Administrator, 'Shall we flee or not?' He glanced at her briefly and said: 'Cars with the orders to flee have been on their way to you since 1230.' As the lady of the manor made her way back, the people on the street were calling out: 'No further! All go back home! The Russians have been beaten back near Gilgenburg.' Several Gilgenburgers actually turned back and ran straight into disaster.

Ella Brümmer whipped up her horse. She was in a hurry.

At this point the Seythen trek together with Romalm had already been waiting for three hours in the big courtyard between the barns, ready to move. Eighteen wagons were packed, the horses harnessed, the people keeping warm in the servants' quarters – but still no order to evacuate came. Inspector Romalm tried every ten minutes to ring the District Group Leader. No one answered. Finally towards noon he sent a rider to Osterschau to discover what was happening. The man returned after a good half hour. The District Group Leader had taken his wife and children to the station and had himself gone on the train – the last from Osterschau.

Angrily Chief Inspector Romalm ordered the people to hurry. Half an hour later the trek moved off. Romalm had selected side roads for the route to Osterode as he had already seen from a distance how the main road was hopelessly blocked. But it was difficult for the horses pulling the fully packed wagons over the hilly ground and icy hills. Again and again extra horses had to be harnessed in front to get the wagons through.

At nightfall Romalm had all the wagons stop and with a few assistants threw out all the superfluous gear – sewing machines, pieces of furniture, sacks of brickettes. There was a frightful clamour and only the threat of leaving the unwilling ones behind achieved his aim. Afterwards they moved faster. Romalm wanted their next stop to be on the Osterode Heights on the Sunday morning without any further delays.

By this time the Schwirgsteiners had also lost their patience, setting off at about 1730 hours on the Saturday afternoon. The first to leave her farm was Christa Dux, after she had fed the animals again and fastened all the doors and windows. The big covered wagon was driven by her old father, while Christa Dux sat with her mother and both children on the bedding behind the driving seat. They had to go about 1,500 metres to reach the main road, where they had to wait a long time before they were able to work their way into the treks rolling past.

In Hohenstein the Schwirgsteiners discovered that the road to Osterode was blocked.

'There is fighting there. You must go north between Allenstein and Osterode,' said a man in Nazi Party uniform. Without protest, thankful for the good advice, the Schwirgsteiners turned towards Locken. The lies the man had told them were because the road to Osterode was blocked. For Christa Dux this was to mean salvation.

While the Schwirgsteiners and the Seytheners sought to get away from the Russians in the stream of many thousand others, time had passed in Seefeld. On the Saturday evening the lady of the manor returned from her failed attempt to make purchases in Osterode. In the Kraplauer Woods she met the treks of Gumbinnen refugees that had been accommodated at Seefeld. The old accountant from the manor was with them and she shouted at him to hurry.

It was getting dark as she drove into her courtyard, which she had left all neat and tidy that morning. Now everything was in an uproar. She went from house to house. Everywhere there was quarrelling about places in the wagons. Frau Brümmer had meanwhile seen how the horses had to struggle on the roads and how many overloaded wagons had ended up in the ditch.

'Don't load the wagons so full!' she warned them. 'Not everyone can take a sewing machine!'

The manor house was swarming with soldiers. A sick man was sitting at the piano in the drawing room, the seventy-year-old not understanding what was going on. Following a heart attack several weeks earlier he had yet to return to his senses.

The lady of the manor put him to bed, from which she first had to clear the pack items of a strange officer. Even the guest rooms were overfilled with sleeping soldiers. The kitchen was full of soldiers. Strange cooks and their assistants surrounded the large stove. The water supply was no longer working, the toilets were running over and water was dripping through the ceilings.

Soldiers were standing around outside and talking among themselves. Everywhere one stumbled over men and packs. The lady of the manor went across to the distillery where her supervisors had gathered. She got the impression that they were drunk and not caring about anything. The woman had to struggle to get the men moving to shut off the water so that the pipes would not burst in her absence. 10,000 litres of spirit were released into the stream because of the danger of an explosion. Over the distillery ditch one could see far to the south. There were houses on fire this side of Gilgenburg.

But the supervisors hesitated to leave before midnight. Finally, at about 0330 hours, 19 trek wagons left Steffenswalde Manor on the Sunday morning. Leading in her Hindenburg carriage was the lady of the manor with her sick husband, who kept falling over senseless left and right. The Chief Inspector brought up the rear of the trek.

They had hardly crossed the manor boundary when they learned from soldiers they were overtaking that the enemy had taken Gilgenburg at 0330 hours.

Wedged into the stream of treks and overtaken on the open left side of the road by military convoys, they slowly moved on to Osterode. Shortly before the town they discovered that the enemy was already in Collishof. The Russians were advancing twice as fast as the treks. Everyone was trying to drive where they could. At about 1230 hours that afternoon the Steffenswalder Trek was stuck fast at the gymnasium in the middle of Osterode as the first shells burst in the town.

At this point the people from Seythen, who had had a much longer journey, reached the Osterode town boundary and rested in a brickworks. Chief Inspector Romalm and the accountant stood outside at the entrance and watched the street to look out for late-comers. They smoked and talked about the way ahead. Tanks approached along the street with trucks behind them. They overtook the columns of trek vehicles on the street at speed and Romalm was about to say something about their lack of consideration when the first tank stopped alongside the brickworks. The turret turned in their direction and the first shot was fired.

'Russians!' cried Romalm, horrified.

The two men raced back into the house and alerted the women. Romalm grabbed a fur and a blanket, shouted at the others to follow him and went out through a back door. A clump of pines 300 metres away offered the first cover, and beyond it was a gorge into which Romalm slid. He was followed by Frau v. W. with her daughter and two other women with their children. They could not see what was happening in the brickworks, but could hear the tanks firing uninterruptedly at Osterode. The refugees waited in their cover until dusk so as to circumvent the town in the dark and make their way to Mohrungen, 30 kilometres to the north. Frau v. W. with her daughter and the Senior Inspector set off, but the two other women did not think they could survive a night march through the deep snow with their small children, and turned back to the brickworks.

The firing had created fearful panic among the people crammed together in Osterode, but the Volkssturm and a few soldiers still had the situation sufficiently under control to keep the left-hand side of the street open for withdrawing military convoys. The refugees in their horse-drawn wagons could only make a metre at a time. The Steffenswalder Trek needed exactly three hours to cover the few hundred metres from the Gymnasium to the Locks Bridge over which the route to the west led, but then the military again forced the refugees to one side. As a herd of captured panje horses was being driven past, Frau Brümmer lost her patience. That these unkempt, miserable horses should be saved and she should be handed over to the Russians was too much for the lady. Angrily she grasped the reins, raised the whip to her horse and drove past a soldier into the middle of the stream of trotting ponies, unconcerned about the others as they complained and shouted after her.

Next morning she reached Liebemühl on the Oberländer Canal. It was Monday the 22nd January 1945. The crush was almost as bad as in Osterode, but the Hindenburg wagon was able to cross the Locks Bridge to a half-timbered barn, the horse's hooves crunching over the crushed ice of the chaussee leading towards Saalfeld. Ella Brümmer could see the Bienau Mansion once owned by her grandfather through the frosty clear air of this sunny morning in the far distance, where she wanted to stop. Her husband sat sunk together next to her and was unapproachable.

She had only gone several hundred metres when a shell exploded in front of her close to the road. The trek ground to a halt. Women began screaming, most of them leaving the wagons and running left to a nearby wood. Then Ella Brümmer saw the long row of white snow shirts coming towards her from the right. Hastily the slight woman pulled her senseless husband from the wagon and let herself slide into the ditch alongside him. Then the Russians were over them. Without a word they ripped the clothing from those lying in the snow and took all the valuables for themselves. One waved a dagger about when Ella Brümmer's swollen fingers would not let her rings slip off quickly enough. Then it became quiet. Ella Brümmer crawled forward cautiously on her hands and knees. The Russians were already engaged in throwing the baggage out of the wagon. Then one tapped the other on the shoulder and off they went with the wagon that bore a silver plate on the front commemorating the laying of the Tannenberg Memorial foundation stone. Later two Poles took the Brümmers in a box cart to the Amalienruh Manor, where the Russians were already waiting.

Lily Sternberg left Gross Nappern Manor with her trek on Saturday the 20th January. She was about six hours ahead of Ella Brümmer. In her landau sat her three children and 81-year-old mentally deranged Aunt Käte, who whined almost ceaselessly. By dawn on the Sunday they had Osterode behind them and that evening they left Liebemühl. At about 1500 hours on Monday afternoon they were standing in the market square in Saalfeld.

They needed only four or five hours more to get to temporary safety beyond the Nogat.

They were stretching their legs in the market square, the coachman standing by the horses, when suddenly a tank rattled and roared across the square. Lily Steinberg pulled her children into the wagon. Machine-gun fire broke out and the coachman cried out: 'I've been hit!' Lily Steinberg could not help him, as Aunt Käte was striking out madly around her. A second tank rammed the landau. The shafts broke and the horses ran off. The wagon hit a plank wall at speed, then the corner of a building, and finally tipped over. Michel, a French prisoner of war from the manor farm, ran up to the wagon and helped those trapped inside to get out through the roof. Aunt Käte had to be left behind as she was lashing out with her hands and feet.

Lily Steinberg was able to take refuge in a nearby house with her children and a quickly grabbed blanket, while outside tank after tank rolled by. When it was quiet again and she dared look out, the horse and wagon had disappeared.

The Steinbergs were able to get out of burning Saalfeld and found shelter in the bunker of a market garden until they were driven out by the Russians. The Russians then drove them back the way they had come. There were Russians everywhere.

Among the thousands over-run between Osterode and Elbing was also the trek from Seemen. They had left on the Friday and had made good progress. Their undoing was two policemen at a crossroads in Maldeuten, 25 kilometres north of Osterode, who directed the treks west for several hours. Obediently, the Seemeners turned towards Saalfeld. After about ten kilometres they realised that they were driving towards the Russians and turned back again. As they approached Maldeuten once more in the late evening, wild firing broke out behind them and to one side. There were gun flashes everywhere. They reached the village just as two armoured cars appeared out of the darkness near them and opened fire. Somebody shouted: 'They are Russians!'

The women snatched their children from the wagons and sought shelter behind walls and house entrances. The uproar only lasted a few minutes before the armoured cars turned round and vanished in the darkness.

The refugees did not waste a minute. They whipped up what horses were left. To their distress was now added snow showers that became thicker and thicker. The children in the wagons slept from sheer exhaustion. A thick covering of snow lay over the bedding and luggage in the open wagons, and the horses' manes were crusted with ice. The brakes were long since frozen solid and when there were hills, the coachmen helped to block the wheels by putting chains and cudgels in the spokes. This was particularly dangerous for the women little accustomed to such travelling, who had to get down among the harness in dresses and shoes. But these brave women proved themselves as good as the men. In fact they often showed themselves calmer and more courageous.

Although they could hardly keep their eyes open from fatigue, they pushed along the Maldeuten–Preussisch Holland road to the north. They travelled all through the night, reaching Grünhagen in the morning. They passed Grünhagen Station without noticing the pedestrians gathered there, and then stopped in Grünhagen for an hour to give the horses a break before going on. The snow had stopped but they did not get very far. A few hours north of Grünhagen a rider caught up with them and overtook them shouting: 'The Russians are close behind us!' A woman shouted angrily after him: 'Bloody man!' as if she could gallop after him with her heavy wagon. Several minutes later the Russian tanks arrived, rolling past the trek as if it was the most natural thing in the world, following close behind one another with trucks in-between full of Mongolian infantry. The infantry appeared to be drunk. They were laughing and bawling, and kept calling out: 'How far to Berlin, Gospoda?'

At first the farm wagons jogged on, uncertain what to do. But when the convoy alongside them became even denser, they stopped. Their flight had become pointless.

Soon the first Russians came alongside the trek on foot. Trembling with fear, the refugees gave them their jewellery and valuables as the Russians waved knives and guns in their faces. Suddenly, from under the hoods of several wagons came the cries of children and calls for help. The Russians were raping the younger women. Somewhere there were rifle shots. No one could help them.

Later in the afternoon on this disastrous Tuesday the Seemeners' wagons reached Grünhagen village. There were Russians everywhere. The Nagel family with their three children left their wagon standing in the street and went without it to a house set apart from the others, where an old woman lived who had remained behind. They were able to spend the night there peacefully, undisturbed by the Russians.

When they went back to the wagon in the morning and harnessed up, they found that it had been completely ransacked with some bags and foodstuffs missing. Behind the wagon they found the body of a woman, about 40 years old. They could find no injury on her, and no one knew who she was. Several of the men carried her to the nearby cemetery. They could not dig a grave in the hard frozen earth so after covering her with twigs, they left her body lying between the graves.

When they returned, they discovered the body of a farmer who had been shot by the Russians during the night lying in a wagon. However, his wife refused to let his body lie there on the ground, wanting to drive on with her two children and father-in-law, and to bury her husband in the home cemetery herself.

Slowly the trek moved on again. They were no longer in a hurry, as no one knew whether their homes and farms would still be there.

By midday the trek was back in Maldeuten. Russians and Poles directed the wagons to an empty site. Only those who spoke Polish or declared themselves as Poles could drive on. The others remained in the icy cold for the rest of the day and the following night on this empty site. Russians and Poles kept coming to help themselves to whatever they fancied from the wagons, and the East Prussians dared not protest. Silently and powerless, they let all this happen to them.

With nightfall the cries for help increased. For what it was worth, the women tried to hide themselves in the wagons, not that this was of much use to them. It only became quieter later in the night. The Nagels tried to warm some frozen milk for the children from a big churn they had with them. This was only possible after they had shaved off some of the ice inside the milk churn.

At noon next day they were allowed to drive on, but Russian sentries were standing at the exit to the site, who sorted the men out and drove them off in a small group to the Kommandatura, where they were supposedly to get a document. The wagons were searched for further victims and then the women were allowed to drive on. The women stopped at the edge of the village, anxiously awaiting the return of their men, until the Russians drove them off with rifle butts. These women never saw their men again. No one knows what happened to them.

From the 60 kilometre wide path of the Soviet advance, only those who had left very early or had a motor vehicle managed to save themselves. From Gilgenburg at least one trek reached Elbing, which it entered on the 23rd January, so it must have had a 24 hour head start before the mass of treks set off.

Some treks were able to turn off to the west and escape over the Vistula. The pressure of these refugees was particularly noticeable in the Stuhm area, where the necessity to flee had not been so prominent. Only the panic haste of the treks passing through caused uncertainty among the inhabitants.

In Honigfelde, about 60 kilometres southeast of Elbing, the 72-year-old Farmer Richter was shooting hares in mid-January and sacked a Polish dairyman for contaminating the milk. Looking back, they were laughing while here and there the German troops were having to give way to overwhelming

Russian superiority. Two of Richter's sons were in the field. Their unit was 200 kilometres to the east, and the eldest had said he was coming for the weekend. One cousin was a soldier in Kurland and another was at a military physical training camp near Elbing. His wife had died here years previously and the house was looked after by a daughter as well as the wife of his eldest son.

Father Richter was at one with his farm, which had belonged to his family for 300 years. There were 50 cows in the stalls, the best breeding cattle, and 15 splendid horses. 'Lisette' would foal any day and he was as pleased about this as if it were a child. He would have preferred to have had her covered two months later so as to have had the foal on the meadows. However, the Wehrmacht needed the stallions, and therefore he would not travel as far as Bartenstein. The harvest had been good, only the threshing had not gone so well, as the Party had taken the men off to dig the East Wall! What sense was there in that? They should have let the Wehrmacht do that. They would finally defeat the Russians at the Masuren Canal – at the latest near Tannenberg – as once Hindenburg had done. The Party had made a lot of the digging and now everything was snowed over and frozen hard. There was too much of the State in this. And nothing good came out of Danzig. Basically this did not mean so much to him; there was no comparison with Kaiser Wilhelm, under whom he had served in Königsberg.

School had resumed on the 13th January after the winter holidays, and he missed the chattering of his grandchildren a little. On the 18th they were back again, the schoolmaster having gone off with his family, and they would soon all be packing in Stuhm. '1914 was just like this', said Father Richter, 'and then they all stayed.'

But the sounds of battle in the distance came nearer and now they could clearly distinguish between the firing and the explosions. Early on the 19th German troops passed through on trucks and carts, some wounded with them, and they did not look good. Father Richter was not very friendly towards them, but he himself did not know why. The women cooked ersatz coffee for them and gave them some buttered bread. This was how they learned that the German front had collapsed.

Father Richter could not take this in until midday, when a troop of frozen, exhausted soldiers appeared on foot, twelve men, the remains of a field artillery battery. They wanted to rest, sleep, warm themselves, and asked how far it was to the Vistula. When they heard that it was only a few kilometres away, they wanted to move straight on, but the women heated a room for them and scattered straw around. Shortly afterwards a trek of 18 wagons arrived, having lost their way after being brushed aside by a military convoy. No sooner had they unharnessed than more soldiers and civilians arrived. Soon the farm and the village were crammed full. All wanted to warm themselves and have something to drink. Even when some moved on, others moved in after them. Richter's barns were crammed with strange wagons, baggage and sacks of fodder. Military vehicles were parked between the cow stalls and the midden. There was a light artillery battery on the meadow behind the house, but not deployed as it had no ammunition left.

The Richter womenfolk had moved the furniture aside in the rooms and scattered straw on the floors. There were so many pots and pans on the big stove in the kitchen that one could not have got a spoon between them. And more and more mothers came wanting milk for their children.

The thunder of guns to the south drew alarmingly close. More to calm the womenfolk than as a necessity, Richter had three trek wagons made ready. One would be driven by the Pole, one by an Italian and the third by himself, should it come that far. They stood just behind the barn and were almost ready packed. One of the children kept an eye on things so that nothing was stolen. The women were baking bread, but they never finished as they were always sharing it out among the others.

At noon on the 20th January a Wehrmacht convoy drove up. In the trucks between the soldiers were a dozen women and children and a few old people who did not move from their places. A sergeant jumped out and ran into the house. 'Quickly, people, get out of here! There is nothing more behind us, only the Ivans!' Early that morning the Russians had surprised a village a few kilometres to the south, and the convoy had had to get away at the last minute, with only a few survivors.

This news caused panic in Honigfelde. Harnessing took place in great haste and everyone pressed through to the road leading north, regardless of the icy storm that was raging. Within 30 minutes the Richters' yard was empty. Only Farmer Richter remained, waiting for the order to evacuate to arrive. One could feel oneself abandoned by the Party when it came to organisation, and the evacuation was supposed to have been planned down to the finest detail, as Farmer Kotusch, the Local Farmers' Leader, had once stated at the table reserved for regular customers. Of course, deadly secret! He would soon call if the matter was really serious. Actually, Farmer Richter was thinking of 'Lisette' and her foal, which for him were more important than the Russians.

In fact the Gau administration had worked out precise plans for a possible evacuation of the combat area in the autumn of 1944. In the inconceivable case that fighting should take place on German soil, the population from parts of the Gau of Danzig/West Prussia and the Gau of East Prussia, especially in the rear areas, were to be evacuated over the Vistula. Only those tending cattle were to remain with their herds and look after them until their owners returned.

The evacuation plan for Honigfelde lay in the safe of the district administration in Stuhm. When on the 21st January the news of the Russian advance on his district became ever more pressing, District Leader Franz called Government President Huth at the Gau Headquarters in Danzig: 'Herr Regierungspräsident, I think we have to evacuate, the Russians are in Deutsche Eylau.'

'That is nonsense, comrade. According to our reports, the situation has been stabilised and our troops have already counterattacked. There are absolutely no grounds for concern. Calm down your people!'

'Yes, certainly, Herr Regierungspräsident. I will pass this on.'

'The District is not to be evacuated!' Huth hastily added before hanging up.

District Leader Franz did not know what to do. Apart from the Volkssturm, there was nothing in the area that looked remotely like offering any resistance.

'One people, one state, one leader'. Twelve years of 'Leader order, we obey!' And suddenly everything was blown away. There was only the fear of attracting unpleasant attention, and fear of the Russians.

The evening of that same day he rang the Gau Headquarters once more. He received the same reply. For the first and last time the District Leader protested: 'Listen, if you don't believe me about what is happening here, then come and see for yourself. What treachery is there here? Have I invented the Russians myself? If you want to take over the responsibility, please do!'

Angrily he stamped out of the room. Then he summoned his District Propaganda Chief, who had meanwhile been destroying his speech on 'holding out'.

'We won't get an order to evacuate,' said Franz in a toneless voice. 'I can't be responsible for the people any more.'

'I have already seen about a wagon, Herr Franz. We can leave in two hours.'

Franz nodded. 'Pass on to the local Party group leaders and the local farming leaders that the order to evacuate will not be given. It is up to the decision of the individuals to take the necessary measures as long as they are prepared to take the responsibility for them.'

The District Leader left the town with his retinue at 0400 hours.

The local Party leaders handled matters according to their assessments and characters. Several cleared off, others swore their belief in ultimate victory, remaining loyal until death, and took many others with them to ruination. Only a few instituted evacuation in their areas.

In Honigsfelde Farmer Kotusch went from farm to farm, begging those remaining to get going. A parish trek formed up on the road leading north. Richter's wagon stood harnessed up and ready loaded in front of the big manor house.

Father Richter went to see 'Lisette' in her stall. It would take hours to deal with the mare. He chatted to the animal and then sat down on a bale of fodder. He did not look up when his daughter came into the stall to get him. 'If they are Cossacks, they will make a good job of it,' she tried to placate him.

'Cossacks,' the old man said contemptuously. However, he went outside and put the reins into his daughter's hands. 'Take the wagon. I will follow with the one-horse carriage.'

But he first had to get out the wagon with the Italian and fasten the harness before his daughter believed him. She silently lifted the reins and the three wagons moved off. Father Richter did not watch them go. He vanished back into the stall. The Russians later took the one-horse carriage with them.

Chapter 3

The Last Trains

There was unbelievable confusion at most of the railway stations, but as long as the tracks were not intercepted by artillery or tanks, the trains continued to operate. It was as if every railway official wanted to prove that this was his very own private railway and that the railway was faster than an enemy tank. The people hung on to these last trains in thick clusters, standing on the running boards and the buffers. Passenger carriages, good wagons, open wagons, everything had to be used. Baggage was simply left lying in heaps on the platforms. Many were unable to accept this, and resignedly turned back home.

At Hohenstein Station, about halfway between Allenstein and Osterode, about 2,000 people waited for a train that was due from Allenstein that Sunday morning. Several empty Wehrmacht trucks drove past the waiting crowd to the nearby Tannenberg Memorial, and shortly afterwards the memorial entrance and vault tower flew into the air. The coffins of Paul von Hindenburg and his wife, which had been laid there in everlasting remembrance of the victorious Battle of Tannenberg, were taken on the trucks to Königsberg and from there by ship to West Germany.

The local Party leader and the railway authorities whined endlessly about the evacuation orders. Together with the railway personnel they assembled 30 goods wagons and passenger carriages into a train with an old, weak shunting engine to pull it. This took hours. Meanwhile some elderly Volkssturm men prepared the wagons, filling them with straw and setting up stoves in each of them with a supply of briquettes. As the water works were no longer functioning, the fire brigade supplied the engine with water. The train left the station late that evening and was able, only just ahead of the Soviets, to reach central Germany.

The last normal passenger train left Osterode on Sunday the 21st January, at about 1300 hours, just as Soviet tanks fired on the town. The compartments and corridors were so full of people and baggage that force had to be used to close the doors from outside. Some were still able to jump on the running boards after the railway personnel had previously pulled away many of them from this dangerous position.

The train reached Dirschau over the Vistula, but was then inadvertently diverted eastwards to Pelplin and stopped there. For five days and nights the people on the tiny platform were exposed to the icy wind. No one dared go to the nearby houses in case they missed the departure or were the last in the storm for places on the train. Eventually a horse transport arrived for the front. The horses were unloaded and, not bothering about the ankle deep manure, the people stormed the wagons, as it was said that the train would be returning immediately to Dirschau.

But after only a short while the engine was uncoupled, and for two days the refugees were left without either water or heating. The sides of the wagons became covered in hoarfrost. The crying of the many hungry young children was almost unbearable. When the train was at last brought back to Dirschau, fourteen of the refugees were dead, most of them children.

Even worse was to happen to occupants of a goods train that was standing on the departure track at Mohrungen, 25 kilometres north of Osterode, on the Sunday evening. One of the many women that were pressed together freezing in a cattle wagon with children and old people was Dorothea Gerlitzki from Marienfelde in the Osterode District. She had seen to her house and packed up on the Thursday. The Party welfare organisation had announced that in nearby Marwalde there was a train ready to take on mothers and children. The promised trucks that would take her and her three children aged 4, 5 and 8, as well as her 53-year-old mother, to the station did not arrive, and the train had left Marwalde half empty on the Saturday morning.

Dorothea Gerlitzki tried to get a lift on a farm wagon. But those that had offered places days before were now apparently overloaded and had not a single seat available. Making a quick decision, Dorothea Gerlitzki packed her two youngest ones, both girls, on a toboggan, threw a rucksack with the minimum necessities and food over her shoulder and pulled the toboggan with her mother. The boy had to ski.

So they mixed in with the treks. From time to time they were able to hang on to a moving wagon, but after five hours on foot they were exhausted from the cold and effort. Dorothea Gerlitzki was about to turn back when a military vehicle stopped near them. The driver could only take them for a short distance, but then found them another truck, so they were able to reach Mohrungen on the Sunday evening at about 2200 hours. There they waited at the station in a vast mass of people until 0700 hours on the Monday morning when a goods train arrived from which Volkssturm were unloaded. Without any request to wait, the waiting mass stormed aboard the train, which was supposed to go to Saxony. It was a very long train. The little family climbed into one of the last wagons and waited for the train to leave.

During the course of the day the town and station of Mohrungen were cleared, and in the reigning confusion the people in the rear of the train did not notice that the front end of the train had left the station. The whole train was too long for the engine in front to pull, so the train had been uncoupled in the middle and the train conductor had unobtrusively given the signal to move off.

In the evening a locomotive arrived with four railway men aboard. They had escaped from Zichenau at the last minute and had already been three days under way without eating and were dead tired. Nevertheless, they were prepared to take the rest of the train to Dirschau. Scarcely had they been fed, the engine moved off under a rain of sparks. It was a weak, elderly engine, with poor brown coal, and had to keep stopping to make steam. On one of these occasions they were fired on across a snow-covered field from the edge of a wood without anything coming near the wagons. Dorothea Gerlitzki thought she saw soldiers in white snow smocks. Some of the frightened refugees wanted to quickly get off from the far side of the train, but then the train moved on and they seemed to have escaped the danger.

In the engine cab at the front the four Zichenauer railway men took it in turns, two working and two sleeping. Franz Koscyk, 62, stood on the driver's platform at the window and fought against his overwhelming fatigue. His eyes kept closing. He failed to notice that the steam pressure was falling and that they were gradually losing speed. Karl Weitenbach, the stoker, had his shovel in his arms as he dozed.

Franz Koscyk stared at the snowy landscape in the night, over which there was a pale light. Gradually the black tracks in front of him curved in a wide dead straight alley. It was a summer evening, the leaves of the tall birches on both sides hung quite still. It was warm and he was only wearing his shirt and trousers. Suddenly a thick, dark shape appeared in front of him in which glow-worms were moving to and fro. The track made a curve, but so sharply he too turned to make the bend, his feet taking him straight into the bushes. Then something hit him rather hard on the forehead.

Karl Weitenbach woke with a frightful pain in his chest. His ribs had run up against the shovel handle. He could not breathe for a moment. Then he crawled over to his colleague and shook him. Outside there was screaming, cries for help, cries for medical orderlies. The stoker cautiously looked out and then fell unconscious from pain onto the railway tracks.

They had driven into the back of a stationary hospital train. There was not much to be seen, only that the last two wagons had been knocked off the tracks. Their slow speed had prevented a greater disaster. In the penultimate wagon of the refugee train they had only noticed a sharp bump. Dorothea Gerlitzki was knocked against those standing in front of her, without causing any pain. Most people jumped out of the wagon thinking that the Ivans were there.

Slowly they all calmed down and climbed back aboard, as soldiers said that the damage would soon be removed. Grünhagen Station, they said, was only a few hundred metres away. They waited patiently until long past midnight. Then they had to get off. A recovery train was coming and would take them all on. Tired and freezing the refugees made their way along the track and camped on the platform. No train came. Instead, early on Tuesday morning the Russians arrived. They fired with machine guns and tank guns into the waiting mass, which dispersed screaming. Russians soldiers drove the fleeing people back together and had then assemble on the road. All men in uniform were taken aside, after which they and also the civilians had all their valuables, especially rings and watches, removed. Trembling, the women waited for what was about to happen.

Some of the Russian soldiers shouted: 'Davai – damoi, davai – damoi' and then chased them along the road to the south. They could not turn back home. For Dorothea Gerlitzki and her three children this was a 70–80 kilometre march on foot.

Sunday the 21st January 1945, at about 0700 hours in Allenstein. The Russians were only seven kilometres from the town. The District Leader, the town mayor and District Leader of the NSV got together in the District Headquarters. They discussed the result of the latest telephonic communication with Königsberg: evacuation transport for Allenstein is not important. Nobody knows what to do except wait.

Towards 1400 hours the District Leader tried once more and this time received a less certain reply. The evacuation of the civilian population could begin. However, there was no transport available. The station was empty. All available wagons had been commandeered by the NSKK regimental commander for Ortelsburg days before, presumably for the evacuation of the population there. The owners of a few carts had long since attached themselves to various treks and left the town.

Nevertheless, it was possible early that afternoon to send a goods train to Allenstein. The station was crowded with people, who since morning had pressed on the ice-cold platforms. Loaded with misshapen bundles of bedding, suitcases, boxes and rucksacks, they stormed the train and consequently blocked the way. It was 1800 hours before the train was finally loaded and ready to leave. Lots of luggage was left behind on the platform, especially empty handcarts, perambulators and sledges that had hampered the crowd.

Karl Becker stood with his wife and his 10- and 13-year-old daughters on the platform and watched the departing train disappointedly. Two years earlier he had lost a leg and a hand in Russia and was back home after convalescence, where he ran a small tobacco business. They had first come to the station that afternoon and had only just got as far as the platform.

When the next train arrived at about 2000 hours, a frightful scrimmage broke out. Becker was angry because a whole horde of newcomers had come in from the side and pushed in front of them. Among them was administrative assistant Hildegarde Aminde with her 81-year-old father and 71-year-old mother. They had only got away from their house on the Hangsee that afternoon. Laden with suitcases and a bundle of bedding, they had to go three kilometres to Allenstein and then through the town to the station. For two hours they had waited patiently in the cold on the loading ramp in the goods station until the sudden announcement: 'Everyone to the main station!' In the crush they had to leave their bedding bundle behind and then the women discovered that the old man had disappeared.

Hildegarde Aminde was able to get her mother into a goods wagon and at the last minute was able to get herself into the next wagon. Behind her a young woman was pushing three young children into the wagon. Hildegarde Aminde just got the last one in her arms and looked around when the train moved off. The young woman made a helpless gesture, being stuck in the crowd. 'I'll come after!' she called to her crying children. It was 2230 hours.

The Beckers were now standing right forward on the ramp. They would certainly get on the next train. In all five were supposed to come, but no more arrived.

At 2245 hours something crashed in the direction of the town centre. Several voices started crying hysterically: 'Air raid alarm!' Becker looked at his wife. 'That was a mortar. Ivan could be here in a few hours. We must get out of here. We will not get away by train.'

They pushed themselves to the side and got away easily as they had little luggage. The old soldier had explained that they could only take food and clothing with them, as everything else was ballast.

A railway policeman ran excitedly here and there on the tracks trying to prevent the people from crossing them. Then the light went out and a dreadful screaming arose that, however, soon died down as nothing further happened.

The Beckers got away from the swarm of people that were pressing into the station bunker or towards the sheds in the goods station, where at least shelter from the snow and cold could be found. Through the dirty windows one could see the mass of soldiers and civilians making themselves comfortable between the piles of luggage. In one corner a vast iron stove rumbled pleasantly. At the bar an NSV Sister and a member of the Party were serving ersatz coffee. Becker was not going to let himself be deceived by the sense of false security.

'We have to get out of here. On the road to the north – even if we have to go to Elbing on foot.'

Allenstein was the seat of South Prussian Government. Government President Schmidt was at this time practically no longer functioning. Connection with the other towns was broken. Most of the Sunday he had been on the telephone to Königsberg, but this had not led to anything. He took action on two occasions: at 2100 hours he prevented the District Leader from paralysing the public utilities so as not to disturb the loading at the station. At about 2300 hours he had then done this himself when the lights also went out at the railway station. Shortly before he had called Deputy Gauleiter Dargel in Königsberg and informed him that the District Leader had decamped as the first shells exploded. The fate of the population still remaining in the town with the mayor bothered neither Schmidt nor Dargel particularly: 'All that remains is for the population to go off on foot.' More important for Schmidt was Dargel's agreement that he should now move his seat of government to Seeburg, about 35 kilometres northeast of Allenstein.

Ten minutes later Government President Schmidt was sitting with five of his officials in a vehicle and driving to Seeburg. The refugees on the roads respectfully made way for them. Next morning these gentlemen reached Braunsberg on the Frisches Haff lagoon – 100 kilometres northwest of Allenstein.

The only responsible person to remain behind was Mayor Schidat. He placed himself at the head of a long train of inhabitants that would have to flee on foot. With perambulators, handcarts and carrying suitcases, they went through the icy night to Guttstadt, 27 kilometres to the northeast. Many gave up soon after leaving Allenstein and had to turn back. Others remained in the villages on the way or had at least to take long pauses. The majority marched on patiently and silently between the ever increasing number of trek wagons abandoned on the roadside.

Berta Rubenbauer had already been several hours in the queue of trek wagons. She could hardly feel her feet any longer. Behind came her 17-year-old daughter on a farmer's hay wagon with her 85-year-old mother and the little hand luggage for which they had found the necessary space. During one of the numerous stops an almost empty Army truck drew up alongside her. The soldiers yielded to their pleas and picked up as many pedestrians as possible. The Rubenbauers went on like this to the next station and then from there by goods train to Bartenstein.

The Beckers were luckier as they caught an empty ammunition truck that took them to Heiligenbeil on the Frisches Haff lagoon.

But also the others that had to trudge on reached relative safety. At the Wadanga River they passed the main front line, where the *Grossdeutschland*

Panzer Division would yet hold on for another week. Among the many others on foot moving between the military vehicles and the trek wagons from Allenstein to the northeast, doggedly and silently dragging their few belongings over the icy country roads, were the inmates of the Allenstein Women's Prison: petty thieves, illicit butchers, women that had opened their mouths too wide and some whose relatives had been involved in the 20th July 1944 plot.

Already that afternoon they noticed that the prison staff had lost interest in their charges. There reigned a constant coming and going, bags and boxes were brought into the prison and stored in the washhouse. Towards 1900 hours the prisoners had had to parade in the corridor with blankets and eating utensils. One of the wardresses handed out their civilian clothing, but they were not allowed to change. The women were cheered by the nervousness of the staff. Now that the Russians were coming, things would be different. There was no evening meal before going on the road. They were led to the road at about 2300 hours and then suddenly the escorting officials vanished. Some women turned back again. They preferred to free themselves rather than walk about outside in the night and cold, and perhaps even be shot by mistake.

Shortly after midnight three Volkssturm men tramped through the now empty town: Alfred Springer, Hermann Koschinski and Paul Harder. They should have been defending the Masuren Settlement, but there was no ammunition there and they had been sent home. They wanted to spend the night in their homes and meet up again in the morning at the 'Kronprinz' pub to discuss what they should do.

As Springer got near his home, the wife of a neighbour came towards him. 'Your wife went to the station. I don't know if she has come back. I am going to my cellar. The people are suffocating in the station bunker,' she said, and hurried on.

Springer's house was completely dark. He suddenly had no wish to spend the night there. He looked around the cleared rooms by the light of his pocket torch. In the dining room he found a bottle of beer, bread and bacon, and after he had had his supper he moved on. He met the other two at the 'Kronprinz'. The same had happened to them.

They were unable to agree as to what was the best thing for them to do to get out of this mess, when quite clearly machine-gun fire was added to the bursting of mortars. Shocked, they ran off in the opposite direction, over fences and walls and through backyards until they reached Kaiserstrasse at the Labour Office. Panting, they lumbered down the steps to the air raid shelter. Shortly afterwards three soldiers came from the railway station and took up a position on the corner of Bahnhoffstrasse and Kaiserstrasse, setting up a machine gun in the entrance to the Commerzbank looking down Kaiserstrasse. Springer wanted to go up to them and find out something about the situation, but just then the sound of tanks could be heard at some distance. One of the soldiers picked up the machine gun and said, shaking his head at the Volkssturm man, 'We can't handle that!' Slowly, without turning round, they went away down Bahnhofstrasse. Springer envied them their long, shapeless, padded coats, for he was cold in his short jacket. When he returned with the news to the cellar, Harder was of the opinion that they were perhaps German tanks. Koschinski thought as Springer did, it would be safer if they ran off. They grabbed their briefcases and packs and went past the station along the deserted Wardangerstrasse towards Jadden. Springer was only a hundred metres from his wife when he passed the station bunker.

Frau Springer was asleep sitting on her suitcase. Shortly before 0200 hours she was woken up roughly as dozens of people crammed into the already overfilled cellar. Some men called out: 'Stay outside! Close the door, can't you see that it is completely full here?'

The call stopped immediately as Russian swearing came from the door and a repeated: 'Davai! Davai!' was heard. The Russians had occupied the town and it was 0200 hours.

The train from Königsberg was due at 0202 hours. Signalman Kleinke had already set the signal at go – the train was reported to be on time – when he was hit by a bullet from a Russian machine gun. A Red Army man had taken him to be a soldier.

At 0215 hours the train from Königsberg, overfilled with refugees, arrived, but before the people with window seats had scraped the ice from the windows, the doors were torn open by Soviet soldiers. Firstly the men were hauled out and gathered together, and immediately began the long journey into captivity, together with captured soldiers. Nobody had asked them whether they were soldiers or civilians. The women were driven into the station bunker, where there was no longer anyone to look after them.

By 1700 hours on the Monday afternoon Frau Springer could no longer take any more of the bunker. The stink alone was unbearable. There was no water or cooking facilities. Several women had already slipped out with their children to go back to their homes.

She had joined up with an elderly couple from Gymnasiumstrasse who wanted to try to flee over the fields. They got out of the cellar without difficulty and strolled unobtrusively to the level crossing. A Russian ran towards them with a machine gun across his stomach, but he seemed to be interested in something else rather than concerning himself with these poor figures. He spat a sunflower seed at their feet as he went past and said something that sounded like a curse. They carried on, climbed over the signal cables behind a shed and reached the fields. Something cracked close behind them and they threw themselves down in the snow, but nothing further happened. They went on and next morning reached Guttstadt.

Others tried the same thing next day, but were caught by the Russians in a nearby village and had to go back to Allenstein on foot. There the Russians separated the fit young women from the old ones and put them in the prison, ten to a single cell, before they were driven off on a march of several days on foot to Zichenau, where they were loaded on trains for forced labour in Russia. Most of them were to spend years in the anthracite coal mines of the Donetz Basin.

Chapter 4

The Fall of Elbing

The fate of East Prussia was decided during the week of the 22nd to the 29th January. While the German 4th Army was able to slow down the Russian advance on its southern flank, the enemy broke through to the north towards the Frisches Haff lagoon in its rear. For over a week Captain Michail Diatshenko and his crew only had a few hours outside their tank. They hardly noticed how painful some of their bones had become. They were winning and they had as much schnaps as they wanted. The town of Osterode lay burning behind them. To the Frisches Haff lagoon in the north was still 70 kilometres as the crow flies. At the command conference on the evening of the 22nd January, Captain Diatshenko heard himself say: 'I would like to take over the assault troop to the north, Comrade Commander.'

At sunrise on the 23rd January he had set off with nine T–34s. His task was to drive north until he came up against determined resistance. They had already done this a dozen times before and seldom had the pleasure in it lasted more than an hour or perhaps two.

On this morning it had already been light for some time, and they had put at least 20 kilometres behind them without having been fired at by the Fascists. They were driving along a country road on which hundreds of horse-drawn carts were moving. Comrade Diatshenko was experienced. He had given his crews strict instructions to drive carefully, not to shoot but to wait until they made room for him. Their patience was hard pressed. Often the farm wagons only made room reluctantly. Many fell out in giving way and their drivers, mainly women, raised threatening fists behind them. But it also happened that the women waved them on. Twice they over-took German military convoys, which drove to the side and waited until the Russians had gone past, the soldiers taking no notice of them. Were they blind? Towards noon they drove through Preussisch Holland. Captain Diatshenko let the sweat fall in streams down his face. For two hours no one had said a word in the tank. They carefully made their way through the traffic in the jam-packed town. Even when a tank crushed a two-wheeled cart, not a shot was fired.

They were already a few hundred metres outside the town when Captain Diatshenko checked his crews. All answered except two. He opened his hatch and looked back and in fact two tanks were missing. They had perhaps gone astray in the jam-packed town.

'Should we turn round, comrade?' asked the driver.

'Nonsense, we drive on to the north.'

At the same moment there was an explosion. Shells exploded near him to the right and left on the snow-covered fields. The civilians on the wagons in front of them began screaming and throwing themselves into the roadside ditches. The firing stopped. Apparently the Germans had become aware that they were killing their own people. The captain tried simply to break away. They had been spotted and something was bound to happen, but nothing did. By 1600 hours the seven tanks were in front of Grunau, eight kilometres from the centre of Elbing. They were wedged in between a number of other vehicles, for this was the only southern entrance to the town through the anti-tank barrier. They shuffled forward metre by metre until at last they could drive into the town at the normal speed.

Captain Diatshenko was ill. It was as if the nerves in his stomach had knotted. That could not be correct; before him was a full tram and the shops on the edge of the street were open. Everywhere were pedestrians and civilian cars. The scarcely darkened street lighting had been switched on. Was this no-man's-land, were they sitting in a trap, or was the war already won? They drove doggedly on in a northerly direction. They came to a large square with a building that looked like a town hall. They drove to the right of it and came to an even larger square. Captain Diatshenko looked at his compass. Opposite a broad street went straight north.

'If it goes on like this, we will soon be in Sweden' said the driver of the third tank. At that moment there were several explosions. 'Tank Seven has been hit,' came a message from behind. 'Open fire!' shouted Captain Diatshenko. The tanks fired with all their guns aimlessly into the surroundings. The street was swept clean. They pressed forward at top speed, and now fire was coming from all sides. Before they were out of the town another tank was left behind. About seven kilometres north of the town they reached a vast area which clearly rose above the snowy landscape, the frozen-over Frisches Haff lagoon. The Soviets wheeled off the road and took up positions in some empty buildings. They stayed there three days until their comrades picked them up.

The army radio auxiliary Alice Bendig was about to leave her home at this moment to go on duty. In the corridor she met a neighbour. He had already finished working in the tax office and had run past the grey Minster. He was quite out of breath. 'Now we are in a mess. And two days ago they told me there was absolutely no danger!'

Alice Bendig left the man standing and ran back into her apartment. 'Maria, pack a few things and take the children. Go to my mother in Vogelsang!' They would be safe out there on the Frisches Haff lagoon. Maria, who had been with the Bendig household since Frau Bendig's husband had been called up and looked after the four- and six-year-old children, was an older, simple woman from the Danzig plain. She just nodded and got on with her job. Alice Bendig ran back to the street. The ghost seemed to have gone. She made her way through the hastening people and vehicles in the crowded streets and reached the Alten Markt in a fully crowded tram that was already moving off. In her office, the operations unit of the *Feldherrnhalle* Division in the Unger Barracks, was in an uproar. The female colleague that she was to relieve had vanished together with the other civilian officials and on the switchboard candles were burning like on a Christmas tree.

For three days and three nights Alice Bendig was unable to get away from the switchboard. The defence of the city was feverishly being directed through here. On paper three divisions had been foreseen. In fact Colonel Schöpffer, the city battle commandant, had only the replacement units of the *Feldherrenhalle* Division in about regimental strength, a Volkssturm battalion and a Volkssturm battery with 88mm guns from the Schichau Works at his disposal. In the end this amounted in all to about 10,000 men because various regiments and combat units had withdrawn from outside the city. They were sufficient to defend the inner city from well inside the anti-tank ditches. Anti-tank units were stationed in the empty buildings and machine-gun nests established, while the artillery observers occupied places on the rooftops of apartment blocks and the barracks.

Mayor Dr Leser did not leave his office on this decisive 23rd January. Shortly after the tanks had broken through, the District Leadership had ordered Evacuation Level 3 (all civilians and persons not required for the defence were to leave the city immediately via their local assembly points). Dr Leser looked about him. Apart from a few old officials who did not wish to commit themselves to the stress of the flight, the town hall was quite empty. Across Friedrich-Wilhelm-Platz civilians were making their way in droves with handcarts, suitcases and haversacks towards the railway station and the Elbing Bridge. For most of them there was no stopping them any longer and no one was asking for a permit to leave.

Shortly before midnight the District Leader called again: 'The evacuation order is rescinded. Everyone has to stay!'

Dr Leser said cautiously that his people had long since gone.

'Gauleiter Forster has told me that he will have every official shot that does not remain at his post!'

On the 24th January it was still possible to evacuate the hospitals and the prison to Danzig, but during the course of the day all order was lost. Refugees, withdrawing units, staffs, stragglers from the east and south streamed through endlessly, choking the only bridge leading to the west over the Elbing River. Unwanted items discarded by the refugees – suitcases, boxes, bedding, typewriters, small items of furniture, items of clothing – were strewn across the streets. It was a dismal train of old, totally exhausted people, crying children, young women with screaming babies.

In front of the Unger Barracks an officers' patrol stopped every Wehrmacht vehicle, hauled fleeing soldiers off and let aboard the mothers and children waiting on the roadside. But only a few got out of the city this way. Cold and hunger caused many to despair. They squatted in empty buildings and apartments in the hope that it would soon all be over.

On Thursday the 25th January two naval petty officers appeared at the Mayor's office. They had the task of taking two newly completed torpedo boats from the Schichau Works to Eckenförde via Pillau. 'We can take quite a few refugees with us,' said one of them, 'But we are leaving in about three hours.'

The news immediately spread among the Elbingers and thousands stormed the Elbing River bank to await embarkation at the torpedo boat slipway. At the same time the Russians began firing on the town with Stalin-Organs. Some of the rockets landed among the waiting crowd, leaving several dead and wounded while the remainder ran about screaming. The shipyard staff let go the mooring lines in the fear that the boats would no longer be able to leave, but about four hundred people managed to get on board before the boats moved down the Elbing River towards the Frisches Haff lagoon.

On the 26th January the Russians had already thrust through on a broad line to the Frisches Haff near Tolkemit, east of Elbing, so that now only the Frische Nehrung strip connected East Prussia with the west. To the south and west the Russians stood between Fichthorst and Zeyer. The city was enclosed on three sides. At the Drausensee Lake, a nature reserve, a Russian 170mm battery had been deployed and was firing ceaselessly at the city. Even the remaining free part of the Vistula marshes northwest of the town lay under enemy fire. The stream of refugees ceased.

Several artillery hits had put the electricity plant out of action, and the electric pumps serving the water supply were also not working. The ever increasing fires spread unimpeded.

The fire brigade had disposed of all its vehicles. When several of the state's own fire engines had had to be returned to Danzig, the brave lads with their vehicles had simply packed up. Also, with the exception of the air raid doctor, there was no longer a single civilian doctor left in the city. And since the departure of the torpedo boats, the whole district administration had disappeared.

On the 28th January the artillery fire eased up noticeably. The Soviets had to aim their guns to the east and west instead of the north. To the east three divisions of the German 4th Army were thrusting into the Russian pincers to clear the army rear and to re-establish connection with the west. In the west the German 7th Panzer Division had started a counterattack.

Mayor Dr Leser and Colonel Schöpffer drove to the left-hand bank of the Elbing River to watch the liberation. They met an advance guard of five tanks. After a brief greeting to the tank men, Schöpffer and Dr Leser made a short drive of inspection further south. Within a few kilometres they were already back under enemy fire and had to turn back home on the ice of the river under cover of the buildings. The situation was anything but rosy. Almost everywhere the Russians had gained ground and were in the suburbs, where the defenders had to withdraw from building to building.

They made their way back past the rubble of shelled buildings. In the city park the 'peoples' kitchen' run by the tireless NSV helpers was still in action. In front of the long barrack block stood a queue of soldiers, distraught women and children taking their portion of potato soup in all manner of receptacles. The Kreissparkasse Bank opposite the town hall was burning brightly.

When Dr Leser reached the town hall, there were two bright red double-decker buses, from which a crowd of people, civilians and uniformed, were climbing out. The buses came from Danzig and had driven past the Russians under cover of the tanks of the 7th Panzer Division. Some one-hundred-per-cent fighter to the last in the Danzig Gau Headquarters had arranged this transport. Among the occupants were Elbing's complete fire brigade, three doctors, several nursing sisters, policemen, a platoon of Volkssturm with Panzerfausts and a number of Party officials, whom apparently Danzig wanted to get rid of.

The most important person among these arrivals was the returning director of the Elbing Electricity Works. He set off immediately for the works with some workers. And shortly after nightfall something happened which nobody had foreseen: the lights went on all over the city. The Russians reacted immediately. A hail of fire descended on the city, as if Elbing was an illuminated target, and Colonel Schöpffer had to send two motorcyclists to the electricity works to have the power switched off again.

After the Soviets had occupied the suburb of Grubenhagen on the left bank of the Elbing River for the second time on the 30th January, Elbing was hermetically sealed in. For three whole days the Soviet 48th Army was under severe pressure from the attacks of the German 4th Army and had to withdraw about 30 kilometres. One day it looked as if the German troops could break through south of Elbing to Marienburg and thus break the ring around East Prussia. But the German attack became stuck well before Elbing, as the Soviets threw several corps and five tank brigades into the endangered front and finally drove the German troops back.

Alice Bendig sat indefatigably at her switchboard and connected with the combat headquarters. There were now only a few lines open since the Russians had concentrated their fire on the city centre. From her window she saw how a lieutenant and a few NCOs from the invalid company dug a mass grave in the garden between the barrack walls and the barracks and buried 25 of those killed there. It was not much more than a gesture, as dead soldiers and civilians were lying everywhere in the streets. Alice Bendig only once went back to her home. It had been plundered and the cellar was full of strangers. She was pleased that her children had got away in time.

There were about 20,000 refugees and homeless persons in the cellars of Elbing. Those who had found shelter in the deep brewery cellars or in bunkers were somewhat safer than those living in permanent fear of the building over their heads being fired on and having to find shelter elsewhere.

The worst torment was the lack of water. They boiled snow and the brackish water from the fire buckets. The bravest armed themselves with buckets and made their way to the brewery, whose deep wells were still intact, while others sought to get water from holes in the ice.

Mothers with their crying children fought their way dead tired to the barracks and hospitals to get at least some milk or porridge.

In the cellar of a private house opposite the Catholic Church were sitting people from Baumgart, which was very close to Elbing.

'It is safer in the city,' someone had said to the three old men and seven women when the Wehrmacht cleared the place. They had not dared to go any further and join the stream of refugees going west. By candlelight and with the provisions they had brought with them, they had already been sitting a week in the gloomy hole waiting for the storm to blow away. The children hardly stopped crying, wanted to go upstairs where one could hear the voices of German soldiers in the empty rooms. They could not look outside because of the air raid blinds over the windows and could only hear the sounds of fighting getting nearer. Machine-gun fire and exploding shells were close to the house.

A voice shouted down the cellar steps: 'Everyone out, it's burning!'

The women began to wail, the children to scream. Two of the old men went first to look around. Thick smoke met them on the stairs. They could just make out the holes in the open front door, where shadows were moving. Then there were some shots and earth-brown figures climbed over the bodies of the two old men.

'Germanski Soldat? Germanski Soldat?' they overwhelmed the women, behind whose skirts the children and the remaining old man hid. They went back up the stairs, where there were a few more shots, then everything was still.

On the morning of the 4th February artillery fire woke the mayor from his sleep. He quickly got dressed. He had hung his brown uniform in the wardrobe days before, and now wore his officer's uniform as a captain of the reserve. When he came down into the cellar of the building, there were several officials sitting there from the city administration and refugees. In the cellars of the new building, the District Headquarters, in which the police and air raid centre were housed, he found no one. Nobody knew anything.

On a desk stood the telephone with the only still intact connection with Danzig. Angrily he lifted up the receiver. At the Danzig end naval Captain Hartmann answered, who informed him in flowery language that the newly declared commander in chief of Army Group *Vistula*, Heinrich Himmler, had in a conference at Marienburg shown him on a big map the direction of attack of several new panzer divisions that would stabilise the situation. In any case Elbing would be held as a bridge between East and West Prussia. Dr Leser only said: 'That is very nice', and put the phone down.

That Elbing was lost was certain. The question was only whether one could get out of this mess. Towards noon there was a pause in the firing. The Russians sent a captured German NCO with a demand for the immediate surrender of the city. Colonel Schöpffer wrote: 'Acknowledged. Schöpffer' on the paper and sent the man back.

The pause in the firing was used by occupants of the Unger Barracks in Königsbergerstrasse to withdraw to the Gymnasium, which lay about 600 metres from the bank of the Elbing River. Alice Bendig made the journey in an armoured reconnaissance vehicle, while most of the soldiers sought to make their way on foot. Later the occupants of the town hall and the command post of the town commandant also moved to the school.

Communication with the fighting units was by means of a communications platoon which was constantly busy repairing the shot-up telephone lines. There was no longer a switchboard. The brave signals auxiliary was assisting Regimental Medical Officer, Dr Kretzschmar, who could hardly stand on his feet from fatigue. She applied bandages, gave injections, comforted, and closed eyes whenever someone died. When she could take this no longer she slipped down to the side entrance in Ziesestrasse. There formerly the janitor had stood and guarded the big school door during classroom breaks to ensure that no one escaped into the city. Now there was only dirt and smoke as the Russians reduced the city with artillery and machine-gun fire.

On the way there Alice Bendig had seen wounded lying on the street. She crept out under cover of the building's walls. She went to the first one, took his belt and hooked on to it, dragging him centimetre by centimetre to the school. Hardly had she drawn the attention of the medical orderly to him than she was back out again and bringing the next one back to safety in the same manner. Alice Bendig worked doggedly, hauling in man after man until a Soviet sniper spotted her. She threw herself down under a stairway entrance while close above shot after shot crashed into the door panels. The biting smell of the explosive bullets filled her nostrils. With a mighty leap she crossed over to the other side of the street and vanished into the entrance of an air raid shelter.

The cellar was full of people: old people, women and children crouching apathetically along the walls in the candlelight. On a pile of coal lay several wounded soldiers begging for water. One whispered to her: 'Get out and leave us here to die. Everything is over.'

The stink was frightful. Alice Bendig made her way back and saw that the northern gable of the Gymnasium had been torn away by a heavy shell. The tram power lines were lying on the street. Everywhere there were glass splinters and rubble, clouds of smoke and ear-shattering din. The Russians sent several more messengers that for various reasons had to turn back again. Once it was a group of inhabitants from Russian-occupied Nordstadt. Among them was a woman who had been raped several times by the Russians and who had been let go again. Later she was able to save herself and got on a boat to the west from Danzig in March.

On the morning of the 9th February Colonel General Weiss called Colonel Schöpffer and told him that he could break out to the northwest. Himmler had ordered a big bridgehead to be built on the west bank of the Elbing River opposite the Schichau Works through which the forces in the city could be brought. No one in the city believed this possible.

The soldiers were still fighting for every building, for every street. From the Heinrich-von-Plauen-School came a call for help: the Russians had occupied the buildings around it and were preparing to storm the field hospital. At about 1800 hours a wild screaming broke out in the school. 2,400 wounded and four doctors with their orderlies were subjected to a hail of shots from the attacking Russians. No one has explained their fate.

The defenders of Elbing no longer had any choice; they had to abandon the badly injured and the thousands of helpless civilians. Several could not take this and shot themselves, like the battery commander of a flak position in Lärchwalde. Others turned around and simply ran into the Russian fire.

When Colonel Schöpffer broke out with his staff at 1800 hours, a tank and two armoured cars were to shoot the way clear past the big Elementary School, but the attack was checked by the fire from the Russians. The only way now was through back yards and allotments. Unit after unit trickled through the complex terrain. The noise of fighting increased on all sides as the remains of the German units disengaged from the enemy and fought their way to the river bank. The Russians had not yet discovered the Germans' intention, but the fire was so strong that they kept having to take cover for longer periods.

The crossing point on the river lay in the glow of a burning wood store. After several futile attempts to construct a raft out of planks and beams, a sapper sergeant came up with the idea of floating a coal barge that lay there. The sappers raised the anchor with a frightful din. As a towing rope they used a shot-up cable that swimmers took across to the far side.

Alice Bendig had joined her soldiers and had met Colonel Schöpffer's group in the allotments. The light from the fires around them threw ghostly shadows. Again and again shells burst and machine-gun fire whistled round their ears. The young woman was armed to the teeth – she would sell her life as dearly as possible.

Silently the soldiers fought their way forwards. Suddenly a captain fell near the female auxiliary. It was only a graze. She pulled him back to his senses and supported him along. There was no point in calling for a doctor. She could still hear the cries of the wounded. There was nothing to be seen except fires. As she then found a doctor she helped him along as best she could. It was almost morning when Alice Bendig crossed the river and set her feet on the other bank. She had only gone a few hundred metres when a shell took off the left hand of a sergeant near her. She helped bandage the man and set off again. Nothing seemed important anymore. It was all vague, quite frightful.

Bargeful after bargeful was pulled across the river. Towards 0500 hours – about 1,200 men of the fighting units and 500 wounded had been brought across – there was a nasty surprise. The vanguard had entered a barracks that was not occupied by the 7th Panzer Division as expected, but by the Russians. The Russians were chased out with wild shooting. Later German artillery fired into the crowd moving northwest when a young artillery observer mistook them for Russians.

Again there were dead and wounded.

By midday it was all over. Among the last troops on the ferry there had also been a number of men, women and children from the cellars of Elbing. Then a Soviet anti-tank gun sank the barge.

About 4,200 men made their way to freedom. On their way to the north-west, towards Danzig, they could still hear the firing behind them in the carnage of Elbing, but they could no longer hear the cries of the women and children in the cellars.

In Danzig they encountered a life full of activity like that they had known in Elbing before the 23rd January; the trams were running, people were strolling along the Langgasse and shopping. The cinemas were showing the same film as in Elbing, *Opfergang,* and the refugees were blocking the streets to the harbour. Several buildings were already empty. Fritz Leser had a fearful feeling and he avoided looking into the cellars.

In the Life Hussars' barracks in Danzig-Langfuhr a small celebration was organised for Alice Bendig, who was awarded the Iron Cross. Two weeks later she was on her way to Hungary, where she experienced the end of the war. She only found her children again long after the war.

Chapter 5

The German 4th Army's Breakout

Army Group *Mitte*, which was later re-named Army Group *Nord* under Colonel General Reinhardt, consisted of the 3rd Panzer Army, which was fighting in Samland and in front of Königsberg, and the 4th Army, which was involved in the Heiligenbeil cauldron with its back to the Frisches Haff lagoon.

Without waiting for Hitler's permission, on the evening of the 26th January Colonel General Reinhardt had withdrawn the front to the Alle Line, as a result of which Hitler immediately sacked the general, who had been wounded the previous day. Meanwhile the commander of the 4th Army had made an even more drastic decision: while abandoning the southern flank at Königsberg, he wanted to break out to the west with all his available forces. In this unstable battlefield he would take the majority of the surrounded German troops with the civilian population in the middle and fight his way through to Pomerania.

The plan was quite Utopian, bringing a vast number of soldiers and civilians through the Russians in a running battle in an already uncertain area, but at that time it really seemed the only chance of avoiding total destruction. In any case the announcement of the plan filled the troops and the civilian population with new hope.

The 28th Light Division under General König, the 170th Infantry Division under General Hass and the 131st Infantry Division under General Schulze would form the wedge and break through between the besieged towns of Elbing and Osterode to the Vistula. On the 26th January these formations reached their start point after making a forced march right through East Prussia, and immediately struck out, being able to force their way deep into the flanks of the surprised Soviets. The Soviet 90th Guards Division was cut off for days. But about 30 kilometres from Liebenau the German attack came to a standstill. General Hossbach was lacking the two divisions that he had been obliged to hand over to the 3rd Panzer Army on the Army Group's orders shortly before. The Soviets threw the German troops back towards Mehlsack and the ring around the 4th Army was now drawing tighter by the day.

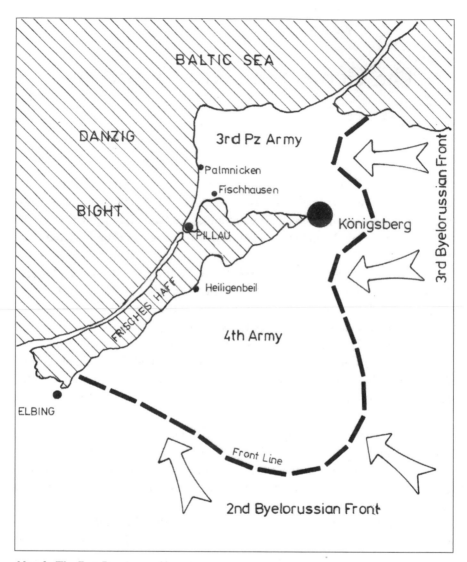

Map 2. The East Prussian cauldron

These events had a devastating effect on refugee movements. Towards the end of January almost all the main roads were blocked to civilians. The fleeing population in the course of making their way north to the lagoon were first forced to return to an east–west direction and must now take to the flimsy roads and tracks with their heavy wagons, soon losing their sense of direction. In the western part of the cauldron many treks became involved in the fighting, suffering heavy losses, or found themselves unexpectedly behind the Russian lines again.

In Friedland, 67 kilometres southeast of Königsberg, Farmer Emil Mischke had already been following the troop movement for the breakout attempt since the 23rd January. Freezing cold and stamping his feet, his hands stuck deep into his greatcoat pockets, he had seen the German formations as they rolled through this little town towards the west. Under his much-too-tight military greatcoat the stocky mid fifty-year-old was wearing the uniform of a Party official.

'That is now all that can crawl out of their homes – and we are watching the retreat,' he said to District Group Leader Döbel standing next to him. They both came from Böttchersdorf, nine kilometres away. Mischke was commander of Volkssturm Company 4/210 *Friedland*, which consisted of inhabitants of Böttchersdorf and Friedland.

'Just a while ago it was said in the Wehrmacht Report that Allenstein had fallen,' said Döbel and one could see clearly how helpless he looked.

'I've said it before, it's the last ones that the dogs bite,' answered Mischke and went back into his guardroom. In mid-January Mischke had parted from his wife and ten-year-old son. He was even a little proud of his role in the Volkssturm, although in civilian life he was not exactly a nobody. In Böttchersdorf he had eleven officials working for him. He was trustee of the Winter Help Organisation, registrar of births, marriages and deaths, representative of the NSV, he issued ration cards and animal slaughter certificates, and organised Party events. His responsibilities had increased three-fold in October when refugees from Tilsit-Ragnit had increased the population of Böttchersdorf by 1,200 souls and 650 horses. He could not understand how everything could be blown away with one blast.

When the District Leader from Friedland appeared that afternoon with a bottle of schnaps, in order to drink to final victory with him and the District Group Leader, he drank dutifully with them. It was all the same to him, and by evening he was dead drunk.

Next day things began to happen in a rush. That morning a commanding general stopped with his train and Friedland became the command post of the 50th Infantry Division. Hours later came the 61st Infantry Division and the Replacement Brigade *Hermann Göring*. Retreating troops swarmed through the town. Across the fields came soldiers armed with sticks, from which hung food bags. Rounding-up teams gathered them in and sent them back towards the front.

Mischke was a real soldier now. He was a Prussian and knew his duty. His company was guarding the railway bridges, the station and several other objects, apart from which there were several men assigned to traffic control. There was not much else left to him since all his men with driving licences had been taken away.

Indefatigably, he was on the way to inspect his sentries. At the station he met Captain Sauvant, the town commandant.

'Have you already taken your family to safety, Mischke?'

'I cannot do that before all the others!' replied Mischke, half sadly, half indignantly, and went on. Between the station and Aachenerstrasse he got hold of two soldiers that apparently wanted to slip away.

'Don't you want to defend the homeland any more?' he raged at them.

'What is the homeland here? The British and the Americans have ours, and that is where we are now going,' shouted one of them at him. Mischke was so taken aback that he let them go.

At noon his quartermaster, Klann, came back from a two-hour leave in Böttchersdorf. Mischke was close to tears, but he would have been a real swine if he had simply let his wife and ten-year-old son come too. From his point of view, this was defeatism. Finally the bridge was closed to civilians. Emil Mischke gave his heart a nudge and signed a pass with which the family could leave Friedland that evening.

Others were less duty conscious. Several of his Friedland Volkssturm men had simply filtered away during the course of the day. When next day, the 25th January, he held a headcount again, fifteen men were missing. Only the Böttchersdorfers remained faithful to him. The refugees seeking to leave made no sense, since the latest news that the Russians had reached Thorn and were well on the advance to Berlin in the west; they had crossed the Deime River and were moving on Königsberg. At the same time a Böttchersdorfer brought the news that Mischke's wife had driven off on a sledge towards Königsberg. 'That is almost into the arms of the Russians!' cried Mischke, holding his head with both hands. But he could do nothing for her. Now it was time to think about his own escape. He got hold of a supply wagon; as the Wehrmacht did not want to supply them, he turned to self-help. What was the point of the cheese factory at the station belonging to his duty area? Soon the wagon was loaded with butter, cheese and peas, as well as a freshly slaughtered pig. He commandeered the wagon to take the posts to the west and to wait there for their comrades.

That evening there was a scene at the Alle Bridge. There crowded hundreds of refugees from Allenburg, because the Wehrmacht sentries had not only rigidly blocked the roadway but also the footpaths and would not give way to requests or threats.

When Mischke arrived there, he recalled that he had been told at noon that no danger existed. Two hours later he persuaded the Wehrmacht to evacuate the town within half an hour. Old folk, women and children of all ages came up to him and complained about the Wehrmacht and the

Party. Very few of them had a wagon. Most carried hand baggage, pushed perambulators or even overloaded sledges.

'What if they shoot me!' called Emil Mischke. He took off his greatcoat to show his uniform, stood the military sentries to one side and channelled everyone across into a queue on the footpath. Next day Mischke wrote in his diary: 'No praying helped. The world kept turning and opened up the day of our misfortune.'

At roll call there were only 40 men. But they did not have to guard the railway bridges any more: they sank into the Alle River at 0930 hours. Consequently towards midday all the firemen were brought to him, 18 men that shortly afterwards drove off to the north with their fire engines. The noise of fighting came noticeably closer during the night. On the way to the cheese factory suddenly splinters flew past his ears. A battery of guns was being destroyed in the Schiller Park.

'Why do that?' wondered Mischke. On the way to the station settlement there were more explosions, this time shell bursts.

At this point Böttschersdorf finally broke up. Before being called up into the Volkssturm, Mischke had sat all night long putting together an evacuation list. On clean, blue-lined paper he had recorded all available horses and wagons and for each vehicle had written the names of those who would take it. He had secretively pressed it into Döbel's hand, as nothing urgent, to play down this example of a defeatist attitude.

When the breakout came, everyone only thought of himself. The bigger farmers packed armchairs and settees and all kinds of household goods into their wagons, instead of considering those who had to go on foot. Richard Döbel led the trek – he was one of the few who took other families in their wagons. Determinedly those on foot pulled their sledges and handcarts behind the horse-driven vehicles – mainly young women with children. Only a few old people dared attempt the march in the cold. Among them was Hermann. Since his retirement ten years earlier as a road worker he had been general handyman in the village. Hermann will do it well, it was said, and for a slice of bread and butter and a schnaps he had done things like a young man despite his 78 years. Nevertheless there was no room for him in a wagon with anyone. Farmer Ankermann said: 'You will get through all right. Ask the soldiers, they will certainly take you with them.'

Straight across the scarred ice of the nearby lake the Böttchersdorfers took the shortest way to Schönbruch, where they lost sight of each other in the press. Frau Mischke had already got through with her sledge the day before. On the 25th January neighbour Heise had called from the railway station to say his wife should come immediately because the railway employees were able to load their household goods and leave on the last train. The railway bridge in Friedland would then be blown up after it. Frau Mischke began to panic; if the bridge was being blown up that meant that the Russians must be in front of the gates. She called Michel, the Russian civilian busy in the yard, and made him get the sledge ready. She could not load much: the wooden box from the kitchen full of ham, some underclothing, three sets of bedding and a few blankets with her son settled between them. They set off at about noon. Michel took the reins. It seemed quite natural that the Russian would flee with them.

Much later it was discovered that the fate of such Russians – whether prisoners of war or forced labourers – was hardly any different from that of the Germans. Without exception they were sent to forced labour camps. The grounds for these inhuman measures lay in the erroneous assumption that these Russians had been impregnated with fascist ideology and that they had to be isolated. Already in 1941 Stalin had ordered that all prisoners of war must be treated as traitors.

Michel, Frau Mischke's Russian, was in a hurry. The trek wagons from other villages going before them had churned up the snow and ice with the dirt of the unmetalled road. The runners creaked in the sand and both towing horses had to work hard. Four year-old 'Fuchs', who as reserve horse was harnessed next to the towing horse on the right, took no pleasure in the whole thing and showed his impatience with pranks that kept holding them up.

At nightfall they came to a settlement on the road to Domnau. Frau Mischke ordered Michel to pull out of the convoy. She wanted to bed down here for the night. Michel began to complain, wanting to go on. Frau Mischke remained firm. The child needed his sleep and the horses a few hours' rest. Stubbornly she helped Michel to unharness the horses, then he took the little cloth bag with his possessions from the sledge, threw a strap over his shoulder and went off into the street to look for another wagon. There were many women that were having to drive alone and were more than thankful when someone took over the reins for them for a few hours.

She had to leave the horses out in the yard, while she was given a small unheated room. She got no rest that night. 'Fuchs' kept breaking free and she spent most of her time re-catching him. By morning she was so exhausted and frozen through – the boy only stood there howling – that Frau Mischke decided to turn back.

The return journey went slowly and she did not reach Stausee, 3½ kilometres from Böttchersdorf, until midday. There she met Eschmann coming towards her, only banging his hands together when she told him that she wanted to go back. Frau Mischke then overcame her fears and set off resolutely on her way once more.

Böttchersdorf seemed to be deserted. The yard was empty. There was nobody in the house, but it looked chaotic. All the cupboards were open and furniture thrown about. The radio was on in the living room playing marches at full volume. Frau Mischke did not bother to switch it off. She unharnessed and fed the horses. The wagon that had been loaded days before for the family's evacuation with china, underwear, clothing and jars of preserves had vanished. There was only a small cart loaded with fodder for the five horses. She loaded her things from the sledge on it. At about 1600 hours three soldiers came cautiously along the trench between the buildings, seeking cover in the yard and complaining about her presence. One helped her to heave the heavy box of ham onto the wagon, and then Frau Mischke drove off again towards the west. At the village exit two soldiers pushed Döbel's Frenchman on the wagon to drive it. He had apparently been working unconcernedly in the cow barn just as on any other day. The Frenchman finally made it home to his country. Döbel was taken by the Russians and died on the way to Siberia.

While Frau Mischke was leaving Böttchersdorf for the second time, Farmer Mischke was sitting in the cellar of the Friedlander Cheese Factory counting the explosions of Russian shells. One hour earlier he had gone to the Kommandantura. Apart from Captain Böhm, everyone had disappeared. Mischke made his report. 'Another one reporting: unit disbanded!' snarled the captain, leaving Mischke standing astonished before him.

'He had a thousand rights to complain,' murmured Mischke to a sergeant who was leaning exhausted against a wall in the room. 'But I have not lost my company! Its decimation was not my fault!' And with that the honest Volkssturm man stumped back under cover of the walls of buildings to the cheese factory to the last six of his company.

The explosions of the Russian shells were in the direction of the railway station, where there was an ammunition train. If that blew up, then it was good-bye to the cheese factory. His deputy, Klann, was having similar thoughts. Suddenly he said: 'Emil, the war is lost – we must get out of here.' Mischke nodded and stood up. One of the Friedlanders had found some bicycles and in less than two minutes the seven men pedalled away through the gate with all their might. Mischke had problems handling his because it would not steer straight and kept threatening to throw him off. Despite snow and ice they made good progress, inspired with the thought that their supply wagon was waiting for them in Postehnen. They had not eaten since the previous evening.

In Postehnen several of the houses were occupied by soldiers. There was no trace of their supply wagon. They found accommodation in a draughty stall.

Next day they continued their search for food and finally reached Domnau. Mischke found his battalion commander there and at last was able to unburden himself of his responsibility for the pitiful remains of his Volkssturm company. They were all given leave to look for their families. Captain Laza said that they should not let themselves be caught. The area was swimming with military police and other persons that thought that something could be saved with 'captured heroes'. Laza had only one concern: how can one do one's self in painlessly? Mischke was unable to advise him.

Emil Mischke went through Domnau with a churning stomach. He headed for a field kitchen, but because he was wearing a Party uniform, the duty NCO demanded a chitty from him. Angrily Mischke moved on and ran straight into the arms of Farmer Robert Krause, whom he knew from the Volkssturm in Friedland. Krause took him to his house, which was full of drunken soldiers who had brought everything they could carry – schnaps, butter, conserves, chocolate – from the huts of the Domnau supply camp. A large cauldron of Glühwein stood on the oven. Frau Krause and her daughter had their hands full cooking and baking for the soldiers. Mischke found this doom celebration to be too much and withdrew with Krause to the barn, where they ate a large piece of sausage in peace.

'My wife does not want to leave here,' said Krause. 'The lad must look after the farmyard, the animals have to be looked after and sleeping in the cold along the road – he is not the healthiest. Only my daughter, who will be nineteen, I must take away with me before the Russians come. Tomorrow perhaps.' Krause was a post office driver in his other role and used to driving in all weathers.

As Mischke told him what had happened to him, and that his wife and his boy were on the way to Königsberg with the sledge, and that he was now looking for Böttchersdorfers to find out the details, Krause remembered that Böttchersdorfers had come through Domnau the day before and gone off towards Preussisch Eylau. Mischke could not be held back any longer. He helped his host dig out a 60 litre barrel of rum from the dung heap, and a barrel of butter from the compost heap in the garden, which was the only place on the plot that was not frozen solid. Then he set off on his bicycle.

An endless column was moving along the Domnau-Preussich Eylau road, wagon after wagon loaded with muffled figures and mountains of luggage; they could hardly move forward faster than walking pace. Mischke was still having problems with his wobbly bicycle, but nevertheless he checked the wagon name plate and the inmates of every wagon as he overtook.

A few times he hung on for a rest. Shortly beyond Kapsitten, half way to Preussisch Eylau, he saw a familiar sight, old Hermann Braun. Tired and drawn, he was hanging on to a wagon, pulling a toboggan behind him.

'Hermann, how did you get here?'

'These are Rogenbergers, they let me hold on. The others all chased me away.'

Tiny pearls of ice hung in the old man's beard, and he had difficulty speaking.

'And the Böttchersdorfers?'

'The farmers simply drove off and left us sitting there.'

'Do you know anything about my wife?'

'She must be up ahead, as she drove off before me.'

'Drove off? I thought she was going to Königsberg with a sledge.'

'No. She had a wagon, that was what Frau Kolkan told me, who is also on foot.'

Mischke pulled a packet of biscuits out of his overcoat pocket and gave it to the old man, then pedalled off as if possessed. If there was a hold up, he would bring old Hermann forward and take him with him. Emil Mischke was in a sweat. He checked wagon after wagon with redoubled attention and was always anxious that he might go past his wagon. He had to pedal for a whole hour before he recognised the two crossed planks and the plywood roof that he had fashioned a few weeks previously. He threw his bicycle into the ditch and jumped into the driving seat, as one could not stop in this stream of traffic.

The situation proved a disaster for Robert Krause, Mischke's acquaintance, the following day. He had said goodbye to his wife and had gone off on a light sleigh pulled by two horses with his 19-year-old daughter towards Lindenhof. An officer had promised to get a travel pass from the regimental staff for the girl, and did so. They arrived exactly at the right time to load the girl with her luggage on a military truck going to Pillau. But when Robert Krause wanted to drive back, he realised that he could not drive against the stream of refugees coming towards him. When he tried to get out of the way, he was forced back into the stream by soldiers and torn along with it against his will. When it started to thaw and his sledge could not go on, he looked for a wagon for his two horses to carry on. Somewhere before the lagoon he wanted to break away and let himself be overtaken by the enemy. To the coast of the Frisches Haff lagoon was only 80 to 90 kilometres, but for this short trek that Krause was stuck in, it took a whole three weeks.

The village trek from Schwirgstein that had wandered northwards between Allenstein and Osterode was also caught up in this millstream. In two days it had hardly advanced 12 kilometres. It reached the village of Podleiken on the evening of the 21st January and the freezing refugees sought shelter in the overfilled farm buildings. Next morning as they were preparing to leave, soldiers ran past and shouted at them: 'Hurry up! The Russians are attacking the village!'

Shocked, women and children left the trek and ran over the snow-covered fields to the nearby woods. Some of the farmers wanted to drive on with their wagons, but could not cross the frozen furrows of the ploughed fields and had to go back to the road, where meantime a panicky flight to the north had begun.

The women and children hid for over an hour in a copse. When they saw that the trek had not broken up and had resumed its normal speed, they ventured out. No shots were to be heard, and they cautiously returned to the village. There was no trace of their trek, only the wagons of strangers. They continued on foot and were later picked up by military trucks.

The men of Schwirgstein had turned off the main road further north in order to reach the copse, but lost their way and landed in the hands of the Russians. Most of them were shot.

Those who had fled during the night had driven on to a vast camp on the meadow before Gross Peisten. Everywhere cooking was taking place on small fires. Nearby was a herd of bellowing cows. The lady of the manor, Annemarie Kniep from Klein Wisch, set off with her daughter and two buckets. At the meadow fence a lame, tired bull was pushing along. Nothing could have been more dangerous. Loudly mooing cows stood beside newly born calves. The hoped-for milk did not exist. The animals' udders were frozen and festering from many wounds. There was no longer any hope for the cattle.

The whole night long they could clearly hear sounds of battle coming from Landsberg. When they dared to set off on the Landsberger Chaussee in the morning, they did not know which direction they could go. Nervous military police forced the refugees from the road to the east. Across a meadow the land rose slightly. They could hear German commands coming from a depression. The drivers speeded up their horses. Of all things the Knieps' wagon now lost one of its rubber tyres. There was a feverish search for a wagon jack. While the coachman was putting the wheel back they could see the glow of fires over Landsberg mixing with the dawn. Behind them, flares rose over the chaussee. The wagons were now only making slow progress, wire fences and ditches holding them up. Most of the people were now going alongside their wagons with rucksacks and bags ready in case they had to leave them to go across country.

Only when the first wagon reached the Landsberg-Preussich Eylau road and got onto it did the convoy move. But now refugees were streaming out of Landsberg in this direction and soon the road was blocked by vehicles wedged into each other. Nevertheless, the wild flight continued over the fields.

Among the wagons setting off one could clearly distinguish the individual coupés of the surrounding estates making their way over field tracks known to them aside from the main stream to the lagoon. Count Eulenburg-Wicken was driving in a wagon with his wife Jeanne. The old gentleman had been lying in bed with severe influenza until the very last minute before the flight.

It had been a very brief farewell when he left his home wrapped in a very thick fur, with a last look in his bedroom at the two valuable wooden plaques with the family portraits of 1580. Outside in the passage were rows of pictures from 1640 and 1750. Past the vast four-poster bed of 1604, whose headpiece consisted of such a richly cut triptych that it formed an altar to honour. The antlers on the wall behind were of no great significance. They were hunting trophies like those that hung on the walls of all East Prussian manors. The four-poster was not the only valuable piece of furniture in Haus Wicken. When the first Russian officer had entered the house in 1914, he had exclaimed: 'Mais, c'est un musée!'

Proud of their estates the East Prussians might be, but they were not sentimental about them. Count Eulenburg closed the ironwood doors to the house carefully behind him, and immediately afterwards the wagon crunched its way over the circular drive.

On the driving seat sat the Frenchman Lecomte and the Belgian Oury. Lecomte was the estate gardener and had tended the magnificent park with its 11 metre high clipped hedge. For him and several thousand of his countrymen the flight meant the end of their time as prisoners of war, and the sooner they got to the west the better.

They crossed the hard frozen surface of the mill stream in its swampy depression at speed. At Lompf, five kilometres away, the manor trek was supposed to assemble with 14 wagons and 35 horses, but there the steward persuaded the count not to wait for the others, but to drive on. With the Landau leading, the trek would also not advance any faster. The Eulenburgs drove on.

No one had thought that the count's luggage and all the foodstuffs were stored on the wagons. Nevertheless the Eulenburgs and their drivers suffered no hunger along the way. They followed familiar routes from estate to estate aside from the main stream and were well received by friends and acquaintances. Despite the complete chaos that reigned all round, the journey went as well as any previously made by Count Eulenburg.

The two prisoners of war brought the Eulenburgs almost straight to the 90 kilometre distant coast of the lagoon without any unpleasant incidents or delays.

This was an easy journey in comparison to that experienced by the estate trek from Garbenicken, which lay twelve kilometres directly northwest of Gross Wicken, the seat of Count Eulenburg. It was thus not only nearer the coast, but had set out a day earlier. There were eleven wagons, including the Macketanz's hunting cart.

The long ladder wagon of the Deputy was drawn by three horses. Because of constant air activity, they had decided only to move along the roads at night. But they were very slippery and the wagons slid on the narrow roads. They arrived at the big village of Schmoditten on the Königsberg-Preussich Eylau road at about 0600 hours on the 27th January and found accommodation in an overfilled farmhouse at minus 20 degrees Celsius.

They set off again on the evening of the 28th January heading northwest towards Kreuzberg. From there people came towards them with the news that the Russians had broken through. They therefore turned south, passing through barricaded Preussisch Eylau with difficulty. From there they continued parallel to the coast to Landsberg. They needed six hours to pass through that town and once they were through it they were held up in an open field as elements of the *Grossdeutschland* Division passed through. Despite all the distance they had travelled, the Garbenickers were no closer to the coast.

At this juncture Count Eulenburg's landau was already in Labehnen, 30 kilometres from Heiligenbeil and the Frisches Haff lagoon. The mother-in-law of the owner of Labehnen had not yet fled. She entertained the Eulenburgs as in the old days and their proposed stay for one day became five. The Soviet advance had slowed down during the first days of February and had almost come to a standstill in several sectors of the Eastern Front.

The treks, finding themselves in the middle of a cauldron at this point, had a rest. The Garbenickers reached Müngen and stayed there for six days. For the first time they were able to sleep in an abandoned farmhouse and tend to their sick. Cystic catarrh, dysentery, heavy colds – hardly anyone was spared. Furtively the dead were carried to the nearby wood and covered with brushwood, as the ground was still deeply frozen.

The attempt by General Hossbach to break out of the Russian trap to the west had soon become known to the refugees and gave them new hope. At least the immediate threat from the Ivans had diminished. But as all attempts to break out failed, and the Russians counterattacked, the treks in the western part of the cauldron fell into the combat area.

In the middle of a panicky fleeing mass northwest of Landsberg, the trek from Gross Wisch was torn apart. For Annemarie Kniep and two other wagons from Gross Wisch the journey ended in a hollow completely blocked by other vehicles.

There was no going forward and no going back. The Russians were not only behind them but three kilometres ahead of them at Eichen. Resignedly, Annemarie Kniep and the people still with her packed some food together and set off to find a building in which they could wait for the end. Close by they found a lonely farm in which hundreds were already packed.

The rooms and passages in the farm were all crammed. In the candlelight the people had pressed close together as if awaiting at any moment an unavoidable natural catastrophe. A strange silence reigned – no complaining, no crying.

Annemarie Kniep and her family still found a place in the barn, where there was more life. Most had buried themselves in the straw stacked in places up to the roof beams. There were Hindenburg Lights and lanterns everywhere, spreading a pleasant light, throwing no ghostly shadows as in the narrow rooms of the farmhouse. People were smoking, but the straw did not catch fire.

There were many soldiers there: 'stragglers' and wounded, and crying children. In the entrance between piles of luggage lay the sick and frail that were unable to climb up into the straw. The people from Gross Wisch had to climb a long way to find a place. Further up a few women or girls had got in with soldiers. Subdued laughter and giggling, the drawing of corks, later panting and groaning. Not a thought for the husbands of these women, the sweethearts of these girls, presumably in the field; Annemarie Kniep was indignant. Like all of them she was much too tired. And who knew what tomorrow would bring? Perhaps those up there only wanted to live once, if one could call it living.

Not far away one of the wounded was delirious. Two other soldiers tried to quieten him down, ending in an argument with some refugees over whether they should carry him out into the cold. It took a long time before the overtired trek driver found sleep.

When she awoke, it was 1000 hours. And the Russians were not there, although the artillery fire was dangerously close. Annemarie boiled the last of her pure coffee that she had been saving for an emergency. There was bread and sausage to go with it. Then she went on to Bornehmen, where she came across an assembly of German troops. She could not go any further, nor on the next day.

On the 5th February she was awoken by an artillery barrage. The frontline was at most only five kilometres away. The weather was clear. At about 1000 hours Russian aircraft appeared over the little village and fired at the farms with their machine guns. The treks quickly broke away, but only got as far as Quehen, three kilometres away. The road was completely blocked. And like every time they halted, some went off to appraise the situation.

With this opportunity, Annemarie Kniep found the missing wagons from her trek. They had been overtaken by the Russians and were behind the Russian front for three days awaiting a suitable opportunity to get away. But the wagons were empty, having been plundered, and the horses towing them were strangers found along the way.

The long train of treks moved on again and was in Angam by evening. The Gross Wisch wagons had to spend the whole night at a busy crossroads in the middle of the village. A young woman ran up to the fence nearby and shouted: 'Let me out. What's happening here?' No one bothered about her. The trek drivers would very much have liked to find quarters here, but the fear of missing the chance of moving on kept them fast to their wagons. Many had trek-psychosis, which usually set in on the ninth or tenth day of the flight: strong anxiety, headaches, vertigo and sleeplessness, with harrowing restlessness. It was like a dead point, which, once crossed, turned the individual refugee into an old hand.

Emil Mischke's trek wagon rolled along in the great maelstrom, which first went in a south-westerly direction, then moved north-westerly on the edge of the great cauldron. They passed village after village, again and again diverted and mainly at a walking pace. Mischke had long since lost his sense of direction and only knew that they were under way towards Landsberg–Mehlsack.

Like many others, he believed that the Wehrmacht would hold the bridgehead until the arrival of the wonder weapons that Goebbels was always talking about. Nobody knew what these weapons were. Some thought they were rockets, others wonder aircraft, and new submarines, that would hit the enemy for good. They would all appear in a few days. The ice theory had many adherents. Carbonic acid and liquid oxygen, when fired at the enemy, would fossilise all life.

When the stream reached the lowlands near Landsberg and overloaded wagons became stuck or turned over, Mischke realised that his wagon was not free of unnecessary ballast. While his wife drove – the Frenchman had long since made his escape from the authoritative man in the Party uniform – Mischke set about inspecting the wagon. He was annoyed with his wife for leaving the real trek wagon behind and driving off with the supply wagon. He found twelve sacks of oats. One after another he dragged them to the rear of the wagon and let their golden contents pour out on the dirty snow, retaining only three of them. Next followed a hundredweight of briquettes and then a sack of hard frozen potatoes. The wagon began to jolt violently, but for the horses it was noticeably lighter. Farmer Klann on the wagon behind had followed Mischke's activities with interest and did the same after him. He also threw the big chaise-longue overboard that had been serving him as a storeroom. Only the following evening did he realise that with that piece of furniture had also gone his smoking stuff, sausages and ham. His wife had carefully packed this valuable freight between the feather mattresses and then forgotten about them.

They made good progress with the lightened wagons even in the strong snowstorms of the 30th January. The drivers determinedly followed the tracks of the leading wagon, which became snowed up every so often when the distance between became too big. They went like this for 30 kilometres and that evening reached Frauenburg am Haff. They were through! Either side of the frozen lagoon lay the narrow strips of land of the Frischen Nehrung, from where the way led to Danzig and Pomerania – the only remaining land connection to freedom.

Chapter 6

Over the Ice of the Frisches Haff

The over 70 kilometre long and about 10 kilometre wide snow-covered, iced-over Frisches Haff lagoon was the last possible way out of the Heiligenbeil cauldron. The refugees had hardly any idea of what awaited them there – only very few had seen the lagoon, which they believed was no more than another of the many large East Prussian lakes that in winter were as secure to drive on as firm ground.

The inhabitants of this strip of coast had more respect for their little sea. Even in summer, if the white lagoon steamers brought loads of holiday-makers and trippers to bathe, sail and stroll around their lagoon, north-eastern storms and ice-cold rain could change the mirror-like lagoon into a seething cauldron. Several swimmers had already been drowned and even the fishermen fled to the nearest harbour.

The lagoon was eerie in winter. The first strong frosts quickly froze the two to four metre deep water. Normally the ice was a good half a metre or more thick, and the inhabitants of the depression and the coastal strip knew only too well that the ice was alive. The stronger the frost, the greater was the stress on the ice. It pressed against the banks and thrust big blocks groaning and moaning over one another. Cracks appeared and at times the mist and fog over the ice was so thick that one lost all sense of direction. On a fine sunny day one could see the depression from Karlsberg to Frauenburg with its little hillocks and woods quite clearly and even make out a strip of the Baltic over the treetops, but in winter there was often no view at all. Among the lagoon inhabitants there were stories about people who had got lost crossing the ice and then for hours – in the East Prussian love of fables – even day- and night-long tapped around them blindly.

In the villages of Tolkemit and Frauenburg, and in the hilly landscape of the southern part of the lagoon coast, most of the occupants had remained at home, even when the Russian tanks were quite close. One of the few to break out on the 23rd January was Prince Louis Ferdinand of Prussia, who administered his manor farm in Cadinen on the lagoon. His people wanted to remain and so he drove by sledge accompanied only by his coachman over the lagoon and reached Danzig.

Also the fisherman, Jakob Klein, at first had no intention to run away head over heels. The widower, who lived together with his daughter and two grandchildren, had been accommodating a sergeant for a fortnight, who had been telling him day after day to at least prepare a pack for his escape. This achieved little against his will although he knew that, apart from the fog and cracks, the lagoon had another snag to it. Two icebreakers had made a passage from Elbing to Pillau that they were keeping free of ice. That was far off, closer to the Spit. Who had a boat that could take him across?

But he was swayed when he heard that the prince had got across on his sledge. And what the prince had done, he could too. Shortly afterwards a neighbour brought the news that Russian tanks were already standing in front of Cadinen only three kilometres away and Tolkemit was to be evacuated.

Jakob Klein immediately ran out into the dark street. It was deathly still and a light south-easterly wind drove fine snow into his face. The thermometer had sunk to 18 degrees below zero. Nevertheless muffled figures with rucksacks and baggage were on their way to the lagoon with sledges and small carts.

The fisherman lost no time. Together with his daughter, he made his pre-prepared pack ready and dragged it to the beach, where his sailing sledge was. Supper was left lying on the table in the little kitchen, and in his haste Klein forgot all his documents, for now he could hear the alarm sounding. He hastily made his 7 metre long vehicle ready.

Klein's preparations had not gone unnoticed. Without asking, other people pressed on to his sledge. Finally he had to fight for his own place at the helm before they could set off. After some preliminary fluttering, a freshening breeze filled the sail which cut like a plank through the black sky. Klein felt relieved as the sledge speeded up, despite the overloading. Some distance away he could see other sailing sledges, and between them long rows of pedestrians, all streaming across the lagoon.

After travelling for half an hour, Klein saw what he had secretly been fearing. Over the ice in front of him stretched a dark, wide strip of open water, and before him the silhouette of both tugs that kept the channel open as icebreakers. Klein steered towards them and let the sail drop at the last moment, but was unable to prevent the sledge shooting into the water. Klein let the sledge stay where it was and climbed off with sack and pack to one of the two ships that bridged the channel. After about two hours of marching on foot the group reached the Spit safe and sound.

A few days later the mass of refugees from inner East Prussia were pressing on the banks of the lagoon. The Soviets had drawn the ring tighter. By the end of January they had the southern coast of the lagoon between Elbing and Frauenburg, including Tolkemit, firmly in their hands.

Russian troops had also reached the north-eastern part of the lagoon near Brandenburg, so that only the about 30 kilometre long middle part of the lagoon coast between Balga and Frauenburg was still free.

Thousands had driven to Sonnenstuhl near Braunsberg, Deutsche Bahnau and Leysuhnen, and were waiting patiently to go on. On some roads the treks stretched 16 kilometres back into the hinterland.

The greatest number of refugees reached the lagoon near Heiligenbeil and the small harbour of Rosenberg. Here lay the headquarters of the 4th Army. Supply vehicles and ambulances mixed with the treks in a complex tangle. Although the Wehrmacht sought to direct the stream of trek drivers past Heiligenbeil to Leysuhnen, the civilians thrust their way between the army convoys with threats, complaining and clawing their way through. Whole trainloads of refugees were still arriving in the town during the last days of January. Among them were also those that had left Allenstein on the last train but were unable to get out of the East Prussian cauldron. The train had been driving purposelessly here and there in the still free area.

Hildegarde Aminde had already been sitting on paper sacks with her old mother and hundreds of fellow sufferers for three days and three nights in the ice-cold goods wagons. Inside the walls were covered with a centimetre-thick hoar frost and there was an indescribable stench. There were constant squabbles about the few foodstuffs available and drinking water – all were hungry and thirsty.

They had already driven past the Braunsberg station sign twice when the train finally stopped one late afternoon. The line ahead of them was blocked by a boundless line of stationary goods wagons. 'Everybody out!' shouted soldiers and railwaymen going along the train. Only reluctantly did the exhausted people, stiffened by the cold, obey. Children cried and some of the old people fell on the track when getting off. Mother Aminde broke a wrist this way and her daughter quickly made a sling with a piece of cardboard and some thread.

The few belongings were thrown off, then the dead and severely ill were taken and laid down on the track alongside the signal wires. A marching column formed itself up and set off stolidly. An icy wind drove knife-sharp crystals into the refugees' faces. Heiligenbeil was about three kilometres off and the way went across the snowy fields and meadows alongside the railway line.

The rust-brown Reichsbahn wagons reflected the same criminal inflexi-bility to becoming victims as the civilian population. Together with the evacuation of the population, the 'withdrawal of economic assets into the Reich territory' had been planned with Prussian thoroughness the previous autumn. When the situation became serious, Gauleiter Koch did not give way to his brother's earnest request to move his wooden shoe factory to safety.

Only when the Russians had already surrounded East Prussia did Koch give the now completely senseless order to evacuate. In all haste valuable machinery and other goods were packed together and sent off on the short journey. Everyone knew that the trap was at Elbing. In the end the whole track of the Brandenburg-Braunsberg line parallel to the lagoon coast was lined with goods wagons – ready packed booty for the Soviets.

The Allensteiners entering Heiligenbeil at nightfall knew nothing of this. Hildegarde Aminde could only carefully set one foot after another. Her mother hung on tightly to her daughter's shoulder with her sound hand. Nobody in the column spoke and even the children were quiet.

Towards 2000 hours they reached the first houses showing dark against the snow in Heiligenbeil. In the glimmer of the winter night, Hildegarde Aminde could see herds of cattle that had found their way into the gardens in search of food. The people, refugees and soldiers, had withdrawn into the warm buildings. A few foreign labourers were roaming about the columns of trek wagons, having apparently been looking at the baggage. Nobody was looking after the wretched convoy.

The Allensteiners were a good half hour in the cold before they found a Party representative in a packed, but warm, school.

There were no buildings left along the coast of the lagoon in which the refugees on foot and the trek drivers were not trying to get warm. But the cold and fear of the Russians drove most of them on without taking a break. Many did not realise that they had already begun to freeze.

From the Dom Hill in Frauenburg Mischke had been able to see the apparently endless extent of the lagoon. The grey-blue line of the strip one could only just make out, barely dividing the lagoon's dull white expanse from the grey sky. Then they rumbled over a railway crossing to the near bank of the lagoon, where they became stuck in a vast traffic jam.

In the wagon little Gerhard had become curious. He wriggled out of his bedding, crawled to the rear and jumped down from the wagon. Mischke first noticed when he heard Gerhard calling pitifully. Angrily he jumped off the driving seat. What was wrong with the boy? Once he had had diarrhoea, then he was thirsty, then he wanted to eat. He found his son on his knees behind the rear wheel, vainly trying to pull himself up.

'Now what is the matter?' Mischke demanded.

'I can't stand, my legs seem to be dead.'

'Damn it! One must see to everything. That is the cold. Why have you kept your boots on when you are in the wagon?' He pulled him up and pushed him into the wagon, where Mother Mischke removed his boots and rubbed his ice-cold feet. It was of no use, but where could one find hot water here? So she tucked him back in his bedding and told him to keep massaging them, but Gerhard soon fell asleep and dreamed of skating on the village pond.

Meanwhile Mischke had gone on ahead to check the situation. A woman called out to him from a strange trek. She was wearing a military greatcoat and a dirty white headscarf. It was the Pischalske woman, wife of a day labourer from Böttchersdorf. Mischke walked closer.

'Everything all right?' he asked her.

The woman shrugged her shoulders. She was alone in the wagon. On the driving seat was a Frenchman, who turned his head briefly towards Mischke.

'Where is Karin?'

Frau Pischalske waved towards Frauenburg: 'With the people.'

Five-year-old Karin had Polish blood. Frau Pischalske was a minx and nobody in the village wanted to have anything to do with her, but little Karin, whose mother scarcely bothered about her, had been adopted by the villagers as common property. It was possible that someone had simply taken the child, but perhaps she had been left sitting somewhere to drive on with the Frenchman. Mischke was sorry for the woman because she belonged nowhere, but he could not show this, for he was an orderly person. So he only said to her: 'Hopefully!'

From a creased pack she offered him a cigarette, which Mischke stuffed into a tin box. 'In front there they are taking the men from the wagons if they don't have a pass,' she said with the thin trace of a smile on her pursed face. Mischke had the feeling that she wanted to repay a debt, but he did not know what it was. He nodded at her thankfully. He did not need confirmation any longer, as at that moment he saw a group of about 20 men being led aside from the landing stage by military police into the town. Mischke ran back as fast as he could, dodging between the wagons, people and baggage, to reach the town command post, which was being besieged by men of all ages. It took a whole hour before Mischke got inside. He gave his old pass to the office clerk without a word. Without asking a question, he placed a banknote between the pages and beckoned the next man. Outside Mischke read: 'Under the orders of the Wehrmacht at the XXth Corps General Headquarters, Danzig.' Beneath were two stamps and two signatures. Mischke nodded happily and stuffed the important document into his pocket. The press within the town had increased considerably during the past hour, and the artillery fire from the west was much closer.

Several buildings in the Weststadt part of Frauenburg were already on fire. As the Russians pressed closer with mortar and machine-gun fire and the German defence was forced back, panic broke out among the refugees jammed into the town. Berta Rubenbauer was standing in the cathedral square next to a Wehrmacht panje wagon loaded with soldiers' packs that had been brought here. She watched helplessly as the driver and a few men tried to bring one of the horses back to its feet. It had collapsed from exhaustion and was showing no signs of life. On her wagon were sitting her 85-year-old mother and her 17-year-old maid. Her husband, with whom she had met up again, had vanished two hours previously.

She was about to suggest to the driver that he drive on with just one horse when a military patrol intervened. They wanted to know to which unit the cart belonged and why the driver had not reported in. Apprehensively, Berta Rubenbauer got her mother and maid down from the wagon and unloaded her baggage, two rucksacks, two suitcases and two bags. Then she had to watch as the fallen horse was dragged away and the wagon was driven off. The air was full of the smell of burning and dust. The shell bursts were noticeably closer, but she could not risk a march on foot with the old woman.

Berta Rubenbauer ended up in a flour and corn barn between the wounded and other refugees. From time to time she went out into the chaos on the streets looking for her husband. Hours later a Wehrmacht unit began clearing the barn. The wounded were carried off, then prisoners of war loaded trucks with sacks of flour and grain. Some of the refugees were able to climb on these trucks and were taken off to the east, among them also the Rubenbauers.

While the Rubenbauers wanted to be taken to Heiligenbeil, most of the other refugees got off the trucks in Braunsberg, wanting to get over the lagoon as quickly as possible at any price. It would take only a few hours before the Russians held this side of the lagoon.

The refugees now crossed the ice in long columns at five places. The endless chains of black spots from wagons and pedestrians became lost in the haze in the distance where the channel had meanwhile been bridged over. On the 26th January the refugees from the Heiligenbeil area had completely blocked Ice Road 1, which the 4th Army's engineers had laid as a supply route. Lieutenant General Niebenführ of the Lagoon Quartermaster Staff had had another road constructed by the engineers from the level of Deutsche Bahnau and the open water of the channel bridged over.

Shortly afterwards further crossing points were made near Leysuhnen, Alt Passarge and Frauenburg. Sappers, policemen and firemen bored holes in the ice along these routes and planted frozen fir trees as markers so that the road could not be missed. Farmers brought long planks from the nearby sawmills to the 15 metre wide channel. The planks were then nailed together in threes and laid in 4 metre wide strips across the obstacle. Cross beams and approach ramps reinforced the bridges, which soon froze solid.

On the near bank the gendarmes ensured that the wagons only drove at intervals of 50–100 metres across the ice so that the surface was not too heavily loaded. Once Mischke had crossed the embankment, he noticed for the first time after a few hundred metres that there was no sign of the crossing point under the firm snow.

The wagons made such good progress that Mischke had to take a seat to keep up. Only two hours later they were at the channel, which many believed would be broken up to stop the Russian tanks, and they felt much safer on the far side of the channel.

Afterwards it began to snow, in light flakes at first and then thicker. A strong wind from the south signalled a change in the weather. Mischke stared desperately at the man in front in order not to lose his tracks. At last he saw the outline of the Spit, but at the same time the trek spur turned to the left, a chain of posts preventing the approach to land. They had to continue south on the ice several hundred metres from the secure Spit. The farmers complained, not realising that they were now practically between the front lines. The chain of posts was meant to deter enemy scouts from the far side of the lagoon.

The refugees went on in the snowstorm, which was blowing straight into their faces. Mischke had to climb down and lead the horses. The drifting snow was up to 30 centimetres deep in places. The wall of snow absorbed the failing winter light and Mischke could hardly see where he was going. Before him appeared several figures in long military greatcoats pushing bicycles. When he tried to overtake them, they threw away their bicycles, which were obviously a nuisance. One of them climbed up angrily until Mischke, like the others, made room for them in the wagons. They were Belgian or French prisoners of war.

It stopped snowing as they drove through the reeds on the bank of the Spit. A clear winter's morning awaited them. Mischke anxiously looked along the coast of the Spit. The outline of the burning buildings of Tolkemit showed up clearly on the horizon. The artillery explosions flashed like sheet lightning and the salvoes echoed over the ice to him. The whole lagoon coastline seemed to be in flames as far as he could see. Also towards Frauenburg, now far behind him, he could make out fires, and he felt sorry for the people having to sit fast in that inferno.

Mischke had come over the lagoon in good time, not having experienced the main assault and what followed it. Hour after hour ever more treks pressed to the coast. Four deep they lined the roads between Alt Passarge and Braunsberg, lying somewhat further inland. Braunsberg itself, like the surrounding villages and farmsteads, was so densely occupied that a wagon could hardly get through. The thin columns moving painfully and slowly over the icy desert from Alt Passarge did not appear to relieve the situation in the slightest. The carts were only moving at walking pace at the crossing points.

All order had collapsed in Braunsberg. The officials had long since left the town and only a pamphlet posted on all the notice-boards remained of the District Administration: 'The military situation gives no grounds for anxiety. Keep calm. Don't listen to wild rumours. Packheiser, District Leader, 22nd January 1945.'

The town hall was empty. In front of the door of the neighbouring church lay a row of corpses, their faces covered with cloths; there was no longer anyone to bury them. Only the Gendarmerie Lieutenant Otto Loppnow had remained with his men, who manned the barrier at the crossing point so that the wagons kept regular intervals, renewed the road markers and assisted the carts to move along. Day after day passed without the mass of waiting treks appearing to diminish.

The manor trek from Garbenicken reached Braunsberg at the beginning of February in a light thaw that had been replacing the strong frost for several days. There was a light drizzle. Frau Mackentanz led in a hunting cart, followed by ten other wagons driven by Poles and Russian civilians. They had advanced at walking pace for a whole day, and finally they stuck fast in front of a pub outside the town.

Two soldiers emerged from the building and went up to the hunting cart. One moved in front of the horses and stopped them at the fence. The other, an NCO, went up to Frau Mackentanz: 'You must take the wounded with you.' He made an overexcited, nervous impression. 'But we have absolutely no room,' replied the lady of the manor. 'Nonsense! They must get on the wagons!' He pointed to eight wounded soldiers being carried or supported by nursing orderlies coming from the building. They were hastily loaded on the wagons, two on a baggage cart and the other six shared out among the remaining wagons, being laid across the bedding and luggage, as the refugees shyly made space. The NCO assured them that they would be transferred to other vehicles at the lagoon.

When at last they could move on and the lady of the manor wanted to jump back on, the drivers had vanished. No calls for them to return or looking for them helped. They had used the opportunity to set off for the south and plunder their way through Poland. The trek had encountered many such bands on their way.

There was only Piotr, a Ukrainian, left leaning against the wall of the building, apparently uncertain about what he should do. 'I'm not going to drive. No water. No soldiers.' The women did not know what to do until Frau Macketanz spoke authoritatively. She appointed the 14- and 15-year-old boys and one girl of the same age as wagon drivers. Some of the women protested, not wanting their offspring in other wagons for fear of losing them, but in the end they had to give in and the trek moved on.

The trek approached the bank of the lagoon near the little fishing village of Alt Passarge, where there were no military, so dozens of 'Golden Pheasants' stumped around in the dirt looking important. Some were directing the traffic with snorts, and when one cried 'Halt!' another shouted 'Move on!'

One sniffed around ensuring that 'everything was in order'. One of the old farmers took an axe and a saw from a wagon, when the same tools were fastened to the wagon behind. 'Theft!' cried the Party man and threw both items down on the roadside. He had hardly turned his back when the farmer unconcernedly reclaimed his property. When one wagon became stuck in a hole, it was: 'Drive on you old donkey!' or, 'If you don't move on, I'll shoot the horses and you can go on foot!'

Other Party officials supported the Gendarmerie when it was necessary to lighten the heaviest wagons: 'Unload half of it, you fat pork farmer. Now you too can sense what war is!'

An angry Party man approached the Garbenickers' baggage wagon and shouted: 'I'll smash everything in it if you don't take women and children!'

He ripped off the cover and pushed in two of the women standing around with three children in with the wounded in the wagon.

The roadside was heaped with refugees' property that had been thrown out. Suitcases, boxes, sacks, grandfather clocks, sewing machines, prams, sides of ham and bundles of linen. Hundreds of preserving jars and frozen potatoes that had been carried carefully for weeks through snow and ice. Now they lay in the dirt. Such things did not seem important for survival in this hasty breakout. A great deal of this disappeared at night.

At about 0300 hours the Garbenicker trek rolled over the lagoon meadows on the ice. To the south the Frauenberger trek route was indicated by the silhouettes of toppled and half-sunken wagons. The driver of the hunting carriage used the time to count the number of horse cadavers lying there, only distinguishable as black dots. He counted over 80. At one spot there were six dead horses around one stationary wagon.

It was a clear day, but the sun had no strength. The wet winter air hung heavily in their clothing. They had already come halfway across when they heard the sound of aircraft engines. Horrified, they looked up but could not see anything. At the same time they heard explosions and machine-gun fire from the direction of the Leysuhn ice road and saw several fountains rising. The Soviets were attacking the crossing from the air. It lasted only a few minutes and the horror was over. The Garbenickers urged their horses on faster and finally reached the Spit unharmed.

As it cleared, the Russian aircraft were back, not letting themselves be chased off by either the German fighters or the heavy flak. Scouts were constantly in the sky and fighters dived on the gatherings on the coast and swept the ice with their weapons.

The sun was already high in the sky when the Domnau post driver Krause crawled out of the empty bunker on the Heiligenbeil lagoon bank in which he had spent the night, having left his wagon standing in Heiligenbeil, wanting to cross the ice on foot. In front of him the dunes fell steeply to the bank. The lagoon presented a dreary picture. Now sails were skating over the frozen surface as in the old days. But the dead and wounded were collected along the trek routes that lay across the ice like black streams. Through his telescope he could clearly see abandoned wagons, horses and people, baggage lying around everywhere and the circular marks of bomb holes in the ice.

While Krause was looking for a convenient route to the crossing points, flak bellowed behind him. Six low-flying machines were coming right at him from the south. He was already too far from the bunker entrance, so he simply let himself drop over the crest of the dunes, hearing the rattle of the machine guns and the bomb explosions as he fell.

Out there on the ice the Kosches were driving with two wagons in the Herzogswalder trek. Father Paul Kosche drove the leading wagon of the two with his sister sitting next to him. The other was driven by the Frenchman Charles, and with him were Kosche's wife Anna and the two children, 15-year-old Ilse and 13-year-old Klaus.

As the aircraft came near, Anna Kosche turned around shocked. She saw how her two children jumped out of the wagon and ran off. At the same moment a tall fountain of water rose near the wagon in front. The horses shied away and went off at right angles across the ice. In the shower of rain and mud now pouring over her, she still saw how the body of her husband fell back off the wagon, while her sister-in-law lay collapsed and lifeless on the ice. 'Stop, Charles! Stop!' she shouted to the Frenchman. 'Nix stop!' he shouted back. He had his hands full stopping the horses from breaking away and steering past the bomb crater. Anna Kosche saw how the belts of machine-gun fire were scoring tracks in the ice. The milk cans fastened to the outside of the wagon clattered under the shots, then the near horse collapsed. The other horse tugged and pulled at the blocked shafts. Charles jumped off to calm him.

Anna Kosche climbed down awkwardly after him and ran over the ice towards where she thought her children were. The attackers had flown off, but anxious people still lay seeking shelter behind suitcases and bundles of bedding. Medical orderlies came across from the other ice roads and tended to the wounded. Anna Kosche found her daughter lying unconscious on the ice beside a toppled wagon with blood running from her mouth.

Later medical orderlies established that she had been shot through the lungs. She died on the lagoon the next day. The son remained vanished. Apparently he had fallen into a hole in the ice and drowned. Her husband and sister-in-law also failed to survive the day.

Anna Kosche got a second horse from another shot-up wagon and drove on with the Frenchman.

Robert Krause dared not stay any longer on the ice that day. In the evening thick fog arose, which gave him courage and he went slowly over to the departure point in which his wagon was in a jumbled line ready to depart. However, things did not go any faster, as the police and Party officials indiscriminately went through the wagons taking whatever seemed too heavy or useless – articles of furniture, sacks of oats, boxes and chests – which they stacked up on the roadside.

Finally Robert Krause went on the ice without a word behind a small cart that apparently did not belong to any trek. Grandmother, mother and a child of about five sat thickly muffled on their scanty belongings. When it became quite dark, Krause asked if he could put his rucksack and bag on the wagon. He needed to relieve himself and had been holding back for so long. Most did not wait for such things any longer since it was dark. Almost everyone had colds and were afflicted with cystic catarrh.

Later Krause took over the reins and led the wagon off the ice. The women were trying to sleep. It must have been midnight already when he heard a ghastly howling that was gradually coming nearer. It could only be a few metres from the trek road. As they came abreast of it, Krause gave the woman the reins in her hands in order to go to the source on the ground. He had difficulty finding the spot in the dark and fog. A young woman was standing by a hole in the ice and raking the water with a stick, without stopping her howling for a moment. Two men were there, pulling her away from the hole, but she struck them with the stick and howled even louder. Hopelessly, Krause went back. As he passed a wagon coming behind them he heard an old man croaking: 'Pack it in! Let the poor soul rest in peace!'

The wagons were driving much too closely together from fear of losing the one in front. In front of Krause was the tail wagon of the Bladiau village trek, which consisted of 18 wagons with 40 families. A cracking noise shocked Krause out of his dozing; the wagon in front of him had broken through the ice with its front wheels. Krause was able to stop his vehicle just before the shaft bored into it.

Women and children clambered down from the tailboard, crying. Slowly the wagon drooped forwards and a big lump of ice rose under the right rear wheel. The weight of the wagon dragged the horses under the ice until the rear axle cracked apart. Krause pulled on the reins and drew his own wagon back with all his might. As the wagon stopped again he saw only two metres from himself a vast hole in the ice in which the upper part of an awning was sinking with a gurgle.

From up ahead came the order to stop. They had to spend the night on the ice. The young woman got down from the wagon. She had stuffed straw into her clothes to protect herself against the cold. Krause tried chatting to her, but they were both too tired and exhausted. He only discovered that she came from the Neidenburg area and had already been three weeks on the road. Her husband was somewhere at the front. Most of the refugees stayed close to their wagons, trying now and again to warm themselves with the horses. Several lay down on baggage on the ice in order to get at least half an hour's sleep, but others were alert and made them get up again. Nevertheless, several dead remained behind when they set off again in the first light of morning.

By about 0900 hours they were off the lagoon and had firm ground under their feet again. It was a clear morning and two Soviet bombers flew over the trek drivers' landing place. Robert Krause decided against marching on to Pillau and lay down in a big juniper bush to sleep.

Day after day, night after night, the black queues crept over the lagoon. Thaws and frosts changed over and made the ice mirror flat. At times horses without shoes could hardly move forward and their hooves had to be wrapped in sacking. The unsettled weather nevertheless had the advantage that the Russians could only use their aircraft at times. A concentrated assault on the refugee columns would soon have made the ice impassable. So in the six weeks from the 26th January to the 4th March hundreds of thousands of the 2.3 million people resident in East Prussia were able to use this route to safety.

By mid-February of that year the worst of the winter was over. Spring would be both early and warm. Along the coast of the lagoon the ice became brittle in places. The untiring officials of the gendarmerie guided wagons like pedestrians along the coast to new landing places.

The trek from Klein Wisch had already reached the houses of Neukrug and the lagoon before the drivers had to turn aside. They did not get far, there was a halt that had formed in front of them. One woman called to the others for help; the horses were not pulling. But nobody bothered. The men looked on with their hands in their pockets; the pause was right for them, and the ice was tested by the engineers and would hold. The Klein Wisch wagons were standing in a large pool of water.

The trekkers made their supper of ham and oatmeal as they had dozens of times before. Suddenly the head of one of the manor officials appeared in the door: 'The wagon is up to its axles in water! You must get out!'

The meal stayed where it was. The wagon was unloaded with the help of some Italians and Poles, fur coats, overcoats, blankets, boots and a big chest going first. Annemarie Kniep wanted to get some of the silver; she grabbed a few spoons, then the wagon slumped to the right. Fortunately the coachman had already unharnessed the six horses. She threw a few bits of food into the arms of those standing around. Her father wanted to keep the petroleum lamp – without petroleum it was as good as useless, thought the young woman and quickly drank another deep slug of wine from the broken bottle. Then she jumped off and stood up to her knees in water. Some wanted to go the five kilometres to the land on foot, but then they gave up. It was too slippery and everyone was soaked through. The lantern was also added to the rubbish.

Annemarie Kniep crept on a rack wagon and lay down to sleep. The trek would move on again at 0300 hours. When she awoke her first question was about the living wagon. 'It's been swallowed up' was the laconic answer. That meant the last of her property, even the food, was gone. She was freezing. Her feet were wet. Hunger set in. One loaf for eight people, nothing else. Why hadn't she unloaded the wagon properly and fast enough?

The ice was thinner to Kahlberg. The water was higher and the horses refused to stay still. Nevertheless, the Klein Wisch trek had luck. They reached Stutthof in the Vistula estuary the next night – and ate warm soup.

The trek from Spittehnen was shelled by Soviet artillery when on the ice road parallel to the lagoon opposite Frauenburg. Great fountains splashed up near and between the trek wagons. A panic broke out and all rushed for the bank. The Russians fired another two salvoes between. A wagon was hit in the middle and literally ripped apart; another wagon had its horses shot away. Men threw their arms in the air and fell in the water. Then the horror was over. The line of trek wagons drove on, leaving behind several shot-up vehicles on the ice or half sunken.

Days later Berta Rubenbauer came to this place. With the help of a soldier she had been able to acquire a two-wheeled wagon and a horse to pull it. The horse was christened 'Rosi'. Whilst she and her mother packed the wagon, her soldier looked for fodder for 'Rosi' from a Wehrmacht wagon and was caught by a sergeant. Berta Rubenbauer immediately inserted the wagon between the passing treks. Her maid, Trude, pushed to make them go faster. Behind them the sergeant was shouting something about a court martial, misappropriating Wehrmacht property and being shot.

The journey over the ice went fine until the point at which the trek road turned south and led on along the ice parallel to the coast. 'Rosi' was as stubborn as a mule and wanted to go straight to the bank. About a hundred metres separated them from the sand beach. The ice here was about half a metre under water. Over there was a thick tangle of trek wagons. Soldiers were waving at them to drive on. Undecided, Berta Rubenbauer stood next to the horse. In the distance the rumbling of artillery mixed with the sound of aircraft. Then the Allenstein woman decided to risk everything. She gave 'Rosi' the last crust of army bread and rubbed her nose. The she called out: 'Don't move, mother!' and tugged the reins of the nonplussed 'Rosi'. 'Rosi' made a jump forward and pulled with all her might. Water spurted up, the wagon slid, cracking bits of ice rose up, then the wheels hit the sand with a dull sound and braked the wild movement. Trude hung on to the tailboard and let herself be pulled on shore. Berta Rubenbauer had let the reins drop and fought her way in knee-deep water to the shore, where several women with outstretched arms helped her over the last metres. Hardly had she reached dry land when bombers raced over her head to the nearby wood and dirt and stones rained down on the refugees.

The crush on the remaining four crossing points – Frauenburg had fallen on the 5th February – began to diminish noticeably in the second half of February. At the barriers there were hardly any delays any more. During the first days of March there were only individual vehicles crossing the lagoon. The ice was already deep under water. On the morning of the 4th March the ice vanished and with it everything indicating the great, distressful passage: shot-up wagons, dead horses and the many thrown-away pieces of baggage. The last civilians were brought by the engineers over the water of the lagoon to Pillau in landing craft.

Chapter 7

The Road along the Spit

For the refugees on the ice the few hundred metre wide Spit of the Frische Nehrung seemed to offer safety, but they had not reckoned with the crowding. On the poor 75 kilometre long road between Neutief and the mouth of the Vistula were combined the five refugee ice roads and at the same time it was the last supply route for Army Group *Nord*.

Hardly had the wagons got hard ground under their wheels again and reached the shelter of the trembling pinewoods than they had to find a place to rest the people and horses for a few hours. Wet through and freezing, the many women and children stood around the smoking wood fires or lay in the wagons around. The strain of the journey, diarrhoea, and colds had so exhausted them that even the fear of Russian aircraft could not persuade them to move on.

Those who nevertheless did drive on sought shelter in the few houses. There were no harbours on the Spit, only fishing villages and sleepy bathing resorts such as Kahlberg, Liep and the customs station at Pröbbernau. The modest hotels and boarding houses served as emergency hospitals or had been taken over by Wehrmacht or Party officers. The civilians crowded into the fishermens' huts and houses.

Mischke looked for a warm place for his wife and son in a small villa on the edge of Kahlberg, but a 'Golden Pheasant' met him at the door, blowing a strong smell of schnaps into his face. 'Can't you see that everything is full here, man?' he shouted at him. Mischke could hear a woman's laughter coming from a room, then the Party man slammed the door in his face.

Mischke withdrew without a word. For a moment he regretted having exchanged his Party uniform for civilian clothes before Frauenburg. The women from another wagon had given him a pair of breeches, a waistcoat and a very tight civilian jacket. Unshaved as he was, he felt like a Russian. He no longer remembered from his semi-military past that he had stowed a carbine in his wagon when he wanted to save the fatherland at any price.

The church in Kahlberg was constantly overfilled. Women and children sat in the pews between prisoners of war and foreign workers, warming each other. Someone had strewn sacks of straw in the side aisles, where dozens were sleeping stretched out. Drinking water came from a deep well in the village. Volunteers were constantly on the way refilling the dirty buckets. There was a constant coming and going. Every few hours there was a queue at the entrance where some soldiers dished out hot pea soup from a big tub. Hard words of command and strong use of elbows forced the pack back into their pews to wait for their turn in the queue.

The wretched remnants of the Gross Seythen trek, two adults and eight children, had acquired a corner near the organ. After the Russians had caught up with them near Osterode, the manor inspector Romalm, the lady of the manor and her daughter had broken through to Mohrungen, where the lady's 12-year-old son was at a boarding school. Romalm had organised a hunting wagon and, in addition to the boy, had loaded six other fellow boarders on it. They reached the lagoon at breakneck speed before the Russians got there. Long before Kahlberg Romalm had already noticed that some of the boys' noses were snow-white at the tip. All complained that they no longer had any feeling in their feet.

From the open sacristy door came a surge of warmth and a sharp smell. There, beside the two iron stoves, was a large table on which mothers changed their babies. The minister's wife and an NSV sister helped them. The group did not let this spoil their appetite. On the Spit road a soldier had given them two loaves of bread and each of them a small sausage in exchange for two packets of tobacco. And the hot pea soup soon had its effect on the youngsters. Grimacing from the pain, they rubbed their hands and feet until the blood flowed again.

After an hour, Romalm went out to see to the horses. He had driven the wagon between the buttresses of the churchyard wall in order to give them protection from the wind and snow. The animals were covered in snow and were hanging their heads. While he was brushing the snow off them and talking to them, he heard noises from behind the cemetery wall. He climbed up on the wheel hub and looked over. Three men were hacking out graves with picks and shovels. It was the mayor of Kahlberg with two helpers. During these days and weeks they buried 378 dead.

Romalm did not bother himself further with them. Afraid that the horses might become sick, he urged them to break out. The little group reached the Vistula estuary next morning.

The complete Manor Garbenicken trek had come ashore a few kilometres south of Kahlberg near the Pröbbernau customs station. They were lucky. A bigger trek from the Heilsberg area had already broken up, making room for them. It was the right time. There were three heavily pregnant women among the Garbenickeners and one of them, the senior dairywoman, had already showed signs of labour. Frau Macketanz brought the groaning woman to a nearby medical post where she was taken among the wounded that the man had packed on to the wagons near Braunsberg. Their dressings were full of pus and there was a frightful stench under the wagon tarpaulins.

As they had been unable to cook on the ice, the Garbenickers had fed on cold fruit. Diarrhoea and agonizing thirst had resulted. Therefore they were very happy to get places to sleep at the Pröbbernau customs station but also welcomed the opportunity to cook. Frau Macketanz even found a bed for herself and her husband.

While the Garbenicker people were able to recover to some extent, an endless line of treks was passing by outside, and next day they had difficulty getting into the column. Nobody wanted to stop until ten other wagons had rolled past. It was hours later, when a wheel broke, before they were able to get on the road that now looked like a moon landscape. The wheels slid through deep furrows, rattled in vast craters and the wagons leaned over so strongly that their structures groaned. The Garbenickers had a wagon turn over that was full of old folk and children. The other wagons had to drive round it and by the light of lanterns everyone helped to right and load the wagon again. They remained the whole night in a wood next to the road. They tried using snow water to make coffee and to warm up some meat, but were unable to get a fire going as the wood was too wet. And again and again Frau Macketanz had to make the rounds to ensure that all were still there with the trek.

Most of the treks had dispersed on the way. Wagons had been abandoned, people had gone off and not found their way back, or had simply been picked up by other vehicles. Children who had lost their mothers wandered about until someone took pity on them.

There was also the lady of the manor who had continued on foot with her staff since their trek had been encountered by the Russians near Mehlsack. She had made her way through to the coast alone on foot and finally ended up with three Frenchmen, who had found an ownerless vehicle for her and were 'Trés enchanté' with the attractive young woman.

Those on foot suffered the most, exhausted from carrying their few goods, hungry and without sufficient clothing – many women only had shoes – and having to sleep out in the cold. Several did not stand up again the next morning. Leaning against a tree stump or a bush they apathetically awaited the end.

At one halt an old man had leant tiredly against Count Eulenburg's landau. Count Eulenburg climbed out. 'My heart,' said the man, hitting his chest and trying to smile. Eulenburg took his heavy rucksack and briefcase off him and hung both on the back of his vehicle. When they went on again the man trotted close behind, but before they reached the turmoil at the

Narmeln crossing point he had vanished. Perhaps he had been picked up by a Wehrmacht truck or had collapsed somewhere on the way and been left lying behind.

Later Count Eulenburg was witness to a completely hysterical man begging and threatening a sergeant to let him have his pistol and eight rounds of ammunition. Behind a windshield made of planks were seven of his family. They all had high fever and could not go on. When the sergeant bawled him out and sent him away, the man ran off.

The sergeant was one of several wounded that had been able to save themselves from an overrun field hospital in southern East Prussia. Most of them had been able to cadge lifts on army trucks to the lagoon coast, where they had the choice of either waiting for the Russians again in a crowded field hospital in a town on the bank of the lagoon, or trying their luck in getting back home. Several had over-estimated their strength and fallen down among the dunes, others had got lifts on army trucks, and yet others tried to get lifts on trek wagons, but most failed because of the stubborness or lack of German of the drivers. A woman from Bartenstein remarked bitterly: 'The foreigners, Poles and French were on the wagons. They drove past the begging wounded standing in the way with their bloody stumps without a word.'

Perhaps among these wagons was one driven by a Frenchman in which eleven German children sat. Their mother had received a fatal head wound from a bomb splinter even before they reached the lagoon, and one of the children, a boy, had been shot in both feet. For two days and one night this sad load was on the ice before they reached land at Kahlberg, where the little boy died from his foot wounds. No one knows what happened to the other ten children and the Frenchman.

Many children fell victim to the cold. Their mothers thought that they were warmly wrapped, without realising that even the thickest bedding could only protect them from the cold for a short time. Without being directly affected by the frost, they died from hypothermia. Only a few were really frozen, but for hundreds of small children the general loss of body temperature was disastrous. Their mothers saw no other possibility but to lay the dead children by the roadside or in a nearby bush.

The majority of the refugees headed west. They were firmly convinced they would find safety on the far side of the Vistula. Berta Rubenbauer did not go with the main stream. Military police had directed her to the north like many others. After about 15 kilometres she came to Neutief, from where one could see Pillau on the other side of the channel at the end of the Spit, the entrance to the lagoon.

On the near bank stood hundreds of abandoned wagons. Innumerable ownerless, hungry horses sought shelter from the cold and from the low-flying aircraft to which many had fallen victim.

For Berta Rubenbauer the arrival in Neutief was a relief from the persistent stress. Soldiers were looking after the refugees. They carried their luggage into heated huts, and there was food and warm water to wash in. It was said that they would be taken across to Pillau by ferry and go on from there by ship. Everything that could not be carried must be left behind. One manor owner used the opportunity to share out his treasures: dripping, bread, ham, honey and sausages – and several hungry pedestrians threw clothing and valuables out of their packs to make room for the food.

Next morning they went to the little steam ferry, pushing on recklessly, and only the forceful use of soldiers – engineers stationed on the Spit – prevented people from being pushed into the water. The view was poor and it drizzled as the ferry set off for Pillau.

Chapter 8

The Pillau Exit

The seaside town of Pillau had 12,400 inhabitants in peacetime. For East Prussia, and particularly Königsberg, Pillau was the door to the Baltic. In the spacious harbour, a centre for sea bathing, there was room for overseas liners, bathing ships, a fishing fleet and customs boats. The inner harbour had been developed as a naval establishment. Here were located numerous small naval units, minelayers and minesweepers, submarines, torpedo boats and others. The civilian part of the harbours was known as Pillau I, and the naval part as Pillau II.

In 1941, when sea bathing had long since succumbed, the 1st Submarine Training Division had been moved from Kiel to Pillau. Since then the three large accommodation ships of this unit – the 16,662-ton liner *Pretoria*, the 27,288-ton 'Strength-through-Joy' ship *Robert Ley* and the 9,554-ton African steamer *Ubena* – lay alongside the sea-bathing pier. The target ship, the 5,407-ton *Venus*, was in the inner harbour with 20 training vessels of older construction.

In January 1945 the first snow fell like sugar dusting on the slate–grey winter sleep of the town. Panje wagons rattled over the iced cobble stones here and there, carrying the fish meal from the fish factory to the railway station. In the inner harbour the cranes of a small steamer screeched as they unloaded ammunition. There was hardly any movement on the streets, just a few women shopping, school children, and naval officials and submariners hurrying between their places of work.

Out in the deep waters chugged the ice breakers, keeping the harbours and shipping channels open. Again and again minesweepers operated, as on clear nights the British seaplanes came to mine the shipping ways in the bight of Danzig. Past the black silhouette of the lighthouses of the Seetief, looming plump and black in the overhanging winter sky, went a lonely freighter on its way from Königsberg to Swinemünde. The Seetief is the 550 metre wide breach in the Frische Nehrung Spit that connects the Königsberger Sea Canal with the Baltic.

Even the news of the beginning of the Russian winter offensive had not disturbed the town and harbour from their customary peace. Even on

Monday the 15th January firing outside the town gave no indication of the storm that would break over it in a few days. With one tiny exception: from the funnels of the *Pretoria* curled thin brown smoke straight up into the sky, and from the main ventilators among the superstructure hissed now and then white jets of steam. The *Pretoria* was making steam and the decks of the *Robert Ley* were vibrating under the pounding of her diesel engines. Hot water spurted from the overflow pipes and melted big black holes in the ice covering the harbour.

Submarine officers rushed to the bridge of the *Pretoria*, which seemed to be preparing for a journey. Navigation officers, signalmen and helmsmen were at their posts, the engine-room telegraph rattled, orders were given. The submariners were being taught how to handle a merchant ship. In the engine room and at the winches submarine trainees sweated at their unaccustomed tasks. The rudder moved slowly but the two big screws of the *Pretoria* remained disengaged. It was the same on the *Robert Ley*, the *Ubena* and the *Venus*. The permanent staff of the Submarine Training Division were preparing themselves for a sudden removal of the living accommodation ships if it became necessary.

The training programme had been running since the Soviets had penetrated East Prussia for the first time in the summer of 1944. Steam was raised every week and the emergency tested. In January the submariners were fully trained to handle the ships. The exercise on Monday the 15th January also passed smoothly and without excitement. It would be the last, although on this quiet winter day the emergency seemed as far off as it had been during the previous weeks.

The situation changed on the 19th January with a blow. Refugees from the Samland and from Königsberg arrived in cars and trucks at the seaside town. Treks from the Samland were standing at the Seetief wanting to be taken across the lagoon. The usually only sparsely occupied trains from Fischhausen were crowded in the corridors, on the platforms, with every centimetre occupied in the baggage wagons, even on the buffers and the running boards. In the evening hours the trains were so long that the Reichsbahn had to use shunting engines. The flood of refugees increased by the hour.

The Reichsbahn officials at the little station tried despairingly to control the mass of humanity and do their duty. Lost children, lost baggage and fragile old folk filled not only the Red Cross offices but also the staff rooms. An overfilled waiting room forced the newcomers to seek accommodation in the town. Many stood about helplessly on the pier waiting for a ship.

The onslaught caught the Party offices and the town administration completely unawares. One of them sought to organise the NSV to at least give the people something to eat, the other concerned itself with room in the schools and guesthouses – but this was nowhere enough. Hundreds of people assembled in front of the town hall and demanded accommodation.

In the Economy Office the refugees stood densely packed together in the corridors and on the stairs for ration cards. The queues made no progress in hours. The senior officer in the county economic office in Königsberg was still not clear what to do. Should the refugees be issued regular ration cards for the remainder of the ration period of the 8th January to the 4th February stamped as holiday rations or should they be taken over by the communal feeding service. In the allotted period there was a weekly ration of 375 grams of white bread, 1,800 grams rye bread, 62.5 grams ersatz coffee, 187.5 grams jam, 250 grams of meat, 125 grams processed food, 125 grams butter or margarine, 125 grams quark, 62.5 grams cheese, 50 grams cheese substitute and 1/7th of a litre of fresh milk per person.

At last that evening Königsberg rang through the decision: communal feeding by the NSV. The Gau administration would send a goods train to Pillau with food next day, and at the beginning of the week a barge would follow along the sea canal with the approval of the war committee – the latter to be organised by Dr Ostermeyer in Königsberg. Town Clerk Kaftan told NSV Director Fischer to immediately turn the SA Home in the Hindenburgallee into a peoples kitchen, and that same evening several hundred portions of pea soup with ham were handed out. Later the big kitchen of the 'Golden Anchor' pub on the pier of the first harbour was turned into an NSV community kitchen.

Meanwhile the Naval Headquarters had become aware of the confusion. Lieutenant Commander Dr Schön offered Mayor Scholz naval quarters as emergency accommodation. The old foot artillery barracks in the Hindenburgallee was almost completely empty since Captain Poske, the commander of the 1st Submarine Training Division, had removed the remainder of his people on board the accommodation ships. Several big huts in the Himmelreich and Schwalbenberg Camps, in which naval artillery and flak personnel were accommodated, were cleared for the refugees. Sailors led the refugees from the station to their quarters. The navy took care of blankets, cutlery and crockery, had straw brought in, and Senior Intendant Paulusch opened his overfilled stores for the care of the refugees.

Mayor Scholz was happy to hand over these responsibilities. In his estimation there was room for several thousand refugees. In an emergency the storage sheds on the Holzwiese meadows could also be used. Meanwhile the farmers could drive further over the lagoon and the others be taken off by ships. From Captain Poske he had long since had the consent for the accommodation ships, should they leave, to take a number of civilians with them.

Then on Sunday evening Scholz received a call from the Gau Headquarters in Königsberg that gave him new concerns. On the telephone was an adjutant of the Reichs Defence Commissar called Plautsch: 'Gauleiter Koch demands that the ships of the 1st Submarine Training Division leave immediately. Under no circumstances may they take civilians with them. The Reichs Defence Commissar has discussed the matter with Grand Admiral Dönitz and has his agreement.'

Scholz vainly tried to get out of this – this a military matter and how could he allow – the other cut him off with the words: 'You answer for this with your head!'

Then the connection was cut. Plautsch had put the phone down. The mayor had no choice but to make his way to the citadel.

The old submarine man kept calm as he, a civilian, conveyed the orders of another civilian and that without his supper. 'What's this nonsense, Scholz? Firstly the Gauleiter has nothing to do with giving orders. My superior is the Commanding Admiral of Submarines, Admiral von Friedeburg, and secondly I consider it completely senseless leaving now.' Then Poske calmed down the completely bewildered mayor. 'Take it easy and get some sleep.'

Fritz Poske left matters until the following morning before he spoke over the submarine cable to Kiel. As a precaution, Admiral Friedeburg checked with the 'Lion'. Grand Admiral Dönitz had not spoken with Koch. The Gauleiter was apparently only hindering the women and children from leaving East Prussia. Poske and the Admiral agreed that the little fleet would only leave Pillau on a codeword from Kiel, and would then take as many refugees and wounded as they could with them. Poske could not resist eventually calling Königsberg and explaining this 'misunderstanding' personally to the Gauleiter and describing the appropriate ways of conveying orders in the Navy. It was one of the few cases in which the 'Hangman of the Ukraine' gave in.

On Tuesday the 23rd January the Gau Administration issued the following orders to the responsible civilian authorities:

1. The road Königsberg–Fischhausen–Pillau must be kept clear under all circumstances for Wehrmacht and other important war transport.
2. All refugees coming from Königsberg will be loaded on ships in Pillau. In Pillau no one is to be allowed on board that did not come from Königsberg by special train.
3. The population as well as the treks must remain in Samland.

The perfidiousness of these orders was made even clearer by a call from Adjutant Plautsch to the mayor on the evening of the same day: 'During the night 500 women and children from Metgethen will arrive that are to be immediately taken aboard ship. Frau Kümmel with two children is to be especially looked after and taken aboard the *Pretoria.*'

The refugees already in Pillau were merely included on the lists. Priority for shipping was for pregnant mothers, mothers with toddlers and mothers with several children under the age of twelve.

The expected train came from Metgethen, but among the passengers were prominent Party personages that Adjutant Plautsch had whipped together. Because it had seemed impossible to assemble a special train in the Northern Station, which was besieged by refugees, they had been diverted to the next station along the line to Pillau at Metgethen and their valuable freight conveyed there on trucks. Scholz had no idea who the Kümmels were. The train from Metgethen arrived in Pillau at 0100 hours. The passengers were brought to the *Pretoria* by the shortest route at a time when the streets were devoid of people. No one noticed the embarkation.

The last regular train arrived in Pillau at 2300 hours. On it was the brand new junior army doctor, Peter Siegel, and his young wife. They dragged their heavy luggage through the crowds in the station. They still found room in the pub opposite the station, sitting on their baggage close to the door. All the tables and chairs were occupied, baggage was stacked against the walls and even under the bar people lay stretched out asleep. Nothing was being served any longer and the kitchen was closed, but chamber music on the Peoples' Radio came from the bottle shelves behind the bar.

The Siegels had just got married on the 20th January in Rauschen on the northern coast of Samland. It was a small wedding with five or six guests in his parents' home. On the way to the church the sun had shone on the quiet, snow-covered landscape and spread cheerfulness. With the coffee and cakes after the roast goose, the little company was in the best of form, but then the five o'clock news broke into the idyll: the Russians had taken Neidenburg, where the young doctor's hospital unit was, and also where the bride's parents lived. The young Frau Siegel ripped the veil from her head: 'I cannot sit here as a bride if the Russians are in our home!'

She jumped up, ran out of the room and returned in a few minutes wearing street clothes. They decided to pack.

Next day, Sunday the 21st January, they were still packing. Meanwhile the Soviets were in Osterode. In the morning the Siegels saw behind their house as far as the Cobjeiten Manor a group of Volkssturm men on a field exercise. This did not look very convincing, the occasional eastern breeze bringing battle sounds from the front.

The old Professor Siegel, former director of the County Women's Clinic at Insterburg until he had been chased out by the Nazis, did not want to go with them, however. He himself had never been a Nazi and thus feared no reprisals from the Russians. And German men had to remain in the east, doctors too. The coming and going lasted three days. Meanwhile Allenstein had fallen and the Soviets were standing in front of Elbing. From out at sea the heavy cruiser *Prinz Eugen* was firing over the deeply snowed-under Samland on the Russian positions in front of Neukuhren. On Tuesday the 23rd January the young couple left alone on the regular train to Pillau via Marienhof and Fischhausen at about 1700 hours.

Sometime or other they fell asleep in the smoky pub in Pillau. Only the stirring of others at dawn woke them up. There was no wash place. They ate some buttered rolls that were brought in.

At about 0700 hours the obtrusive sound of marches coming from the People's Radio suddenly broke off: 'Attention! We are interrupting our programme for an important announcement by the Gauleiter and Reich Defence Commissar. The military situation has stabilised. There is no longer cause for unrest. The refugee treks are staying in Samland. No more embarkations are taking place. I repeat . . .'

The refugees listened silently and most of their faces showed indecision. Many had fled from the Soviet artillery and the horror was still reflected in their faces. On the other hand, the announcement was exactly what they wanted to hear. It was all right again, their flight had been a big mistake, and they could go back home.

Nevertheless, only a tiny fraction of refugees set off back – most had complied with the Party's 'stay still' orders once before and then been unpleasantly surprised by the Russians.

Peter Siegel pushed his way out and went across to the pier to make sure. On one of the big accommodation ships he met a young naval officer who apparently belonged to the crew. 'No, we are not leaving, and we are not taking anyone with us. The situation has actually quietened down,' he replied to Siegel's question. And the young doctor believed the comrade, who perhaps did not know that there were already 500 refugees from Königsberg on the *Pretoria*.

Relieved, Peter Siegel went back to his wife. Why should they remain in Pillau when in Rauschen they had every convenience? At about 0800 hours they boarded the train for Fischhausen. It was only partially occupied, most of the passengers being Königsbergers wanting to return to the city. Towards noon the Siegels were back in Rauschen.

But the refugee situation in Pillau had not changed. It had even got worse. Then the stream eased off. Up to the 25th January there were about

20,000 refugees in Pillau. Captain Poske had sent 300 young sub-lieutenants and midshipmen of the 1st Officers' Training Detachment to the Foot Artillery Barracks to look after the refugees. They were to divide the refugees into groups, list them and issue boarding passes to be prepared in the pursers' offices on board.

The timing of the departure was to be kept secret to the last minute, firstly so as not to alert the enemy submarines and torpedo boats, and then to avoid a storm on the ships. Already on Tuesday Captain Poske had let the town administration know that he could take any amount of household goods. The *Pretoria* had vast holds that seemed unsuitable for the accommodation of refugees. In fact soon afterwards big quantities of boxes and baggage were stacked up on the pier, all of which vanished into the stomach of this vast ship.

Meanwhile the icebreakers *Baldur* and *Haff* were keeping the harbour free of ice, and the tugs *Ernst* and *Skirwieht* had both positioned themselves close to the big ships ready to help them out of the narrow harbour.

On Tuesday morning the damaged cruiser *Emden* passed down the canal from Königsberg. As well as 1,300 members of the Wehrmacht and refugees, it also carried the coffins of the former Reich President Hindenburg and his wife, that had been taken on board in a ghostly ceremony in Königsberg harbour. Shortly after came the submarine accommodation ships *Der Deutsche* (11,435 tons) and *General San Martin* (11,250 tons), and the 1,200-ton air defence ship *Greif* with naval personnel, female signal auxiliaries, military equipment and a few civilians. *Der Deutsche* had patients and nursing sisters from the Königsberg hospitals on board – the doctors that originally went with them had been taken back by the SS before the ship sailed.

On Tuesday afternoon the little pilot steamer *Delphin* with 185 refugees, mainly family members of officials of the canal authority from the construction harbour in Pillau, set course for Stolpmünde.

The wounded in the five hospital trains at the sea service railway station had to freeze for another day before the hospital ship *General von Steuben* (14,660 tons) arrived at Pillau. The ship took on about 300 severely wounded and lightly wounded, as well as a number of refugees, and took them to Swinemünde.

On the morning of the 24th January the two freighters *Duala* (6,133 tons) and *Haussa* (2,819 tons) arrived at Pillau II. The *Duala* discharged large boxes of Wehrmacht property, which were stacked on the pier and driven off on army trucks from time to time. The *Haussa* was loaded with 37mm flak ammunition and Panzerfausts. Lighters that were meant to take the ammunition across the lagoon to Rosenberg went alongside. Twenty concentration camp inmates carried out the stowing on the lighters under the supervision of four SS men.

Two of the prisoners, the Czech Frantisek Wlcek and the Austrian Joseph Traubner, stood under the crane at the after hold of the *Haussa* and heaved the cases of 20 shells or 5 Panzerfausts. Frantisek was 25 and Joseph 63 years old. Their movements were slow for they did not have much strength. They ignored the occasional threats of being shot. The guards only carried submachine guns and not the feared oxtail whips. About midday one of the crane cables parted and had to be re-spliced, which took a good half hour. Frantisek and Joseph crept into a corner protected from the wind, while their guards vanished into the interior of the freighter. They knew there was no chance of escaping here.

Wlcek and Traubner belonged to the labour force of the Explosives Arsenal, which was located in Fort Stiehle and on a small hill close to the harbour. Their barbed-wire-fenced hutted camp lay close to the fortress walls, being one of the 90 auxiliary camps of the Stutthof Concentration Camp. Frantisek Wlcek usually worked with 50 others in the Naval Headquarters' motor vehicle depot, but today he had been wrongly assigned and he still had pain in his groin that his protest had earned him.

'Have you seen the people, Joseph? They all have to leave. I heard a navy man say that the Russians had broken through and that the whole of East Prussia will soon be theirs.'

'They will chase them out again, too,' said the older man. 'It always goes like this, backwards and forwards. They now have had five years of war. The one no longer has the strength to do the other in. We saw that in the First World War.'

'But you lost it,' said Frantisek. 'What do you think we should do with our trucks? They drive wounded, wounded, wounded. You have never seen so many wounded in a heap. And should you ask me, they have more wounded than fighting soldiers.'

Frantisek was shivering from cold. He only had two sets of underwear under his blue-striped concentration camp uniform. Joseph was similarly dressed. He had cut a sort of poncho out of a blanket which he wore under his jacket. It warmed him and protected him from blows.

'Minus ten degrees,' said Frantisek. 'I know this precisely, for then the snot in my nose freezes. I already knew that as a child. If the Russians get quite close, I'll be off home, right across Poland – that is the shortest route – will you come with me?'

'You are crazy. They are not coming. And what's the point – I'll not get away from here again.'

What was the point that he had still two years to go to his pension. His wife had died on the transport to Treblinka and he had not heard anything more of his two daughters. Who knew who lived now in his house in the Danube meadows near Melk.

'Will you help me when the time comes?' asked Frantisek. 'It's coming,' said Joseph carefully, as he already knew what Joseph wanted of him.

Frantisek was unable to work on his plans any further as the cables were repaired and they had to go back to work. They were finished shortly before dark. But they could not get back ashore over the ship, as the decks were swarming with streams of refugees, which had increased during the loading. A rowing boat brought the prisoners from the ship's stern to the pier. People stood in dense clumps on the gangway, where the military police were sorting out men of military age. The handcarts and prams loaded with luggage and bits and pieces had to remain behind and were causing obstructions everywhere.

Frantisek could feel the silence in which everything was going on; even where the women were arguing about their places, this went on with silent nudges and inconsiderate but dumb jostling. Above on deck they perched on the railings and looked on at the crowd on the pier. No one helped if someone below asked for a bag or a child to be lifted up.

As they approached the hutted camp, the other work detail from Fort Stiehle came towards them. They had been helping with the demolition preparations for days. There were still the sea mines and torpedo heads to be moved because there was not enough priming cable and nearly all would have to be demolished with timed fuses. Frantisek had learned from a sailor that the timers could run for six days, from which he drew the false conclusion that Pillau would be blown sky high within at least six days.

At about 0800 hours on the Thursday morning – the *Haussa* and the *Duala* had already been at sea for six hours – Captain Poske received the codeword for the transfer of the Training Division to Hamburg. About 20 minutes later the sublieutenants and midshipmen went to the barracks and the other places of accommodation to get their refugees on their feet and to get them to the ships. At the same time the medical units were told to get the wounded from the hospital trains and hospitals on board.

The *Pretoria*, like the *Robert Ley*, stood very high above the water and the gangways were consequently steep and long. This was the only difficulty in embarking: the old and sick had to be carried on like children. Many were dizzy and now and then some women began an appalling screeching. Hour after hour the mass of people advanced four deep to vanish aboard the ships. No one asked for boarding tickets any more. The inhabitants and refugees in the private quarters had soon realised what was ahead of them and had simply adapted themselves to the circumstances.

The first great embarkation of refugees took place in complete calm. There was no trace here of what was to come in the following days and weeks in the embarkation and become life-long nightmares for many. Only when the gangways were withdrawn at about 1700 hours did some unedifying scenes take place as many of those remaining behind took these to be the last ships travelling to the west and thought that they only had the choice of either travelling on them or dying.

On board the ships every bit of space was in use. The big double cabins accommodated up to ten persons, in the lounges, dining rooms and cinemas the people sat so closely together that no one could lie down. Nevertheless there were facilities for bathing the babies. The big galleys on board cooked around the clock and nobody had to go hungry on the whole journey to Swinemünde. But the toilets were inadequate for these masses. The crew were forced to flood them from time to time. Several did not bother to use them.

The ships could only leave at dusk. They were to proceed at top speed towards Bornholm and then turn west in the open sea upon a radioed command. The deep water was significant as there were no mines there. Sea mines are useless in a depth of over 20 metres, and the shallow coastal waters were strewn with British mines. On the other hand, the minesweepers were in a difficult position, as some of the mines could be driven over up to 64 times before coming to the surface.

However, in the open sea Poske had to reckon with Soviet submarines and motor torpedo boats, which were operating in the Baltic with increasing success. This danger could only be lessened by travelling at night at top speed. Poske had arranged an escort of two submarines for each ship, but this was of little benefit as the little vessels could only travel at half the speed of the big ships.

At about 1800 hours the *Pretoria* cast off her mooring lines and was towed out of the Haken by two tugs and taken out of the harbour to the open sea. 22,000 people left endangered Pillau on this small fleet: refugees, wounded and naval personnel. Next day they were delivered safely to Swinemünde.

Captain Poske had remained behind in Pillau. He wanted to follow next day on his 'flag-ship', the ocean-going tug *Wogram*, and to overtake his accommodation ships by steaming along the coastal waters. That same evening he brought his wife and three children, as well as the family of a good friend, on board the tug, in whose little mess in the end 23 people were squashed. Then Poske went to his office in the citadel to check inventory lists, write reports and prepare for a final round of inspections of the harbour on the Thursday.

It had long since struck midnight from the town hall tower when Poske, exhausted, stretched out on a camp bed for a few hours' sleep. Nevertheless he had hardly fallen asleep when there was a frightful clap of thunder. Dirt, stones and glass rained down on his bed. The curtains, instead of providing blackout, were hanging crossways over the empty window space. The night outside was deep black. Poske's wristwatch showed 0130 hours. He got up swearing. Excited voices came from outside. He ripped open the door and shouted in the darkness: 'What's happening here!'

A marine wearing a steel helmet rushed along the corridor: 'Captain, Fort Stiehle has been blown into the air!'

'Right, I'm coming,' Poske replied.

He called Captain Puhlmann, the commander of the defensive weapons arsenal, but he knew no more than Poske did. What had happened and what effect it had had on the town could only be seen next day.

The old town had been badly affected, the blanket of snow coloured red with brick dust. Several roofs had been blown off, almost all the windows destroyed. The prisoners' huts within the fort had been blown away, even those of the naval flak unit on the Schwalbenberg had largely collapsed; others had been damaged by falling masonry.

It was fortunate that so many refugees had left Pillau in the big ships the evening before. Nevertheless, town clerk Kaftan recorded 300 civilians killed, 600 wounded, some badly, and over 2,000 homeless. Among the damage to property the worst was the destruction of the electricity cables and the breaches in the water pipelines, which immediately froze and brought the water supply to a halt. Among the dead was Joseph Traubner. Frantisek Wlcek was the only prisoner to escape unharmed, but he was shot by the SS four weeks later, together with 40 Russian prisoners of war from the naval motor pool near Löchstadt.

The cause of the explosion was never clarified, as no one had survived from inside the fort. Sabotage seemed unlikely, and it was assumed to have been due to carelessness during the preparation for demolition. While the dead were being buried, the rubble cleared and the windows filled in with makeshift covers, chaos continued in Pillau.

Part of the Soviet 43rd Army had thrust past Königsberg and was now deep inside the Samland, from where a constantly increasing stream of refugees flooded towards Pillau. The fortress commandant, naval Captain Jerchel, had the treks met at the 'Grosser Kurfürst' Barracks, as they otherwise blocked the approaches to the Seetief deep water channel. There was hardly any room in the harbour area for pedestrians and ever more soldiers were mixing with the refugees. Already many German units had been wiped out in the first Russian attack. These stragglers were being rounded up on the Holzwiesen meadows and formed into new units. Space had to be made in the military accommodation for the many wounded, and the herded-together refugees put into private homes. Up to 100 persons were crowded into one apartment, while others were housed in ice-cold cellars and barns. Nevertheless, there was still not enough room because more refugees were coming, not only from the Samland and Königsberg, but also from the Haff lagoon across the Seetief channel into the little town.

Chapter 9

Flight from Königsberg

'I would like to live and be buried in Königsberg', Joachim Ringelnatz had written, but all the old tranquil days of cream and marzipan had been shattered the previous August by a British bombing raid. The old castle with its powerful round towers and the elegant university building, which looked more like a palace than a teaching institution, had suffered badly, like many other buildings in the old city.

The city had been tidied up again, but one was now clinging on to everything – not just rushing away. Returning after their not quite so opulent holidays, the Königsbergers were back at work, slaving away for the final victory. They were busy when the first of the refugees arrived in the city in mid-January. There was so much quartering, re-housing, filling and emptying that it was not so obvious if an office here or there, or a family, vanished to the west. Many of the almost 40,000 inhabitants were determined not to flee.

With the number of refugees streaming in from the province, unrest broke out in the city. The refugees wanted to go on, heading for Fischhausen and Pillau, and crowding the Königsberg harbour in the hope of being taken aboard a ship. The bad news accumulated and more and more Königsbergers joined in the flight.

As it became known that the Russians were not only to the east and south of the city, but also to the north, there was no holding back thousands in a city already overfilled with refugees. Well over 100,000 people left Königsberg during the last days of January. At the northern station people fought for standing room on the trains still providing regular services to Fischhausen-Pillau.

On the roads leading there tramped endless streams of people on foot mixed with Wehrmacht vehicles that would give them a lift when they could. There was more traffic than ever on the 40 kilometre long canal connecting Königsberg with the Baltic.

A number of 2,000-ton freighters, coastal motor vessels, picket boats, harbour tugs and whole lines of towed boats were made available to the refugees by the naval authorities and the harbourmaster. The smaller elements ran shuttle services between Königsberg and Pillau, while the bigger ones headed for Gotenhafen, Danzig-Neufahrwasser, Swinemünde and other ports in the western Baltic.

The steamer *Consul Cords* (900 tons) was under repair at the Königsberg shipyards on the 25th January. A damaged propeller shaft had been replaced, but there were tears in the shaft tunnel that had still to be welded up. Late that evening the skipper received orders from the harbourmaster to move to Berth Number One to take on refugees and set off for Kolberg. The skipper protested that he could not be responsible for the safety of his ship or his passengers, but to no avail. At Number One berth a crane loaded several bundles of straw on board to line both holds and the coal bunker. The skipper alerted the helmsman to the risk of fire and disappeared into his cabin.

About 1,200 people embarked, mainly women and children. Several had boarding passes issued by the NSV but no one on board knew what to do with them. Then, before nightfall on the 26th January, the *Consul Cords* cast off and moved slowly down the canal. The skipper had posted a lookout with a signal lamp to warn off following traffic, as they were constantly being overtaken, and each time the swell from the overtaking ships caused the ice floes to crash against the steel plates of the *Consul Cords*. The little cargo boat reached the deep water channel off Pillau at about midnight. One could see the silhouettes of many ships lying in the harbour against the snow. The refugees on board were restless, thinking that they were already at Kolberg and wanting to disembark.

On the straw in the coal bunker a small group had made themselves comfortable by the yellow light of a petroleum lantern. They were the von Weiss couple from the Gross Plauen estate, two of their estate staff and Frau Kuckuk, a Königsberger woman. They had three days of trekking behind them – less than many on board – but this had been enough for Eva Kuckuk.

For Eva it had all started on Sunday the 21st January. A specialist in the office of the representative of the Reich Treasurer for revisionary matters of the Nazi Party's East Prussian Gau, she was a friend of Frau von Weiss and had been invited to Gross Plauen for the Sunday. A carriage had collected her for lunch. There had been pheasant, and Eva Kuckuk had been amused how Emmi von Weiss had sorted out the shot on the edge of her plate as if greeting old friends.

Eva Kuckuk had wanted to return that evening by train, but no more trains had come. Shortly before her departure, at about 1800 hours, came the news that neighbouring Allenburg had to be cleared of its civilian population within an hour. At the same time it was announced that the trains would not be running any longer and that those without transport should walk to Friedland, where onward conveyance would be organised. For Frau Emmi von Weiss and her husband, retired Colonel Otto von Weiss, it went without saying that Eva Kuckuk would join the Gross Plauen trek.

The whole night they packed and prepared. Among other things, Emmi von Weiss gave her friend a capsule of cyanide. 'Should you fall into the hands of the Russians. Absolutely painless. I got it from a chemist.' The Gross Plauen trek set off at daybreak. There were 16 wagons, led by the lord of the manor's coach.

The road to Friedland was completely blocked, so they had to use side roads. Nevertheless, they only progressed at walking speed and after ten hours had only gone eleven kilometres. They spent the night at Klein Schönau at a manor farm whose owners had fled; it was overflowing with refugees. Only by taking it in turns could Eva Kuckuk and her friend get some rest on a chair.

On Tuesday the 23rd January they set off again at dawn. As far as the eye could see there were refugee wagons, wandering people and roaming loose animals. The fear of being left behind and the cutting frost drove them on. The dull growling of artillery filled the air, seeming to come from all directions. That night they reached Lisettenfelde. Instead of the expected rest they were met by a Wehrmacht unit, whose officers urged them to abandon the trek and let the unit's trucks take them on towards Heiligenbeil-Zinten or to Königsberg, but without their luggage, of course. At first the Plauen people and smallholders' wives were agreeable to this, but at 0500 hours next morning the estate accountant appeared and asked Otto von Weiss permission to trek on. So only six of the sixteen wagons were handed over to the Wehrmacht and their occupants climbed aboard the military trucks. The remainder of the estate people trekked on.

About 20 people found room on the wagons to Königsberg with their hand baggage. They stood so close together that they could hardly move their feet, but they made good progress and were in Königsberg by about noon. Eva Kuckuk took her friends to her apartment and then went to her office. Then came the next surprise. In her absence two specialists and two typists had moved camp by steamer to Güstrow in Mecklenburg, taking several of the files. The remainder of the personnel were sitting at empty desks, keeping up appearances. Thus Eva Kuckuk had no hesitation when Otto von Weiss appeared and told her that he had found a steamer. At 0200 hours in the morning she was aboard the *Consul Cords*.

The little group in the coal bunker were confident, feeling secure in the belly of the ship. The engines thumped regularly and they had become used to the cracking of the ice floes, and they had no idea of the other dangers lurking out at sea. Eva Kuckuk was asleep when the next surprise struck: 'Eva, Eva, wake up!' It took a while before she was sufficiently awake to learn the hastily whispered news that Otto von Weiss had brought down from the bridge. About two hours after they had passed through the exit of the deep sea channel on a northerly course for Hela, the ship's engineer had reported water in the engine room. The *Consul Cords* had a list of about ten degrees and the captain reckoned that the ship would only remain afloat for a few hours. He was therefore heading for Gotenhafen and trying to establish radio communication with the port. After half an hour still without a reply, he changed course. Hela lay nearer even though there were only naval ships and submarines there.

Together with the helmsman, Otto von Weiss kept an eye on the people in the holds, who were to make themselves ready for disembarkation as they were about to run into Hela. For three hours they dealt with the anger of the refugees over the supposed delay. No one noticed the danger that the ship was in. But they made it. With its last strength the *Consul Cords* ran into Hela harbour.

Two days later naval engineers had repaired the damage and the ship was able to continue its journey. Most of the refugees left the little steamer in Kolberg in order to make room for a load of aircraft engines and grain, going on by train to Saxony. As the steamer, this time without an escort, set course for Warnemünde, she had 285 people on board. Among them were also Eva Kuckuk and the Gross Plauers.

Two hours from their destination, at about 1200 hours, Eva Kuckuk was taking a midday nap in the cabin of the ship's flak detachment, which the soldiers had generously cleared for her. The *Consul Cords* was quietly making her way at about 10 knots. To port one could see the outline of the coast. Suddenly the ship reared under a frightful explosion. They had hit a mine.

Eva Kuckuk was shaken up in her cot. Everything over her and around her seemed to be broken with an almighty bang and, even before she was fully conscious, it was quiet again. Next moment she heard screams. An emergency alarm was ringing uninterruptedly through the ship. Close by a voice called out: 'Get out quickly!'

Instinctively she reached for her handbag that she had put down on the deck beside her. A vast hole had appeared next to her bunk in which wreckage was sliding about. The remains of the deck consisted of bent, smashed iron plates, whose sharp edges stuck up like spearheads. Carefully Eva Kuckuk felt for something to hold on to. Of the flak standby room only two metres away all that was left was a bit of a wooden partition.

In the wreckage below her feet she saw a paratrooper who was using both his arms to work his way through the tangle of wood and iron. Eva Kuckuk leant forward and was able to reach the sergeant major with one hand and help him free himself out of his dangerous position. About a metre lower she saw one of the steamer's stokers up to his neck in wreckage. She was unable to reach him and had to leave him to his fate.

As quickly as she could, she worked her way to the captain's cabin, where the von Weiss couple had been at the time of the explosion, with their 8-year-old daughter, and Eva Kuckuk's maid. But the cabin was empty. She hurried past a partition against which someone she knew from Insterburg was leaning, dumb and rigid, looking out to sea, with a large, bloody wound on her forehead. Eva Kuckuk was so shocked over her appearance for the moment that she went past without saying a word. She was able to save the woman's daughter, a musical student, who was in the water.

The deck was torn up at the level of the hatch and the ship was sinking very quickly. Eva Kuckuk waded up to the top of her stockings in the water flooding in and swam to a lifeboat that was tied to the ship by a rope. She swung herself over the side and saw that the boat was leaking, with some dead fish floating in it. As she was about to climb in, the boat capsized, forcing her under water. At the same moment she was caught in the under-tow of the sinking ship; luckily it was not very strong because of the shallowness of the sea. Several times Eva Kuckuk was able to work her way up again but kept hitting her head against the lifeboat. She was already seeing black before her eyes when she shot to the surface and saw the blue sky overhead.

Eva Kuckuk swam to a rubber float on which the paratrooper sergeant major had climbed, having been able to get away from the ship with the last of his strength. He was bleeding badly from a head wound, where the glowing iron stove in his cabin had hit his head. Together with another woman and her 5-year-old son, whom she pushed up, Eva Kuckuk hung on tightly to the rubber float.

She saw the von Weiss couple about 200 metres away with their heads sticking up out of the water as they clung on to some object. She later learned from his wife that it was a barrel. Because of the wreckage, boxes, planks, suitcases and clothing floating around, she dared not swim over to them. To the left of them she saw a big steamer at some distance. It was the *Margarete* picking up the survivors.

After about half an hour the heads of Emmi and Otto von Weiss dis-appeared. Eva Kuckuk could feel her own strength ebbing away. She could hardly hold her left arm up. Slowly the rescue boat approached the little group. Eva Kuckuk saw it first and spoke encouragingly to the woman. Then her head fell forward and she lost consciousness.

When she opened her eyes again, she was lying on a picket boat in Warnemünde. Four hours had passed. A sailor was standing bent over her saying over and over again: 'You are saved! You are saved!'

He was beaming, because the medical attempts to revive her, in which he had helped considerably, had at last met with success. Eva Kuckuk had been 40 minutes in the cold water. Of the 285 people on board the *Consul Cords* only 30 had been saved. Some of the survivors later died from their injuries, including Frau Kuckuk's maid, who had been severely injured in the explosion and died a few weeks later in a Rostock clinic from sepsis that had set in after a leg amputation.

Nobody asked about the fate of the *Consul Cords* in Königsberg. Weeks before such a high number of dead would have been the talk of the city, but now the treks streaming in and the wounded transports were bringing in a hundred dead per day. The distress of the refugees brought concerns about their own survival. In this they saw themselves as the most important, and many were ready to risk their lives to get out of the city.

The situation in Königsberg became more threatening from hour to hour. On the 26th January the 3rd Byelorussian Front had strong units eight kilometres north, east and south of the city centre. Königsberg's surrounding ring of twelve old forts and bastions began to form the line of defence. At the northern Fort Quednau, about six kilometres from the city centre, the German 367th Infantry Division was able to repel a strong Soviet attack, knocking out 30 enemy tanks, and at the easterly Fort Stein the 561st Volks Grenadier Division held its positions against the advancing Russians.

The first low-flying Soviet aircraft appeared over the city and drowned out the sound of the artillery with their engines. The offices, factories and dockyards were still working. The vast licensing and distribution administration continued to function. Even Pillau's request for food for the refugees was fulfilled. Dr Ostermeyer had been tasked by the War Association of Food Wholesalers in Maraunenhof. Shifts working day and night filled a large wooden barge with peas, beans, flour, sugar, ham and other foodstuffs. On Sunday the 27th January a harbour tug took the barge in tow from the goods harbour to Gross Holstein at the mouth of the Pregel River, from where it was to be towed to Pillau next day.

Dr Ostermeyer had thought not only of the foodstuffs, but of his own welfare and that of his staff. In a roundabout way he had obtained from the Party leadership written permission to accompany the load together with his staff. He had hardly got the valuable piece of paper in his hand when he was off with the firm's lorry to collect the families of the little workforce and some friends from all over Königsberg and bring them to the barge. His own family had left days before, leaving the city on one of the last trains for the west.

At about 1520 hours the Soviet artillery began firing on the city. The lorry driver now had to make a large detour, but by evening the last people were on the barge in Gross Holstein. The group spent the night in a fisherman's house near the mooring.

On Sunday morning the frost had increased to minus 20 degrees. Freezing, they tramped to the barge, going quickly to get away at last. But their hopes were dashed by the bargees. The barge was too wide to be towed through the narrow channel in the ice. The sharp edges of the ice could cut clean through the oak planking and it would sink within a few hundred metres.

After a long discussion they decided to transfer the cargo from the wooden barge to an iron one lying nearby. This took the whole day and into the night. With the exception of 500 kilos of sugar, the wooden barge was emptied. They could not lift another kilo more and placated themselves with the thought that they had everything on the steel lighter except the 500 kilos of sugar. But the promised tug was not there. Disappointed, they crept back to their camp in the cosy, warm fisherman's house.

Monday the 29th January broke. In the morning half light they saw three ships coming towards them along the canal from Königsberg: an icebreaker, behind it a minesweeper and a small freighter. Despite the cold, the decks were full of people. Dr Östermeyer's people waved and shouted: 'Take us with you! Take us with you!' But no one responded. The crews of the three ships had had virtually no sleep for days. Practically without stopping, they had been travelling between Königsberg and Pillau carrying refugees.

The women and children they now had on board had arrived in Königsberg on the 25th and 26th January from the eastern and northern parts of the province. As the Russians opened fire on the city, they had been sent to the Schichau shipyard to be taken aboard ship. Distraught, they had set off. The Lötzeners, who had been accommodated in an elementary school in the east, set off in groups of 50 to 100 people. It took them about six hours, for on their way they had kept having to take cover and were often detained for long periods in some cellar or other.

The shipyard quays were already full of people waiting when the Lötzeners arrived. It had become dark and the firing had died down. No ships were to be seen, and it was midnight before the minesweeper and the freighter came alongside. The gangways were hardly down before both ships were stormed by the crowd. In the middle of the crush there was a flash of light, followed by the first heavy explosion. Panic broke out. Many ran screaming back into the city, others threw themselves flat on the ground, others pushed the people in front of them into the ship, believing that it would be safer there.

Many were trampled down and injured. The crowd thought that they were being bombed.

In fact engineers were blowing up the secret installations of the submarine construction yards. The minesweeper commander seemed to be the only one to have immediately understood the situation. He shouted down from the bridge through a megaphone: 'Listen! There are people here!' Slowly the people on the quay quietened down and willingly followed the sailors' instructions. Half an hour later the ships cast off with the icebreaker leading to break the quickly forming ice.

When the convoy passed the Gross Holstein moorings, the morale of Dr Ostermeyer's people sank to zero. There were arguments because some wanted simply to leave the supplies and continue on foot, either along the canal to Peyse or across the fields towards Metgethen, where one could see in the far, far distance the white smoke of the trains to Fischhausen. But every time they saw a refugee-laden ship or a barge approaching from Königsberg, they jumped as one man aboard the wooden barge, which meanwhile had become frozen fast to the iron one, and shouted for rescue. Late afternoon they gave up and went back to the fisherman's house once more, frozen through.

On Tuesday the 30th January they were woken up by the sounds of fighting. They could clearly hear the bellowing of anti-tank guns and the rattling of machine guns coming over the snow-covered fields to them from the north. The Russians seemed to be quite close. The people made controversial proposals, having delayed too long, and did not know whether to flee on shore. In fact the Soviets had thrust forward west of Königsberg towards the canal and had already cut the city's last land connection. Königsberg was surrounded.

Ship after ship went past the desperately waving and shouting Königsbergers. This time they had a response. They should go on to the signal station, where the ship would lay alongside. Four men raced along the old towpath and reached the signal station in five minutes, shortly after the icebreaker.

When they explained the situation to the helmsman, he shook his head. Towing was out of the question. The ship was only tasked with picking up the signal station personnel and taking them along the canal to Pillau. And the helmsman was not only concerned about the firing on the land for this was good flying weather and his ship was only armed with two machine guns. He was in a hurry to get to Pillau. But the four men did not give up. One of them was on the board of the shipping company and was eventually able to convince him.

The icebreaker turned round and went back. It needed almost an hour to thaw the frozen hawsers and free the barge's side before it could extricate the fast-frozen barge. Then at a slow speed it went down the canal along the south coast of the Samland parallel to the Königsberg-Fischhausen-Pillau railway line. The firing by the Soviets behind them gradually became weaker; they were, for the moment, safe. Of what was happening in the Samland at this time they only learned later, piecemeal.

Chapter 10

The Soviet Invasion of the Samland

From the canal the south coast of the Samland looked like a broad land-scape of individual marshes and woods looking dead in the glowing winter sunshine. Beyond stretched the most fruitful and densely populated area of East Prussia. The right angle projecting between the Kurisches Haff and the Frisches Haff lagoons fell as a steep cliff down to the sea in the north and west. Bathing resorts and little fishing harbours formed the picture of the Amber Coast, where in the grey times of prehistory this valuable resin fossil had been found. In Palmnicken, the best known source, the amber was excavated in open mines by giant shovels out of the blue-black earth. A granary in the East Prussian bread basket, the Samland was above all a summer paradise for nature lovers, gliding, sailing, and children. The long sandy beaches had attracted tourists from Königsberg and the whole country in peacetime. In wartime the locals had their paradise to themselves until the Russian came in January 1945.

For days it had looked no different than had already been seen in Osterode and Allenstein, Bartenstein and Heilsberg. Thousands of treks from the counties east of Königsberg headed west along the coast near Palmnicken and then south-westwards via Fischhausen to Pillau. Overtaken by fleeing German Wehrmacht columns, with the Russians hot on their heels, the refugees enjoyed no respite.

In the middle of this scrum was also the Volkssturm from the Cobjeiten Estate, which the young Siegel couple had seen on exercise in the fields in front of Rauschen on the 21st January. That same afternoon the Volkssturm men had been taken from their exercise to become a 'hunting commando' with the task of holding open the road going west from the north of Königsberg for the Wehrmacht and protecting it from low-flying aircraft. The landlord of Tyrkehnen, Max Schneege, also belonged to this commando with his people and some neighbours. Some of them had served as officers in the First World War. Now they were being led by a milkman, a sturdy SA man, who had never held a weapon in his life.

They were driven to the Russians past the oncoming treks on trucks. On the roadside were abandoned Wehrmacht vehicles, toppled-over trek wagons, refugee baggage and dead horses. The people were so engaged with their progress, their survival, that they did not notice what was happening around them. Only when they came under fire and everything went crazy did the picture change. And while mothers sought their children, and crying

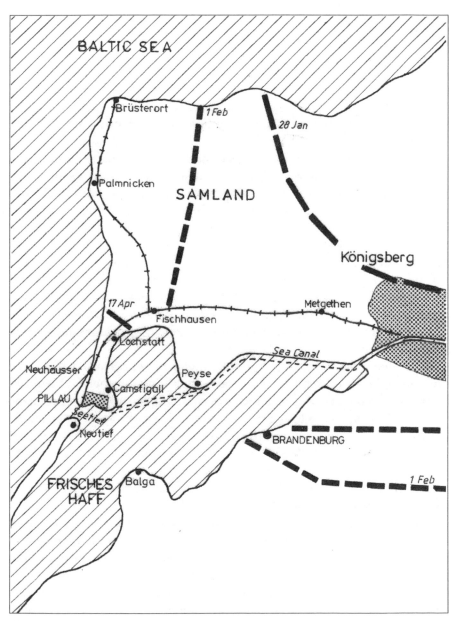

Map 3. The Soviet invasion of the Samland

children their mothers, only then did the wagons stop – until those following simply tipped them over into the ditch in order to take their place.

The Volkssturm men found none of the empty roads that they were supposed to keep free. Driving against the stream, the front only got a little nearer every day and they were already far beyond Königsberg before they became stuck in a small village.

Somebody brought a poster that they had to stick on doors, windows and fences: 'The situation has been secured. There are no grounds for unrest or flight. The District Leader.' There were no civilians left there. The village dairy had been plundered and cheese and butter was strewn everywhere in the snow. Soldiers shot the pigs running around and threw them on a horse-drawn ammunition wagon. The ammunition had previously been unloaded on a dung heap.

The perplexed Volkssturm men were unable to find quarters, they were so frozen and tired. A colonel shouted to the dairy assistants to please immediately march off to the west and provide the treks with flank protection. So the troops turned around and set off with the refugees day after day back to the west. At night they set up their machine guns on the roadside. They could not help them, nor could they protect them. Soldiers laughed at them and Max Schneege bore the brunt of the jeering for wearing an overcoat in Party brown cloth, which he wore as a uniform over his civilian clothing. But there was much of this as it got worse. Once he fell upon a big group of inadequately dressed, neglected-looking pedestrians. They were inmates of the Tappiau nursing home who had no one to look after them and were never seen again.

On Sunday the 28th January the Tyrkehners approached Königsberg once more. During the last two days the sounds of fighting behind them had clearly got nearer and Max Schneege was confused. Early in the morning he went off alone on foot to Königsberg. There was a lot of coming and going in the city. Everywhere there were Wehrmacht, Volkssturm, Hitler Youth and among them refugees with bags and packs. Max Schneege made his way to the office of the business manager of the East Prussian *Herdbuchgesellschaft*, Dr Schumann, with whom he was close friends. Schneege was lucky: Dr Schumann had been waiting determinedly at his post. After a few glasses of schnaps and some telephone conversations, Schneege received new orders. He was to turn around with the Tyrkehners and set up in Rauschen.

By evening Schneege was back with his people. They were now down to six and had no problem rounding up two horses and a sledge with which they could set off home. But already in the overnight location they became hopelessly stuck. A number of horse-drawn gun carriages had forced their way into the treks and brought them to a halt. Schneege felt secure with the orders he had and forced a way between the strange vehicles with the sledge. He knew that they had come along the railway from Rauschen. Nevertheless he still had to go round several fences and inconsiderately force his way through the oncoming treks before he reached the railway station. There they pulled their sledge on to the tracks and drove between the rails of the Samland railway to Rauschen, from where they finally returned to Tyrkehnen.

On the north coast of the Samland between Rauschen and Brüsterort it was still quiet, thanks to the only still-functioning German defence belt east of the Neukuhren aerodrome. The Siegels, who had turned back from Pillau for Rauschen, enjoyed the peaceful winter landscape and liked the deceptive peace so much that on one of the evenings they opened a bottle of wine.

The news of the Russian advance, the pessimism of the soldiers coming back from the front and constantly approaching thunder of the guns gradually changed even the Rauscheners to becoming very uneasy. One after another they set off for Pillau or tried to find a boat in Neukuhren fishing harbour. Now even Peter Siegel's parents did not want to stay any longer, and the young doctor's leave pass had expired.

On the 28th January Peter Siegel reported to the Rauschen field hospital, where they were packing up. Within an hour the field hospital was to move to Pillau. For the elderly chief doctor the new man had come just at the right time. He gave him the job of escorting the train, while he went ahead in his vehicle. All four lugging their baggage, the Siegels made their way to the station. The hospital train was a normal passenger train. The wounded lay on the benches and civilians crowded the corridors. No one had the heart to chase them away. An elderly couple kept climbing in and out, unable to decide whether to use the opportunity to go or not. Finally they gave up and went back into the town.

The train left at midnight and passed five stations but at the Marienhof junction it stopped, for the Russians had reached the Fischhausen water meadows between Peyse and Fischhausen. The staff of the Peyse Power Station had fled over the ice to Pillau and that part of the Samland still in German hands was without electricity. This also meant that the pumps in the stations were not functioning and the locomotives were without water.

The station master heard that there was still water at Palmnicken, 66 kilometres by track there and back. A locomotive was sent off with three tank wagons. It had already been dark for some time and the front line was only 12 kilometres away. Would they get back? The brave railwaymen returned next morning and the train was off again towards Fischhausen before noon. Hours later the Russians were in Marienhof, and at about the same time they were able to cut the direct Königsberg-Pillau line between Seerappen and Metgethen.

In the last train to get through sat the Königsberger Heinz Kroll. He had no idea of what was happening only several hundred metres behind him. Together with his old mother, he had left Königsberg on foot on the 28th January for Pillau, a distance of about 45 kilometres. For this leg-amputee Finance Office official the route over snow and ice was particularly difficult. Nevertheless they reached Seerappen that night, having made 15 kilometres. Mother and son spent the night at the home of an officer. When they wanted to go on next morning, Kroll's stump was so swollen that his artificial leg no longer fitted. He helped by bandaging it and made his way to Seerappen railway station. There he wanted to turn back, but his mother persuaded him to change his mind.

At about 0700 hours they climbed aboard an open wagon of a goods train in whose cattle trucks lay wounded. The train remained all day at the station in minus 20 degrees, during the course of which some 30 wounded died and were unloaded again and placed next to each other in the station buildings.

At last, at about 1800 hours, the train set off. Nearby Kroll heard the firing of Russian anti-tank guns, then machine-gun fire. That night they stayed in the station buildings of the next station, Poweyen, and it was not until the following afternoon that they left the station on an ammunition train, behind which wild shooting had broken out. For several minutes they feared for their lives, then the noise lessened and they were out of the danger zone.

The firing had been at a refugee train from Königsberg as it was passing the Seerappen signal box. The engine stopped with a riddled boiler. A thick white cloud of steam, which hung long in the icy winter air, lay like a shroud over the wagons as the Russians stormed the train, occupied by women and children, firing and shouting. The same fate awaited the two following trains between Seerappen and Metgethen, and hundreds of civilians were killed.

On the 30th January the Soviets had reached the lagoon coast west of Königsberg and thus surrounded the East Prussian capital. They had thrust deeply into Samland in an east-west direction and were soon only three kilometres from Fischhausen and ten from Palmnicken. The German front found itself completely dispersed. Only the miserable remains of the 3rd Panzer Army still existed.

Elements of the Wehrmacht and thousands of civilians were in wild flight in western Samland. The opening of the south-western point of its sack-like shape was not large enough to allow a proper outflow. The roads were choked and Pillau's capacity limited.

The trek from the Tapiau area just 40 kilometres east of Königsberg had already been ten days under way. First they had headed for Königsberg, then they had been forced north past Königsberg, where apparently they passed Max Schneege's Volkssturm unit and, like it, were constantly being stuck in jams with Wehrmacht vehicles, guns and treks. They had finally broken out of the overcrowded town of Germau several kilometres southeast of Palmnicken in order to find quarters on the coast in Sorgenau. Now on their way, they learned that the refugees remaining behind in Germau had fallen into the hands of the Russians. Their wagons had been plundered and they had been locked up in the churches and a barn.

Despite the increased artillery fire on them, the Tapiauers drove on. Ernst Damerau, a farmer from Moterau, led the trek, which consisted of a whole row of relatives, among them Bruno Damerau, the registrar of Tapiau, and his family. They only wanted to move forward as quickly as possible to the next place, to find a roof over their heads before Ivan came. Several men went ahead looking for accommodation. They found a half-empty school that was being defended like a fortress by a burly man. The Tapiauers were not to be intimidated. They drove their wagons into the iced-over school yard and occupied a classroom on the ground floor. Space was found for the horses in a large barn. They were able to obtain straw for them and wood for the little iron stove. Soon a hen was being cooked in the pot.

Towards midnight they were awoken by artillery fire. The men jumped up and ran outside. Towards Germau the sky was a deep red and they could hear machine-gun fire coming from a nearby wood. It could not take long before the Russians were there. Dejected, they returned to the classroom. Some simply wanted to continue on foot either to the south or the north, and it took some effort on the part of the others to talk them out of this nonsense. Awkwardly they removed their wedding rings from their fingers and hid them in the straw with their other valuables. Then they waited for whatever was to come.

But nothing more came that night. The machine-gun fire stopped and soon afterwards the refugees were asleep on their straw nests once more. Daylight lay lead-grey on the snowed-over fields when life returned to the school. Another group occupied the classroom next to the Tapiauers; they had run into the fire of the Russians during the night. One farmer had a minor graze from a bullet on the upper arm and they had lost two wagons, but otherwise nothing had happened to them.

It had become suspiciously quiet on the road. Bruno Damerau burrowed in the straw, unable to find his wedding ring. Suddenly all the people that had been out in the yard rushed hastily into the room. A sledge with laughing and waving Russian soldiers had driven past. Several minutes later it came back and drove into the schoolyard. There were three strapping lads, about 20 years old, with their hands fast on the barrels of their sub-machine guns. They were looking for 'Germanski Soldat'. A Lithuanian among the refugees was able to understand them and showed them over the school from the cellar to the attic. Then he came back with them. The Russians were quite friendly and smiled at the refugees: 'When Hitler finished, we will all be brothers,' translated the Lithuanian. The Russians came from Smolensk and wanted to know why the people were travelling. The victorious Red Army was only against the Hitler-fascists, but felt themselves to be liberators for all the others.

After half an hour's difficult discussion only lack of mutual understanding remained.

The Russians had hardly gone when the sounds of fighting resumed. The Tapiauers crept into the straw and waited for the Russians to return that evening as promised. The men had discovered a ravine where the women and girls could hide, but the Russians did not come back. German counter-attacks had created a breathing space.

Next day the frightened Tapiauers decided to head for Pillau. For the journey they fortified themselves with a goose, which had been brought along alive in a wagon. There was nothing left for the horses, and they had to make an expedition for fodder. Bruno Damerau and his brother pulled a sledge over an iced-up, completely ruined track to the next estate. They saw no sign of anyone on their way. Further off they could hear rifle fire. The estate was deserted and looked desolate. Potatoes, grain, hay, straw, peas, and farming implements lay strewn about in the snow, doors had been smashed in, and a dead pig lay near the dung heap. A sharp wind was wafting fresh snow over the landscape. Both men hurried through fear of being cut off by the Russians. They packed potatoes, hay and a large bundle of clover on their sledge and made their way back to the school.

The roast goose was heavy going. The silence outside made them some-what uneasy, so they set off next morning. The sounds of fighting had increased again, stronger than the previous day, but also further away. The road to Pillau was reserved for the Wehrmacht. The host of civilians made their way over the fields towards the sea with wagons, sledges and on foot to the port.

In the Lochstädter Woods, about 15 kilometres from Pillau, the stream of refugees was even denser and had almost come to a halt. The Tapiauers were lucky, having arrived close to the chaussee. On the other side, only separated by the military convoys driving past, soldiers were cooking. The refugees sent across a delegation to beg and soon had steaming in their bowls, mess tins and other vessels a thick bean soup with plenty of meat –

horseflesh, but that did not bother them. The soldiers not only gave them something to eat, but also informed them about where they came from and how it had been for them on the way. They belonged to an East Prussian Volksgrenadier division and were worried about their own families. The refugees were happy to at last hear sympathetic words and not just be messed about. The fact that they could go no further did not change anything. Their route was crossed by another even stronger stream of refugees pouring out of Fischhausen for Pillau.

The drama in Fischhausen had begun at about 2200 hours on the evening of Sunday the 28th January. It was a cold winter's night when Dr Ostermeyer transferred sacks of foodstuffs from the wooden barge to the iron barge in Gross Holstein, the fresh junior doctor Peter Siegel and his relations travelled on an improvised hospital train from Rauschen to Marienhof, and thousands made their way over the ice roads of the Frisches Haff lagoon.

In the town hall of Fischhausen District President von der Gröben had already thought of going to bed when he received a call from Gau headquarters in Königsberg. The President, Reichs Defence Minister and Gauleiter Erich Koch, was thinking of holding a conference in Fischhausen next morning with several senior Gau officials.

The district president knew his Pappenheimer and he knew how brittle the situation in Königsberg was. This call was the first sign of flight, and the senior Gau officials recognised it as such, most of them arriving the same night. The population of Königsberg knew nothing about it. They made their own version of events and the Russian artillery spoke clearer to them than the silence of the 'hold on' Gauleiter. On this sinister winter night, in which the temperature rapidly dropped from minus 10 to minus 25 degrees before midnight, thousands left their homes and fled head over heels from the capital. Those who could not get away on a train or could not be taken on a cart or truck took to the long road on foot. With sledges, carts, and prams they poured into a gloomy train along the Pillau road. Hundreds of motor vehicles with civilian dignitaries, Wehrmacht staff or specially prominent mortals overtook the refugees or were forced in among them when Wehrmacht convoys and tanks appeared.

The road from Fischhausen was completely blocked that night. Together with the adjutant of the general of prisoners of war, Major Freiherr von Schröter, whom he happened to meet, District President von der Gröben was able to get through the traffic jam. Some of the refugees were sent straight over the ice of the Fischhausen water meadows to Pillau. Trek drivers had to drive their wagons on the snowy meadow banks or leave the wagons and animals standing and continue on foot. The majority headed for Fischhausen, where everyone sought warm accommodation.

For two whole days the flood continued and Fischhausen was hopelessly overcrowded. When the Soviets appeared on the 30th January, they thrust towards Pillau and blocked the way for the refugees coming from northern and central Samland.

As expected, the Gau officials' conference in Fischhausen never took place, the gentlemen having gone off to Pillau. Gauleiter Koch flew with a small staff out of surrounded Königsberg on the 31st January to Heiligenbeil, and then on to Neutief on the Frische Nehrung lagoon, where a command bunker had already been set up for him. From there he sent Hitler his famous telegram: '4th Army in flight in the Reich. Cowardly attempt to withdraw to the west. I will continue to defend East Prussia with the Volkssturm.'

This telegram incidentally had two different consequences. The commander of the 4th Army, General Hossbach, was relieved of his command for attempting to effect a junction with the 2nd Army to the west and transferred to the reserve. General Müller took over the command. And the arrogant offer to defend East Prussia with the Volkssturm led to the recruitment of all men under 60 from the treks. In the course of events this changed nothing, but many of them died.

Chapter 11

The Sinking of the *Wilhelm Gustloff*

Late evening on the 30th January the improvised hospital train from Rauschen with the young junior doctor and his family was lined up at the unloading platform at the harbour railway station in Pillau. A snowstorm was keeping them confined to their wagons.

Peter Siegel only dared get off the next morning. He stumped over the tracks to the station buildings. Already from afar he could see behind them the mass of people forming a thick crowd down to the pier. He went round this crowd and approached the Russendamm, where the outline of a large ship towered in the winter sky. The wounded from another hospital train were already being loaded on the *Meteor* (3,700-ton) hospital ship. Two of the senior doctors that had driven ahead of his train were standing around.

'We are next,' one of the two called out to him. 'You will now have to supervise your unit!' Siegel understood that neither of them was prepared to let him wriggle out of it. But they let him at least show his marching orders to Gotenhafen, where apparently his Neidenburger Hospital was – if the Russians had not got there from the north.

Siegel looked for a ship that would take him to Gotenhafen. As far as he could see lay freighter after freighter. Both of Pillau's harbours were completely full. The naval sea transport detachment had the whole available shipping space of the supply fleet in the harbour on the move. As well as the 13,882-ton wounded transport ship *Monte Rosa* and the hospital ship *Meteor* lying in Pillau harbour that day, there were also the *Göttingen* (6,200 tons), the MS *Gotenland* (5,266 tons), the *Irene Oldendorff* (1923 tons), the *Eberhard Essberger* (5,064 tons), the *Fangturm* (1,923 tons), the training ship *Oktant* (800 tons), the training ship *Nautik* (1,127 tons) and many smaller ships. Peter Siegel forced his way through the mass of people. The people were not only pressing up the gangplanks to the *Göttingen*, but the first mate had let down pallets with a crane on which prams, old people and baggage could be brought aboard. Next to it lay the *Gotenland*, where things were the same. Only the day before the ship had been in the Schichau docks in Danzig for repair because part of the decks had been torn up by a bomb strike off Libau. The *Gotenland*, despite the protests of Captain Vollmers, had been sent by naval headquarters in Danzig without an anchor chain, without a capstan on the foredeck and without a forecastle.

Hitler Youths were loading artillery ammunition on the *Irene Oldendorff*, looking completely exhausted. Peter Siegel discovered that they had been on a ten-day march from a training camp near Elbing over the lagoon ice to Pillau. They had already reserved places for themselves on the ship, but had first to finish loading the ammunition. Then they had to help on board the women and children who were waiting patiently and half-frozen behind a barrier.

Going past another ship he saw a gangway breaking. The picture of an old woman falling would remain with him for ever. With a completely expressionless face, she fell straight down with her many dresses slowing her fall like a balloon. She hit the water without a sound. At the same moment a member of the crew jumped after her and hauled her back on board with the help of his shipmates. It did not always go so smoothly. Particularly at night, with the ruthless pressing forward to the edge of the pier, women and children were being driven into the water and drowned before anyone could help them.

The further Peter Siegel went from the outer harbour closer to the inner harbour so did the mass of people lessen. After half an hour on his way there were only small groups and he could see how city buses were bringing in the refugees. At a naval ship with a most unusual superstructure and a forest of aerials over the bridge, he caught sight of the First Officer and had luck. He could go to Gotenhafen with his family and go on from there to Kiel aboard the night-fighter directing ship *Togo* (5,402 tons), which had been on station until then off Norway. An hour later Peter Siegel and his relatives were on board. They were given a cabin with four bunks and a washing facility and, apart from that, could eat with the crew. Even if the onward journey to Kiel did not take place later, they had it better on the Pillau-Gotenhafen stretch than most others.

When the *Togo* cast off at nightfall, she was followed by the steamer *Göttingen*, sailing via Hela to Swinemünde. The *Göttingen* was carrying about 5,000 people, mainly women and children. The people sat and lay close together in the deep holds that were only sparsely covered in straw, without either heating or water. For toilets they had buckets that the sailors pulled up on ropes. The stink was almost as bad as the hunger that soon set in. Apart from the sparse rations for the crew, there was no food at all on board. What they could spare the crew shared with pregnant women and mothers with children. They were constantly being pestered by soldiers offering rifles, pistols, tobacco and jewellery in exchange for food. It was worst for the wounded, several hundred of whom were lying in an emergency hospital.

An army staff doctor vainly tried to look after them, but he only had a small box of pills, no medical equipment, no bandaging material, and no disinfectant. The journey lasted only three days, but cost the lives of a dozen old folk and babies, and ten soldiers.

The *Göttingen*'s place on the Russendamm and the *Togo*'s in the harbour were taken over by two other ships in a short time. The officials estimated that there were 60,000 refugees waiting to be carried off. And however many ships wanted to take them, however many took the three ferries over the Tiefsee channel to the Nehrung Spit to go on by foot, the great influx kept the numbers constant. The ferries across the Seetief were overfilled in both directions since the people from the lagoon ice had arrived in Neutief.

In Pillau town hall the chief clerk, Hugo Kaftan, sat at his desk and ripped up the instruction he had received from Naval Senior Staff Superintendant Plautsch: 'Minimum occupancy of two rooms eight persons, in three rooms twelve persons, in four rooms 18 persons, and in five rooms 24 persons.' This might have been appropriate two days previously, but now the people were already sleeping in the corridors and in the cellars. Kaftan's four-roomed apartment housed 50 strangers, and he hardly went back there anymore. An hour previously he had picked up the occupants of the old folks' home in Fischhausen, who had been wandering about the town. They were now waiting in the town hall cellars for someone to take them to the old folks' home in Neuhäuser.

The field telephone rang. Police General and SS Brigade Commander Heldig was on the line. Kaftan knew him as one of Koch's bosom friends. He expected nothing good, but he went pale when the voice shouted: 'I shit on you, you bloody sack of shit! If you don't find me suitable quarters by 1400 hours, I'll eradicate you, you'll see! You will get to know me!'

Kaftan only said: 'Yes, General,' and put the phone down. That morning he had moved heaven and earth to find seven of Hellwig's officers a duty room, two offices and a room for the typist. Finally he had put their luggage in the Schiffler pub. They should look around the refugees' quarters again.

Kaftan was not worried about the threat. For several days there had been more generals than corporals in Pillau. Headquarters Army Group *Nord* and Headquarters 3rd Panzer Army that had been driven out of Samland with all their staffs, offices withdrawn from Kurland, reception staffs, and now the Party chiefs from Königsberg. The latter dare go no further as long as Gauleiter Koch sat like a cat in front of a mouse hole in Neutief.

There were just three 'Representatives of the Reichs Defence Commisioners' for refugee matters. The most important had set up his tent in the 'Golden Anchor' on the fore harbour pier. Dr Dzubba, a notorious intimate of the Gauleiter, Regional Commissar Bauer and a number of other 'Golden

Pheasants' stood aside. Dzubba was the Gauleiter's voice in Pillau. Through the District Headquarters he directed the recruitment and deployment of the Volkssturm – and issued boarding passes.

Commander Branneis from the Naval Headquarters gave the various refugee offices, including the District Headquarters, the names of arriving ships and their loading capacities. Each of these offices then issued boarding passes without consulting the others. Few refugees used these cards, many believing they would have to pay for them. And in the press on the mole, everyone was happy when the next ship arrived. There nobody asked for the passes, and with the rapid sequence of ships, many ships were loaded and unloaded again before the issuing authorities had issued them.

The only offices that Kaftan kept in touch with were those of the District Headquarters and the NSV. District Leader Grau was his protector from the Wehrmacht. When a colonel rang the town hall and demanded that in certain private houses latrines should be dug, Kaftan passed the order on to the District Headquarters, which anyway did not know what to do with the constantly growing Volkssturm units.

On the 31st January the town had already been without water for two days. Shortly after the damage caused by the explosion at Fort Stiehle had been cleared up, the Peyse Power Station had packed up. Not only the pumps at the waterworks but the sewage system also did not work. The waste water backed up and in many cellars, including the only field hospital, there was a stinking brew. There was no working water closet in the whole town. The heaps of excreta in the streets were a nuisance. Quite rightly, the Wehrmacht feared an outbreak of illness as soon as the weather became warmer. So in the gardens of private houses and on open ground hundreds of latrines were dug. The excreta lying in the streets did not diminish, however; there were too many people in the town.

Kaftan was already setting up two rooms in the town hall for a 'Mother and Child' delivery station when a drunken police officer went up to him: 'General Hellwig wants new quarters immediately! Otherwise it will become very unpleasant for you!'

He could hardly contain himself, but Kaftan kept his head: 'Of course, captain. I will take him myself.' One hour previously the new Army Commandant of Pillau, Lieutenant General Anset, had issued a circular: 'The commander of the 3rd Panzer Army has tasked me with quartering matters within the fortress area of Pillau. Therefore I have appointed Colonel Pfeiffer as head of the Pillau quartering office, Horst-Wessel-Allee 12.' The town clerk led Hellwig's envoy to Horst-Wessel-Allee and asked an orderly to announce the captain to Colonel Pfeiffer. Afterwards Kaftan heard no more of Hellwig.

The commander of the 3rd Panzer Army, Colonel-General Raus, proved himself a benefactor, without Kaftan and the many thousand refugees knowing it. As the Russians thrust forward during the last days of January on the lagoon and the Fischhausen water meadows, heavy machine-gun and rifle fire could he heard coming from the Peyse arsenal. Captain Puhlmann called the Naval Commandant, Captain Jerchel, wanting to know what he should do. 'Do as you think fit,' Captain Jerchel ordered him.

Captain Puhlmann decided to blow up the arsenal. After the charges had been set, the arsenal personnel were to move to Pillau. The appropriate orders were being issued when Captain Jerchel telephoned: 'Don't blow it up! As far as demolition is concerned, you now come under the immediate command of the 3rd Panzer Army and Colonel-General Raus!'

Puhlmann had the charges disconnected. Shortly afterwards Colonel Ludendorff called and wanted to know what effects the explosion would have on the nearby Peyse Power Station, the towns of Fischhausen and Pillau as well as the ice on the Frisches Haff lagoon. Nobody on the naval side had thought of raising these questions. Captain Puhlmann could give no clear information: 'I and my personnel have no experience with demolition of such proportions, including the demolition effects dependant on many factors – wind, situation, the state of the ground, etc.'

Colonel Ludendorff ordered the demolition deferred awaiting a direct order from Colonel-General Raus. Part of the arsenal was cleared and served as shelter for refugees. The remaining mines and torpedoes later fell into Russian hands. Possibly the shock would not have broken the surface ice, but certainly the flying debris on the vast concentration of people in the vicinity would have had a devastating effect.

At the same time an order came from another colonel-general, apparently less concerned with the fate of the refugees. The new commander of Army Group *Nord*, Colonel-General Rendulic, issued from his headquarters in Neuhäuser: 'No man that can participate in the defence of East Prussia, in whatever form, is to leave the army group's area.'

Town clerk Kaftan had already started thinking about his own withdrawal, but was still sitting fast. He would not get permission to leave as long as Gauleiter Koch sat securely in his bunker in Neutief and the prominent Party leaders practised defence to the end. Hugo Kaftan felt the desire to have a drink in the 'Ilskefalle' bar behind the inner harbour, but this was impossible with the masses of people. So he went to Karl Fischer, who had his NSV office in the 'Golden Anchor' and now was sitting in the snug, and wherever Karl Fischer was, there was also schnaps.

He got the schnaps, but the NSV man was not about to mope, for he was half a bottle of schnaps ahead of Hugo Kaftan and because he had had some good news. A barge full of food had arrived for his NSV kitchen. His only concern was how he could get this treasure from where it lay alongside the 'Ostsee' fish factory to his stores. 'But you have quite a few vehicles in your motor pool, Hugo?'

Hugo put on a thoughtful face: 'If you give the water ways office a tractor, you can bring it straight across.'

'And pull it through the crowds of people on a handcart? We don't stand a chance!'

Kaftan agreed, but still pretended: 'The Kauka truck has a crack in the cylinder block. The tractor would be best.'

One hour later six Volkssturm men were on the way to the inner harbour with a tractor and rubber-tyred trailer to unload Dr Ostermeyer's barge.

Basically, the Königsberger wholesale food merchant was happy to finally leave the barge at the 'Ostsee' fish factory. The icebreaker that had towed it through the canal had simply dropped it off in the outer harbour. Helplessly it had drifted towards the moorings of the big ships and it was already almost dark when a vast ship's side approached. The barge was apparently not visible from the steamer's bridge. A loud cry arose from the pier, alerting the crew to the barge at the last moment. Ostermeyer and his people were staring dumbly at the iron wall that was almost on top of them when a head appeared over the railings: 'What are you up to there with your apple barge?' Then he let loose a fearful cannonade of swearing about them until a tug came and took it in tow to the other side of the harbour.

Next morning the food wholesaler had his next surprise. He had expected the food to be taken to Gotenhafen for safety, but the officials of the district agricultural staff had other ideas and took the load for the feeding of the refugees. Ostermeyer stumped through the snow to the 'Ostsee' fish factory with a bundle of the consignment papers. There he met two senior economic advisers from Dzubba's office that were responsible for feeding within the fortress. These gentlemen were sitting down to an opulent breakfast and were very friendly. No, they had nothing to do with the feeding of the refugees, that was done by Herr Fischer of the NSV. But they would gladly sign for the handover of the foodstuffs to the Königsberg agricultural office.

Dejectedly Dr Ostermeyer returned to his barge that evening after he had dealt with several other formalities and discovered that it was pointless queuing up for boarding cards. It seemed equally pointless to him to join this crazy stream of humanity and perhaps have to wait for days to board a ship.

The seven of them sat in the barge cabin and discussed what to do. They did not want to go out there, trusting in their luck. But to wait until the barge was empty and have themselves towed to Gotenhafen with the barge hanging silently on to something? If it was not so cold, everything would be easier. In the middle of their debate Herr Sonnabend of a competitive Königsberg firm burst in. Dr Ostermayer had brought him along from Gross Holstein out of pure friendship. Thus Herr Sonnabend was so grateful for being brought along as an extra, that he came to tell him that next morning a minesweeper flotilla would be leaving the Russendamm and that there was still room on it. Dr Ostermeyer was not so sure, thinking of the many refugees on the pier.

His concern was unfounded, for the boats lay beyond a barrier. Petty Officer Henkel, commander of boat *02*, would not only take the seven of the group but also another six others that had joined them on the way, and he did not refuse when the Königsbergers invited him to supper on the barge.

The minesweepers were rebuilt 80-ton fishing vessels with a sixteen man crew. They had instructions to each take 50 to 70 refugees each. When Petty Officer Henkel was returning from the harbour office next morning he came across a group of four extremely pretty young girls. One of them, a cheeky blonde, addressed him: 'Captain, can you help us get away from here? If we push ourselves forward, the others will lynch us.'

Henkel said quickly: 'Come one at a time at intervals of ten to fifteen minutes over there to the grey shed. Don't come all four together, that won't work. Then I will get you onboard by various routes.'

Then he went off as if they had only asked him the time. An hour later the girls were aboard the *02*, much to the delight of the crew.

At 1325 hours the minesweepers, all nine of them, were passing through the Seetief channel. They made only slow progress in the heavy seas and the land–lubbers on board were nearly all seasick. At 2135 hours the boats tied up in Harbour I at Gotenhafen.

In the last two days of January the passage, especially for the small ships, became difficult as soon as they reached open water.

A lighter loaded with 37mm gun barrels and carrying hundreds of refugees had just passed the lighthouse on the northern mole when someone shouted: 'The water is coming in here!'

The lighter had a leak and the spaces between the gun barrels gradually began filling with water. Panic broke out in the hold. People were shrieking and trampling on each other as they tried to push the hatch cover up from below. The seamen tried to open the hatch from above while the ship lay deep in the water and was being overcome by it. At last they heaved several of the planks out and let the people on deck. Several thus went overboard. Two swimmers were saved but the others sank.

Frau Pfeifer, who had escaped from the Heiligenberg area several days before with her two children, was still sitting in the hold. She had reached

Pillau via the ice in the lagoon and the Seetief channel. She had stood for hours and was able at the last moment to push her baggage and both children on to a steamer lying alongside. Then she was hit in the chest by a sailor, making her fall back in the crowd while the ship with her crying children moved away from the pier. It was all the same to her if the boat went under. She did not believe she would see her children again.

Automatically she got up when the water reached her thighs and hung on to a pipe, then a man pulled her up on to the deck. The sailors strung ropes from the bow to the stern so that no more people would be torn overboard by the waves coming over. A boat coming to the rescue could not come alongside because of the swell. The captain had no choice but to turn round back to Pillau. In the calm water of the Seetief channel, just before the harbour, a rescue boat took on the refugees. The lighter tied on to the mole and was pumped empty there.

Seamen brought ashore two drowned women who had been fished out of the sea and they were buried at Pillau I cemetery. This was nearly full as the victims of the explosion at Fort Stiehle had been buried there. Town clerk Kaftan had made contact with the Army graves officer and had agreed with him to seek a place for a large new cemetery. Soldiers that had succumbed to their wounds were constantly being unloaded from the wounded transports, and a dozen refugees died every day. For the period from the 1st January 1945 to 31st March 1945, 1,563 deaths of civilians were recorded in the Pillau town records.

On the 31st January Hugo Kaftan heard that the 'Strength through Joy' ship *Wilhelm Gustloff* had been hit by four torpedoes off Gotenhafen and sunk. On the 2nd February naval units brought 123 victims of the catastrophe to Pillau. The rumour of the sinking of the ship went round the refugees. Nevertheless the storm on the ever more numerous ships did not diminish, even if some had found good accommodation and preferred not to leave Pillau.

The actual extent of the catastrophe was not known at the time and the rumours soon died down.

As in Pillau, so in the Danzig-Neufahrwasser and Gotenhafen harbours thousands had waited for ships. As in Pillau, the submarine accommodation ship had set off, with the former 'Strength Through Joy' ship *Wilhelm Gustloff* (25,484 tons) and the *Hansa* (21,232 tons). The loading of the *Hansa* was delayed and later the main steam pipe broke, so that she could not follow the *Wilhelm Gustloff* until a day later.

In the early afternoon of the 30th January the *Wilhelm Gustloff* cast off. On board were the members of the 2nd Submarine Training Division, female naval auxiliaries and a large number of refugees from Gotenhafen and Danzig. Unlike at Pillau, the setting off of the ship was not prepared at length, which had made one feel safe in Gotenhafen. Also relations between the civilian and military elements of the ship's command were not of the best. As soon as they set off, there was disagreement over whether the life-boats should be swung out in their davits or not. The civilian crew were against it and the boats remained on their stocks. At about 1900 hours the *Wilhelm Gustloff* rounded the point of the Hela Peninsula. The only escort was the torpedo boat *Loewe*. Snow showers were being driven across the sea by a wind strength of 5 and a swell of 4. Against the strongly agitated sea and increasing icing of the superstructure, the *Loewe* could not take a zigzag course as was intended. Even the *Wilhelm Gustloff* was taking a straight course as Captain Petersen did not trust the bomb-damaged and weak-engined ship with this strain. Consequently he was not going any faster than 12 knots.

Enemy submarines had not been reported in this area, but they were there. At about 1900 hours the Soviet submarine *S-13* had approached the area of the Hela lighthouse from the east. Its commander, Commander Alexander Marinesko, swore. In this strong sea it was impossible to keep the boat at periscope depth. Either the waves blocked his view or the tower stuck out of the water. The fascists could not have wanted a better target. Marinesko decide to stake everything on one card.

'Blow tanks!' he ordered. Slowly the conning tower rose from the water. Together with his signalman, Marinesko climbed out through the tower hatch. The tops of the waves reached to just under the coaming and kept sending spray over them. Gradually a fine sheet of ice formed over the breastwork and their clothing. They could not go on like this without freezing or drowning.

Marinesko was one of the Soviet submarine commanders that had been commanding a boat since the beginning of the war. In 1942 and 1943 he had sunk the German freighters *Siegfried* and *Helene*. Determinedly the two men stared into the pale darkness. And then they saw, where they had expected, to port, the plump outline of a large passenger ship.

Marinesko altered course and closed in on the ship with increased speed. He had to be parallel and a little in front of his prey before he could attack. He could only surface when he was in a firing position. Over the next two hours the two men changed positions on the tower. Every 20 minutes one of them climbed down to warm himself.

By 2108 hours they had reached the point of attack. The bows of the *Wilhelm Gustloff* slowly pushed forward into the leading edge of the torpedo targeting apparatus. The torpedoes were released from the tubes in a quadruple hiss. Then came three dull explosions. They had hit it! At the same time came the call: 'Torpedo four still in tube!' Marinesko turned away and was busy with it for the next half hour, pulling the stuck torpedo back into the boat before it exploded.

The explosions had caused panic to break out on the *Wilhelm Gustloff.* The ship immediately took on five degrees of list to port and was slowly tilting further to 15 degrees, where it held for about 20 minutes. The boats on the starboard side could not be lowered into the water, and on the port side several davits were frozen fast. Some boats were released too soon and dived into the sea, others tipped over when they reached the sea because they were overloaded. On the upper deck there was a struggle for life-floats and there was fighting at all the exits and shots were fired.

When after 20 minutes the ship no longer appeared to be sinking, the panic died down. Over the ship's loudspeakers the officers called upon the people to stay calm, as other ships were on the way to their aid. Several hid back in the interior of the ship, not least to get out of the biting cold. Others looked for jumping-off places on the starboard side, while others lay about on the promenade deck quite resigned to their fate, and from time to time one jumped into the icy water.

At about 2200 hours a violent shaking suddenly ran through the *Wilhelm Gustloff.* The hull tilted right over to one side so that the decks dived into the water. The water poured in everywhere and the ship sank, gurgling, within a few minutes. Hundreds were able to jump into the water, but it did not take long before they froze and went under. The naval units hastily arriving rescued 937 of the shipwrecked, but over 4,000 died.

It is not clear how some of those saved could have survived. The steamer *Göttingen* on passage from Pillau reached the site shortly before midnight and took on 27 survivors that had been over two-and-a-half hours in the water at minus 15 degrees and in a swell of 3 to 4. Then at about 0100 hours the *Gotenland* passed through the wreckage-strewn site and out of hundreds of drifting corpses fished out a woman and a petty officer who had survived under wet blankets on a float.

Chapter 12

The Sinking of the *General von Steuben*

On the 5th February Pillau had fine weather at zero degrees. The Pillauers used the sunshine to queue at their town hall for the next period's food rationing tickets. Of course there were no longer any monthly rations, only holiday rations for seven days: 2,230 grams bread, then 1,000 grams rye bread, 250 grams meat, 150 grams butter, 70 grams margarine, 175 grams jam, 200 grams sugar, 150 grams baby food, 50 grams ersatz coffee and 60 grams cheese. Refugees received no tickets, but were directed to the community provisioning centre, standing in long queues at the NSV supply points.

That day Berta Rubenbauer with her mother and her maid also arrived in the town across the Seetief channel. They had left her mother with the baggage at the harbour and wandered around the town for three hours looking for accommodation before they found a place between empty desks in the office of a removals firm. There they ate the noodle soup that they had collected from the NSV kitchen at the 'Golden Anchor'. Even as they were eating, their eyes closed from fatigue. The way across the ice and the lagoon had been too much.

The Dameraus from Tapiau arrived in Pillau at almost the same time as the Rubenbauers, but they had been received like an occupying power and at their first attempt found accommodation with an official from the naval laundry. They had eaten their last goose near Palmnicken, but there was still so much ham, butter, eggs, honey and sausage left that the official splashed out as he became aware what a blessing of supplies had poured over him. He cleared beds, a bath and even a kitchen for them.

The Rubenbauers queued up every day for their pea soup, two slices of bread and jam. The Dameraus ignored the community feeding. And it so happened that the Tapiauers met someone they knew from home who was now selling bread in a Pillau bakery. Naturally she also sold to the Tapiauers while the Rubenbauers vainly sought to change their long-invalid marks from Allenstein. And these were the small injustices among the 60–70,000 refugees whose only concern was to get away from Pillau alive!

It was 1400 hours when the weak sound of a siren came over from Neutief. Only a few in Pillau heard it. As the stream of refugees had come to an end there had also been no air raid alerts. Two minutes later the Russian bombers arrived. Panic broke out on the pier, which was packed with people. All ran and fell over each other in an attempt to find cover against a house wall or even to reach a cellar. The crying of the children was drowned by the noise of the low-flying bombers and the engaging heavy anti-aircraft guns from Schwalenberg and the ships below. The Soviets came in several waves with their 60 machines.

Most of the bombs fell in the water. An observer thought that the Soviets had dropped about 120 bombs. Only a few of the people on the pier were hit. In all there were 54 killed, including three members of the Wehrmacht, and among the civilians 41 men, eight women and two children. There were 82 wounded. The steamer *Delphin* sank. An icebreaker, a lighter and two mine-sweepers also disappeared under the surface. The water works pumping station and sewage plant, 28 trucks, as well as a number of town buildings near the inner harbour had been turned into rubble by the Russians. A hit on the drainage ditch caused the Holzwiese meadows to be completely flooded, and the people accommodated there sought in all haste to bring their belongings to safety. Some bombs had hit the Pillau sawmill, which immediately went up in flames and burnt down to nothing. It was a large fire, as army engineers had been bringing in freshly cut tree trunks to be cut into beams and planks for a temporary bridge near Fischhausen. The plan had been to take away thousands of refugees from there across the sea and thus reduce the pressure on Pillau, but it came to nothing.

The encircling of Königsberg reduced the number of refugees, if hardly noticeably. On the other hand, the nervousness and stress increased and hardly a day passed without some disturbance. Shortly after midnight on the 19th February refugees in the mass quarters and in private accommodation were shaken out of their sleep by soldiers and Volkssturm men: 'Open the doors and windows! Everybody out! Put something warm on!'

Obediently, they crawled out of their straw sacks and went out sockless into the snow in their boots, complaining and perplexed. Then bangs came from the Frisches Haff lagoon. Windows rattled, dust fell from the walls, but nothing could be seen. 'Demolitions!' said one disdainfully. 'The Russians,' said another and resumed packing.

In fact it was the German ships' heavy guns that had disturbed them. The Admiral Eastern Baltic had ordered the heavy cruiser *Hipper* to Pillau in order to silence the Soviet artillery on both sides of the sea canal and support the Army restoring the land connection to Königsberg. The *Hipper* had anchored southeast of the Pillau outer harbour in the widened entrance to the canal. A tug held her astern in position and then she fired her heavy guns uninterruptedly for an hour towards Metgethen. Then the cruiser went back to the open sea and anchored far out.

Next day she hauled up her anchor and lay alongside the Pillau 'Peace Jetty', from where she fired at the far bank of the sea canal near Galtgarben. This firing was of decisive assistance to the German divisions that had been moving slowly towards Königsberg in the Samland. The Russian resistance was broken.

Meanwhile in Pillau there was keen recruiting for the Volkssturm. Even the brothers Bruno and Ernst Damerau had been caught. Bruno was 55, Ernst 58. Both were ill and had already become unsuitable for anything. Nevertheless at the District Headquarters they had had a piece of paper thrust into their hands for their medical inspector. They stood stark naked in fives in the examination room, showing their age with hanging shoulders and stomachs. As active soldiers in the First World War they had had to let things pass, but what they saw here was a sheer mockery. Only a few words from the young army doctor sufficed and they were all one hundred per cent fit for active service. Of course one could not blame the youngster, he was only doing his duty – and if he had declared them unfit he too perhaps would have been sent to the front.

So Bruno and Ernst Damerau reported in Kamstigall next morning at 0630 hours. There Bruno went to a group of about 40 men that were so sick and frail that even the overhasty army doctor would have to accept their unsuitability. And as always in life, one must stand in the right queue. Bruno Damerau could return to his quarters with the laundry official and was greeted there like a home-coming warrior. The time for reflection was over. Now he had to find a ship at any price before he fell into the hands of the recruiters again.

They did not wait for lunch. The baggage was put on the little wagon and they went back to the pier. After standing waiting for two hours the ship was declared full when they were only 50 metres from it. Together with the others they ran along the pier to the next boarding point. In passing they saw the name *Hektor* on the bow. But there were sentries standing in front of this ship. Men could not go aboard, only women and children. Bruno Damerau saw how a man on his left had to leave and his wife accompanied him after they had apparently tried to plead with the sentry.

The Damerau women did not want to go on board the ship without their husbands. Bruno stopped talking. He took hold of the sick Franz, who could hardly move because of his open leg wound, grabbed the luggage with his free hand and went round the women and children, coming unhindered past the sentry on board the auxiliary cruiser *Hektor*. Several hours later they were all safe and sound in Gotenhafen.

Bruno Damerau was lucky not to have been sucked into the Volkssturm. He never saw his brother Ernst again.

The Volkssturm was basically the last empty manifestation of the Party's claim to power. With the establishment of battalions of youngsters and old men they tried to demonstrate that they were still the bosses in the state, although their organisation had long since ceased to exist. The Volkssturm remained long after the Party superiors had departed. Poorly armed, without training, mainly dressed in civilian clothes or in Party uniforms, they were delivered up to an enemy that gave no quarter. The Wehrmacht could not or would not help them. Only a few of the Pillau Volkssturm survived.

Fear played a big role in this sacrifice. Summary executions were the order of the day. Again and again in the refugees' accounts appear references to hanged civilians and soldiers, whose bodies often hung for days on lamp-posts and trees with placards around their necks saying 'I am a deserter', 'I plundered', 'Saboteur'.

Meanwhile Town clerk Kaftan had found room for a new cemetery on the North Mole that extended for half a kilometre from the dunes almost as far as the Beach Hall and in the course of time could take over 8,000 soldiers and civilians. The cemetery would be laid out between light clumps of firs in accordance with the Heldenheim scheme. A large wood cross adorned the assembly place in the centre. The inscription has not survived, but it would scarcely have taken account of the thousands of women, children and old people dying every day on the East Prussian roadsides.

But at this time much that was going on made no sense. On Saturday the 10th February the *Monte Rosa* was on the way from Pillau to Gotenhafen with wounded and refugees. On the escorting ship *M204* was the deputy director of the Pillau Saving Bank, Gegner, with several boxes of the bank's most important documents. Among them were also the savings accounts of over 21 million Reichsmarks. He was told that they were going to Swinemünde.

Five days later Hugo Kaftan received a letter from Gotenhafen. The sender was Gegner: 'assuredly you think that we have already been in Swinemünde or Wollgast for some time. Unfortunately fate has decreed otherwise. On the way our boat *M204* received another task and we came to Gotenhafen. The boxes are now standing in the harbour and are exposed to the weather. As the mayor of Gotenhafen has already disappeared, we can expect no help from that direction. The only authority is the Party. The naval headquarters does not help us either.' In the end Gegner got away on a ship, but without his boxes, while Hugo Kaftan had to keep going.

Life in Pillau had become a bit more bearable since there was electricity once more, if sporadic. After the Soviets had been driven out of Neplecken and the Peyse area, a military technical company had become involved with the generator in the naval dockyard. Together they sought to repair the damage. Some of the labour force that had turned back assisted them. It all went smoothly to the point when the plant should start up again, for which they needed an outside power source. One of the naval officials suggested using a submarine generator, but it took a long time before all those involved were convinced and two submarines were brought alongside the generator pier. The naval construction engineers, Weiss and Mombe, and the chief engineer of the Peyse power station, Auerbach, then soon discovered that, because of the lack of synchronisation, only one submarine could be connected, and because of the great loss of power in the makeshift connecting system, this one submarine was insufficient. The chief engineer needed a whole day to reduce this loss of power sufficiently to start up the system. Not only did a part of Pillau have electricity again but also a wide part of Samland that German troops were in the course of counterattacking. There mills and dairies could resume serving both the population and the Wehrmacht.

The supply of foodstuff in Pillau had also played a part. The community kitchens worked all hours and at the harbour Volkssturm shared out bread and sausage or smoked ham as provisions for the journey. Many did not get their share in the press, while others declined as they did not want to lose their place. And the baker who had helped the Dameraus from Tapiau was still exchanging bread for meat. In the Ostsee fish shops on the Graben and in the Langegasse, the NSV had set up fish stalls. Two daring fishermen had gone out fishing despite the prohibition and landed two loads of cod. Within a few hours the fish had been sold without the offer having been announced beforehand.

Meanwhile ship after ship was leaving the harbour laden with refugees. By the middle of February 204,000 people had left Pillau this way. Another 50,000 had been transported over the lagoon on foot or with treks and from there fled on foot towards Danzig. Coming towards them were the refugees that had used both the northern ice roads so that the three little ferry steamers were constantly overfilled in either direction.

Those coming from the lagoon to Pillau had hardly the strength to get off at the harbour. After two or three weeks of fleeing through snow and ice, always in fear and often under fire, sick and hungry, their first thoughts were to find accommodation in which to rest. Kaftan remarked a little maliciously: 'The refugees felt fine in Pillau and did not think of going on to the Reich.' However, at the same time he helped to set up cobblers' shops in Breitestrasse and Predigerstrasse for the refugees, as the boots of the majority had suffered in the icy water of the lagoon.

Together with Mayor Scholz and a police captain, Kaftan inspected piles of abandoned baggage in the sea service sheds. Volkssturm men were to sort it out: textiles (bedding and clothing) for the 'Peoples' Sacrifice', foodstuffs to the NSV for use, papers and valuables to the local police for safe keeping. Kaftan was already thinking how many years it would take the few men to work their way through this immense pile when a sailor shouted through the open door: 'The *Steuben* has been caught beyond Stolpmünde! Mine! All drowned!'

The 14,660-ton former North American steamer *General von Steuben* had set sail at about 1530 hours on the 9th February carrying wounded men. It was her third journey from Pillau to Swinemünde. She had 1,467 severely wounded and 1,213 walking wounded on board, as well as 900 refugees and a large number of doctors and German Red Cross nursing sisters. With the crew, this was about 4,000 people.

The ship had passed Hela and the Stolpe Bank unharmed. The torpedo boat *T196* was constantly circling the big steamer as her only escort. On neither ship was anyone aware of the presence of a third vessel, *S-13*, the Soviet submarine under the command of Lieutenant Commander Alexander Marinesko. Already at about 2000 hours, long before the ships approached the Stolpe Bank, he had started an attack but had been deterred by the approaching torpedo boat. Now it was 0050 hours and Marinesko was lying in a firing position for the second time. Two torpedoes left the stern tubes and raced silently though the night-black, calm sea to their target. Moonlight let their illuminated ripples betray them.

In the former ship's hospital on the boat deck a nursing sister placed a child born only a few minutes before in the arms of a young woman and rolled the bed across to the mother's bunk. The army doctor and a naval medical orderly that had assisted him as midwife had finished washing their hands and were about to look for their quarters. They had reached the door and the young doctor declared, more for himself than the politely listening orderly, how one had to act after a birth, when two heavy blows shook the ship. A cruel flash of light flamed up behind the bridge, changing immediately into a blazing fire. The flames illuminated the results of the two hits: a gigantic black cloud of smoke was rising between the two funnels. The two participants in the birth saw nothing more. A screaming mass of people forced their way out through the door, ripping it off on to the deck, which was already beginning to tilt. The sharply slanting bows with the crews' accommodation broke off first. The loosely fastened equipment for a complete field hospital went crashing and clattering overboard, taking with it into the water dozens of women and children who had been standing on the deck into the water.

There was panic below decks. The wounded sought to save themselves from the rapidly encroaching water through the doors and portholes. They climbed and fell over each other recklessly. Cries of pain bellowed out, and shots were fired. The lightly wounded climbed like ants high on the upper works, trying to get into the swung-out lifeboats or to go up the increasingly higher stern of the ship, while cries for help came from the severely wounded below.

The *Steuben* only held above water for a few minutes and then sank, gurgling, taking most of the wounded and refugees with it. The torpedo boat's searchlights swept over the surface, which was covered with debris, dead and swimmers. For hours the launched boats of both naval craft, *T196* and *TS1*, fished out survivors from the water. 630 were saved, including two German Red Cross sisters, and were taken to Kolberg.

At 0450 hours a convoy in the area received orders to steam to where the *Steuben* had gone down. Although the ships immediately changed course and headed for the spot, they only reached it at 0900 hours. Captain Burmeister of the railway ferry *Deutschland* could only find empty, partly upset lifeboats and floats. Between them were bits of wreckage and some bundles of clothing that they took for dead persons floating in the grey-green sea. The ships searched for almost an hour, then resumed their old course and set off again without having saved anyone.

The *General von Steuben* was generally indicated as a hospital ship and both the Army and the Navy were embittered that the Soviets had no respect for ships carrying their wounded. This deed had to be attributed to the German war leadership. On the 19th July 1941 and again on the 27th February 1942 the Soviet Foreign Minister, Vlatcheslav Molotov, had informed the diplomatic representatives of Sweden, Great Britain, Japan and Bulgaria that, although not signatories of the Hague Convention, the application of this to Russia would be regarded as binding if Germany did the same. Germany had declined to answer these appeals.

Thus the Soviets had not felt bound to honour these conditions and acted accordingly. In the summer of 1944, in the withdrawal from the Baltic, even signed and unarmed hospital ships were attacked. Afterwards the German Navy converted freighters and passenger ships into wounded transports. They wore camouflage and carried 20mm quadruple- and 37mm single-barrelled guns.

Nevertheless, in March 1945 several wounded transports were converted back into hospital ships, like the *Pretoria* and the *General San Martin* – i.e their guns were removed and the superstructure painted with a white stripe and a big red cross on the funnel. Whoever had given this order was aware of the situation. Nevertheless, when the *Pretoria* was attacked by Soviet aircraft off Gotenhafen and badly damaged, and many wounded and refugees were killed, the Admiralty simply cabled the Foreign Ministry with an un-demonstrative request for an international protest.

The *Steuben* belonged to an armada of naval ships that were ordered to Pillau from their moorings in the eastern and northern harbours. They included training ships like the *Nautik*, *Oktant*, *Ostmark* and *Herkules*, target ships like the *Venus* and later the unfortunate *Goya*, small hospital ships like the *Glücklauf*, *Meteor*, *Regina*, *Rügen* and *Oberhausen* and the air defence ships *Greif*, *Boelcke* and *Hans-Albrecht-Wedel*.

Pillau had never seen so many ships. The freight traffic with supplies for Army Group *Nord* had more than tripled with the interruption of rail communications to the Reich. Troop transports like the *Ringe*, *Licentia*, *Fangturm* and *Hestia* brought units withdrawn from Kurland from Libau and then took on wounded and refugees before travelling back to Swinemünde or Kiel.

In the Bight of Danzig the main traffic was between Pillau and the harbours of Neufahrwasser and Gotenhafen. Thousands of wounded and refugees were conveyed in return traffic from the eastern to the western ends of the Bight. The ships and their crews got no rest. The air defence ship *Greif* only stopped to load and unload. Its sole task was the transport of supplies for Neutief aerodrome and the fighter squadron stationed there. After two trips with refugees from Königsberg, the *Greif* made fast at the Neutief pier opposite Pillau at the point of the Spit. She took on 2,000 refugees and set off for Neufahrwasser at about midnight. Twenty-four hours later she was already back in Pillau and tied up this time in the outer harbour. Four hours later she returned with 1,800 refugees. The refugees landed at Neufahrwasser, and the *Greif* took on ammunition for the aerodrome. So it went, day after day. The loads for the east consisted of bombs, ammunition, anti-aircraft guns, once even four new *Me 109* fighters, then again oil, coal and supplies for the pilots. The loads for the west were human beings.

A reciprocal traffic was established between the Spit resorts of Kahlberg and Neufahrwasser to reduce the number of wounded from the overcrowded Spit. The hospital ships *Glückauf*, *Regina* and *Meteor* could not get closer than about 500 metres to the lighter landings and had to anchor in the channel. Artillery lighters, fishing boats and ferry boats brought the wounded, including victims of the low-flying attacks on the ice roads, to the waiting ships.

Chapter 13

Westwards over the Vistula

The flight over the ice was now in full swing. The wagons rumbled over the Spit road with rattling utensils, the horses had white beards and blew little clouds of steam from their nostrils. On the seaward side near Kahlberg and Steegen small ship units also took on refugees. But only the most daring, mainly those on foot with little luggage, used this opportunity. The masses, like the Mischkes, Romalm and his group, the Knieps and the Macketanz, drove on. The mouth of the Vistula was still safe and the way through Pomerania open.

Mischke had reached the mouth of the Vistula in the first days of February and found a stable for his horses and a room for his family in Steegen. After many days he at last could relax and sleep without fear of his horses and wagon being stolen.

Next day they reached the Vistula. The weather was damp, cold and misty. Shivering with the cold they joined a queue of wagons over one kilometre long wanting to take the ferry. About every ten minutes they moved forward 20 metres, and by dawn next day they had reached the water, which flowed black and sluggish between the frozen ice floes along the river banks to the open sea nearby.

The ferry people had already been conveying refugees and military personnel over the river for weeks, day and night, without a break. And they would continue operating the business until the bitter end before they dared the dangerous journey under their own steam over the Baltic to Kiel, although the ferry was not seaworthy and basically consisted only of two floats with planks laid over them.

Mischke wasted no thoughts about the ferry. He was happy that his horses, without making difficulties, had managed the log road and got through easily. There was a second queue waiting for the next ferry, but they traversed the Vistula without taking breaks, as both ferries operated at regular intervals.

That evening Mischke reached the railway junction of Praust. Here everything was peaceful and organised by the Party. Horses and people were accommodated in the stalls of a manor farm. Mischke grumbled: 'The lord of the manor sits in his well lit castle – and certainly is kept warm!'

Mischke was not happy with the direction he had been shown. He wanted to drive on via Danzig and not so far to the south. He had no idea that he had double luck and now found himself where he could get through quickest and safest.

Had he gone north or left a day later, he would have been caught by the Volkssturm that had been posted on the second Vistula ferry just hours after he had gone through. Anyone who came through the barrier on the bank of the lagoon was taken from his wagon.

The sentries did not care if they were crippled or sick. Farmer Motzkus, who had sustained a severe leg injury in the First World War, wanted to know how he was to march in the column. 'We will drive you there – you will not get out again!' answered a smiling Party man, as if he had made a joke. They asked everyone their age, trade and last job, in an attempt to catch out the false ones. But there were no big 'animals' with the treks. Graf Eulenberg apparently was allowed through because of his great age. Also Pastor Mantze from Widminen, because of his office as a holy man, was allowed to stay with his family.

Mischke experienced far less than schoolmaster Otto Lippke from Allenburg. Lippke had got out of his home town with his wife on the 21st January. Then in Friedland his wife had the opportunity of going on by train. Lippke had then driven back alone to Allenburg to help women with children get away until the mass of fleeing German soldiers also drove him out of the town. Going on his bicycle along the snowed roads, he caught up with the Allenburger wagons in Barnstein. The people had made themselves at home in the deserted buildings and stayed there four days. They were still hoping that the Wehrmacht would withstand the Russian onslaught. Then they went on but, despite all good intentions, Lippke was unable to keep the trek together. In the end everyone went their own way.

He crossed the Vistula near Habichtswalde. He had no idea where his wife was, although in fact she was in another trek only a few hundred metres behind him.

One of the military police took hold of the handlebars of Lippke's bicycle, from which the teacher's two briefcases hung. 'Your pass!' They never said 'please', and the demand sounded like a sentence. With trembling hands the teacher took his pass from his worn briefcase. The great crowd of other men that had been rounded up before him had already seen him from the ferry. They stood depressed in front of a shed and stood on one leg after another. 'In there!' said the sentry, and the teacher obediently pushed his bicycle into the shed.

They marched to Danzig in three ranks between the fleeing refugees. At the reporting office near the main railway station they each received a reporting card. On Lippke's card was written: '15th February, Leibhusaren Kaserne, Danzig-Langfuhr.' That was in three days' time. Lippke used it to seek his wife. Aimlessly he wandered through the streets, checking schools and cinemas. At the last minute he found her on an omnibus that was taking women and children to the Reich. There was enough time for a brief farewell and then the schoolmaster was alone with himself and the Volkssturm.

He was assigned to Construction Battalion XXX(V). The commander, Lieutenant Greitsch, was a government inspector from Allenburg. Their task was to dig trenches south of Danzig. On the 17th February at about 0500 hours they went on a goods train, equipped with a loaf of bread and a spade, to Praust. He passed the big manor farm where Emil Mischke had spent the night. But by this time not only was the manor owner away, but Mischke was long since in safety.

Count Eulenberg wanted to find a better mode of transport for his wife, whose health was getting noticeably worse. With the help of his relatives he was able to find a place for her in the sisters' quarters on a hospital train. There was great unrest in Danzig. Of the people known to the von Eulenburgs hardly anyone was there. It would have been easier for him if he could get a train or a ship to the west. The Technical High School had already been evacuated at the beginning of February. Most officials had sent part of their staff and files to the west, but public life still functioned. The newspapers appeared regularly, and the shops were open.

The lord of the manor had always had a weakness for Danzig. When his ancestors built Gross Wicken, Danzig had already gone past its zenith. St Petersburg, Riga and Odessa competed with it for the Russian trade, and the corn trade with Poland went straight to Erlingen, because the country had lost its granary around Smolensk to Austria. In 1540 still 60 per cent of all shipping that passed through the Baltic straits was of Danzig origin. Danzig ships with grain cargoes could then decide wars, save whole provinces from starvation, and gain wealth. In the Hansa war against England, Danzig Captain Paul Benecke pulled off a coup in 1473 of which the Danzig burgers were very proud. To the Prussian Eulenburg the business was nevertheless a bit improper. Benecke had captured an English ship off Sluys, the harbour of Bruges. The ship had the triptych *Das Jüngste Gericht* by Hans Memling on board. The artwork had been commissioned by the Medicis for the Santa Maria Nuova Hospital in Florence. Despite an intervention by the Pope, the Danzigers kept the picture and put it in the Marienkirche. (Today the original is in the Pomeranian Museum of the Ulica Torunska, the Marienkirche retaining a copy.)

The wealth of Danzig was displayed in its buildings. The high, narrow facades were a mixture of Bavarian baroque, Westphalian sparseness, Dutch brick gothic and Kaschubian massiveness. The liveliness of this mixture was what fascinated Eulenburg, like the wealth of the past with which one flirted a bit too openly. It was not the downfall of the Third Reich, it was the rise of Prussia that had ruined this city.

In the first half of the nineteenth century it seemed as if the gradually dying merchant city, which had lost its hinterland through a cruel play of nature, stood another chance. Ships were still being built in Danzig, but the harbour and shipbuilding yards were at the mercy of the moods of the impetuous Vistula. But in the spring of 1840 the ice and high water forced a new bed for the stream in front of Danzig to the Bight of Danzig. The arm of the Vistula that connected Danzig with the open sea became the Dead Vistula, with a constant water level, these conditions allowing the establishment of shipyards on a big scale. The Klawitz shipbuilding yard built the Prussian Navy's first steamship, and the Schichau and Danziger Yards established worldwide fame in subsequent years.

Over the Speicherinsel with its ancient warehouses, the Langen Bridge on the main arm of the Mottlau and the crane tower across the way, one goes through numerous fine gates into the city of Danzig. This jewel of a rich city is so narrowly built and so full of nooks and crannies that one gets through best on a bicycle.

Eulenburg only stayed one day in the city. On the 14th February, a clear and frosty day, he drove on with his Belgian and Frenchman. The journey went from manor to manor. Everywhere he found a welcome reception from friends and relations. Between Köslin and Stettin he changed his direction of travel to the northwest towards Swinemünde-Wollin. The way ahead was not only blocked with refugees, it was visibly dangerous. The Russians had got seriously close.

Eulenburg had it easy, stopping on the way. Wehrmacht staff were often quartered at the manor houses and the officers were mainly well known to him, giving him information on the situation day by day.

After a journey of over 40 kilometres he came to Schwiersen, where he wanted to stay overnight at a certain manor farm, but the village was full of treks. Several hundred metres before the manor they were denied passage by a local official, a weedy little man. They must turn round and drive back almost 20 kilometres before they came to Benz, one of Count Flemming's manors, where they met Administrator von der Gröben, who had directed the Königsberger refugee traffic in Fischhausen. On the 22nd February the landau crossed the Wollin Bridge, thus becoming the first – although they did not know it – to reach safety.

Count von Eulenberg was one of the last to get through on the land route. Many others who had left at the same time as himself and from the same neighbourhood did not make it.

Chapter 14

From Pillau to Gotenhafen

Life was hard for the people who had landed after coming by sea from Pillau. They sat in vast, ice-cold warehouses in Neufahrwasser or Gotenhafen waiting for any of the ships lying at anchor that would take them. Bruno Damerau and the other Tapiauers were also accommodated in such warehouses in Gotenhafen.

When they had climbed aboard the *Hektor* in Pillau, it felt to them as if the flight and all the hardships were over for ever. Everyone had got a bunk. Ham, bread, sausage and coffee were given out to the sound of dashing military music from the ship's loudspeakers. Frau Petereit from Preussisch Eylau brought a son into the world on board. Mother and child were doing well, announced the mate proudly. The crew raised 3,000 Reichsmarks for the new sea citizen, while the refugees passed around the abundantly available bottles of schnaps. Because of the dangers from aircraft and mines, the catholic mother asked the captain for an emergency baptism. He went through the rituals thoroughly and the old bear of the sea baptised the little Prussian with plentiful flowing water – 'In the name of the Father, the Son and the Holy Ghost' – with the name Franz Arno.

The great sober German reality had already confronted the Tapiauers in Gotenhafen. The floor of the warehouse on the pier was only half cemented and on one side a big hole yawned in the wall with a monster of a machine wrapped in sailcloth. As the shed was empty, nothing stopped the icy draught. The mass of refugees streamed in, running madly about, everyone seeking a good place. Finally they fought for every half square metre for themselves and their luggage, until about 2,000 people were crammed in the hall.

No one knew what would happen next. They also found no one who could give them any information. Hungry, freezing and fatigued, they rolled over to sleep on the thin layer of straw. Many remained sitting on their baggage and slept leaning against each other.

Morning had hardly broken when they gave vent to their displeasure. An old man, for whom this was obviously too much, shouted with a highly red face into the crowd: 'You have shouted "Heil!" so long, now you can now bawl "Unheil!" [ruin].'

At the same moment a Party official appeared. His light brown, gold embellished uniform, with gleaming brown leather boots and belt with a golden buckle, stood in strange contrast to the black or brown, torn and dirty clothing of the refugees. He climbed up on a projection of the covered machine and said loud and clearly· 'Heil Hitler! Now listen in!' He conveyed a personal message from the Führer to his beloved, brave East Prussians, and asked them to bring their bowls and eating utensils outside so that he could lead them to some food.

The refugees did as they were bid. They stood a whole hour in front of the warehouse before anything happened. A Party comrade in a less impressive uniform led them. 'It is only ten minutes away,' he assured them. The big wound in Franz Damerau's foot had become worse and the pain brought tears down his furrowed yellow cheeks. The others promised to bring back a good portion for him.

The food distribution centre was much further than they had expected. After an hour's march they arrived at the rifle club's festival place. For 2,000 people? No one there knew anything about it. So the Tapiauers turned back grumbling and hungry. Later the crews of the ships lying in the harbour helped them. They brought buckets of pea and barley soup, bread and sausage to the warehouse. But no one could tell the refugees on what ship and when they would travel on.

The Siegel family from Rauschen had also landed at Gotenhafen. Peter Siegel, his young wife and his parents had had a similar journey on the *Togo* to that of the Tapiauers on the *Hektor*. But upon arrival in Gotenhafen they had not taken the risk of mass accommodation. Peter Siegel had gone off on his own account to find accommodation and brought his family to the home of the milk dealer Gustav Traube.

The young assistant doctor reported to the main dressing station and shortly afterwards was standing in a white overall in the big hall of the torpedo workshops at the end of the pier, now being used as a transit centre for the wounded. Small naval vessels brought them from Kurland, Samland and the 4th Army's encirclement on the other side of the harbour. On the other side was the big steamer that would take them back to the Reich. But there was a long wait, as in the assembly hall lay hundreds of severely wounded, mostly amputees and some with large wounds that had to be dressed twice a day before going on.

Together with a qualified doctor and four assistants, the young junior Army doctor tried to prevent the worst. It did not always work, especially if the threatening secondary bleeding occurred. For this young doctor the situation was a nightmare, not at all what he had expected in his profession.

Meanwhile the two women made themselves useful in the widowed milk dealer's business. The old lady stood behind the counter ladling out the milk, while her daughter-in-law stuck the small milk tickets on big sheets of wrapping paper for the economic office. The old Professor Siegel had long talks with Gustav Traube, who was in deadly fear. He was a Party member and steward and had even taken part in a Reichs Party Day.

The Siegels stayed for over a week with the milk dealer, who did not want to leave his home. Then Peter Siegel found a travelling opportunity for the family. Professor Siegel would travel that same day on the *Lappland* as ship's doctor.

The farewells of the young married couple were brief. Then the three stood alone in front of the big ship. The *Lappland* of 7,644 tons had only been built in 1942 but broad streaks of rust crept over her grey flanks. Steel ropes and hawsers hung over her bulging railings like decorations on a Christmas tree. The giant freighter had never seen better days. It had left the dockyard in its grey wartime shirt and since then had not had a single pot of paint expended on it. The high projection of the bridge deck, which stuck out over the forward third of the ship's length, looked like a block of flats. A flat deck with a bulky funnel extended over the centre section and aft of the after hold the poop rose like a wooden shoe.

A Belgian sailor led the Siegels to midships, where the dispensary was located between the cabins with the badly wounded. This was where Professor Siegel would work for the next few days, while the two women occupied a cabin close by. As from a distance, they heard the trampling of the other refugees coming aboard and disappearing into the holds.

The crew held back and made no real attempt to assist the women and children to climb down the steep ladders with their luggage. They had had enough since the first trip from Pillau when the masses had stormed the ship and several of the crew had been knocked down. Even the sailor Schmidtke had had enough of being helpful. In Pillau he had held back the refugees the longest with his bear's strength and carried old women or two children single-handedly down the iron ladders until someone had dropped a vast suitcase on his head.

The ship was equipped as a troop transporter for 1,000 men. Now 2,000 women and children and over 1,500 severely wounded had to share the same space.

Supplying the masses was the biggest problem. The *Lappland*'s crew recalled their first journey from Pillau to Swinemünde only with horror. Fighting had broken out on board when a large cauldron of soup was brought aboard, and in Swinemünde harbour women had begged bread from ships passing close by. A few dozen loaves were thrown across from a naval vessel. Behind the deck of the *Lappland* it looked like a battlefield with people trampled down in the fighting.

At the beginning of February the refugees' supply situation was mentioned by the commander in chief of the navy at Hitler's daily conference. Hitler had himself ordered that a ship be sent with food to the east and made the Gauleiter responsible for providing an adequate supply. Gauleiter Koch had food brought from Königsberg, which the population was later to miss so much that, following the final occupation by the Soviets, cases of cannibalism arose. In Danzig Gauleiter Forster requisitioned trek vehicles to bring in grain and foodstuffs from the silos and warehouses in the area to the district farming associations. There was no lack of meat. Only the NSV organization was too weak to meet the hunger of the masses of people along the coast.

So the merchant ship skippers dealt with the matter themselves. In Gotenhafen the captain of the *Lappland,* Franz Appel, had sent his first mate, Karl Hillmann, to find something edible. Hillmann was put on the right track by an NSV kitchen and found a full warehouse near the railway station. He returned with a wagon load of army bread, a few sacks of dried peas, beans and sugar. So at least the children and the sick could be nourished with sweet bread and soup.

These difficulties were not noticed in the *Lappland*'s dispensary, as the feeding of the crew continued as normal. The young Frau Siegel and her mother-in-law had set up a kind of out-patient department, handing out cellulose to the women, charcoal tablets and aspirin, taking the temperature of the sick children and giving good advice, which was hardly practical but was of great value to morale.

As a gynaecologist, Professor Siegel was in the right place. Already during the second hour of the journey there was a precipitate delivery, the young woman not having enough time to remove her underclothing. There were five other births without complications. Several old people and two babies died and were laid on the boat deck with the dead and wounded.

The *Lappland* was in a convoy of ten ships that had assembled in the Hela roads. This alone demanded the full attention of the watch, which had no previous convoy experience. They had no fear of aircraft, the freighter, like the other ships in the convoy, being well equipped with 37mm and 20mm anti-aircraft guns. The *Lappland* alone had 40 gun crew aboard. But everyone was aware that a submarine or a mine could blow them sky high.

Shortly after midnight a sailor threw open the door to the bridge and shouted: 'Man overboard!' A child had gone overboard at the stern and the mother had jumped blindly after it. Two men were sent to the stern, but by the time they had forced their way through an escorting boat drew up along-side and asked what was the matter. 'Carry on!' shouted the commander to the freighter. 'We will take on the search.' So the *Lappland* carried on and no one knew whether the two had been fished out of the water.

There was no stay in Swinemünde this time. The convoy tied up and hour after hour the men clattered down the gangways to the pier and across to the waiting trains. A cutter took the corpses of those that had died on the way from the boat deck. The *Lappland* loaded several truckloads of army bread and steamed back to the witches' cauldron in the Bight of Danzig. On the way the first load of bread turned mouldy and had to be thrown overboard, about half a railway wagon's worth. Meanwhile the Siegels were on their way to Berlin by train.

The Königsberger wholesale food dealer Dr Ostermeyer and a few people of his team were stuck fast in Gotenhafen at this point, although they had left Pillau at the same time as the Siegels. Sometime or other Dr Ostermeyer had lost his strength and let himself be swept along in the slow-moving stream of refugees. Finally he had ended up in the Gotenhafen *Stern* cinema in Row 4 of the first central section.

Then it came to him that he knew quite a number of influential people on this side of the Bight of Danzig that could help him on. He shook off his lethargy and set off. Several visits came to nothing because the people he knew had already left. Only bank director Nouvel was still there, and he took in his friend from Königsberg.

Herr Nouvel knew the senior signals officer Wiebeck, who lived in a signal tower at Harbour 4 and knew the times of arrival and departure of all the ships. Wiebeck had a pleasant nature and temperament. He had a very pretty refugee woman and her five-year-old son from Königsberg with him who would be travelling on the destroyer *Castor*.

They played skat the whole evening in Wiebeck's small den. The woman cooked macaroni with ham. Before she lay down to sleep, Nouvel said goodbye. He was sure that all would go well. Next morning the four of them went shivering to the bastion where the destroyer lay. A number of people crowded in front of the gangplank. All had tickets and thus priority, but even more priority was given to the severely wounded that already had been loaded, and the 90 nursing sisters that had accompanied a large field hospital to Gotenhafen. Only ten more people could be taken aboard, whose particulars had already been taken. Then a female doctor upset the whole business by demanding that the Gotenhafen Hospital's children's isolation station should be taken. The captain was annoyed when he heard of diphtheria and measles, and asked whether they wanted to infect 1,200 people. It took a while before the doctor gave up.

Dr Ostermeyer had watched this for about an hour. The business with the personal particulars did not apply to him. He pushed his way towards the steamer *Memelland* lying further away. To his surprise, no one needed a ticket there. The *Memelland*, a victim of engine damage, was to be towed by two tugs to a North Sea dock, so the 6,234-ton petrol tanker could take along 350 people. Meanwhile Ostermeyer had found three men from his team again, and they moved into the boilermen's cabin with four bunks and a small table.

The *Memelland* soon left the harbour under tow. She went without an escort. The crew were on a good thing. The tanker was practically unsink-able, consisting of 36 hermetically sealed tanks. Food supplies had been brought on board by the NSV in Gotenhafen. At noon there was thick soup (peas, noodles and potatoes) with ham or meat, with afternoon coffee and in the evening a loaf between six men, and for every man 50 grams of butter, jam, sausage and the remainder of the soup.

It was a long journey. They lay motionless for almost two days in the open sea 12 nautical miles north of Kolberg because the route had not been cleared of mines. The men spent most of the time playing skat, the women washing shirts, cooking potatoes and cutting each other's hair. In the outer channel off Swinemünde they lost another day taking on provisions and water. After six days they reached the entrance to the Kaiser-Wilhelm Canal in Kiel and with it the end of their journey.

Meanwhile the situation in Gotenhafen had become more desperate. Tens of thousands pressed upon all possible sources of assistance, and every day there were more. The noise from the front line was clearer and unrest spread in the quarters. Everyone wanted to get out of this trap as quickly as possible.

The Tapiauers too sat in Gotenhafen. In the meantime they had been moved to mass quarters in School VI at Gotenhafen-Grabau, about an hour on foot from the harbour. 3,000–4,000 refugees were accommodated in the building's three wings. The Wehrmacht looked after their needs. There was an irritable atmosphere in the classrooms. The refugees were rude to each other, stole from each other, denounced each other, and occasionally celebrated events. On the 23rd February Franz Baum's wife, whose health had made good progress, celebrated her 69th birthday. A feast was prepared for her in the room, for which someone provided smoked ham and someone else the last of their real coffee.

Meanwhile the Dameraus had had a suitcase stolen, the contents of which appeared next day a few rooms away. One female thief, not having found anything, put on the stolen clothing. Somebody shouted: 'Hang the plunderer!' Others wanted to take her before the People's Court. The uproar only died down when the police led away the three female culprits.

During the confusion Bruno Damerau had still found the time to paint two water-colours of the Kurisches Haff lagoon for the two nursing sisters that had looked after old Franz Böhm. But the transport to take them away got no closer.

Gradually it dawned on the Tapiauers that they had been bypassed. People who had arrived long after them received boarding cards and vanished to the harbour. 'Those who have got the money, travel,' Mother Damerau had always said. One of the women slipped the camp leader a bottle of cognac and next morning they had 24 tickets for the *Deutschland*.

The 21,046-ton *Deutschland* had spent the whole war moored in Danzig as living accommodation for submarine trainees. But since the 30th January she had made three trips with 8,000 refugees and wounded each time. The crew under Captain Bruno Feindt had been topped up upon its first arrival in Kiel with a mixture of Germans and Croatians, neither of which could understand the other.

Captain Feindt had abundant provisions on board, including 15,000 loaves and 8,000 kilos of ham. His largest hold was filled with a load of wood and submarine batteries that he now had to take to the west for the fourth time as nobody wanted to unload them.

The very few refugees that went aboard in Gotenhafen with the Tapiauers had never seen such a large ship before and were audibly impressed. Below decks in the labyrinth of staircases and passage ways, bulkheads and doors, the ship seemed even bigger than it did from outside.

A sailor told them to lie down in the gangways on the left and right but to leave the centre of the passage free. They made themselves as comfortable as they could. There were no places to lie down. Big pieces of luggage had to be stowed in a bathroom to make enough room to sit down. They soon realised what 'Betriebsgang' meant: they had been accommodated in the middle of the busy crew and there was a constant coming and going along the gang-ways, forcing them to keep pulling back their feet.

A drunken sailor tripped over the stiff leg of a badly wounded soldier in the gangway. In a barrage of swearing, he started to fall on the old man sitting on the deck, trying to pull him up by the arms. At the last moment, before he could really strike a blow, two other sailors intervened and stopped him. None of the intimidated refugees had moved, their physical strength as exhausted as their spiritual. The same sailor later made unflattering remarks because some of the refugees were chewing bacon that they had brought with them, but this only drew an indignant glance.

The *Deutschland* lay in Gotenhafen for two days. A northerly storm with wind strengths of 8 to 9 made the passage through the minefields impossible. Finally the lines were cast off and she was escorted out by two destroyers and two torpedo boats.

As well as the 6,000-7,000 refugees, the *Deutschland* also had 1,400 wounded on board, for whom only three doctors and a small number of assistants were in attendance. There were no dressings available, and the majority of the wounded had not had their wounds dressed for many days. The dressings were soaked through and naval doctor Hans Pilz found worms under the bandages. Nevertheless all the old dressings had to be reused.

Medicines, especially painkilling drugs and opiates, were also lacking. Whenever a surgical problem was unavoidable, Dr Pilz used a mixed preparation of Scopolamine, Eukodal and Ephetonin to avoid narcosis. He knew this mixture from psychiatry, where it had been used as a sedative for especially unruly patients. Whatever he did, he knew that it was no longer in his hands whether a patient survived.

The refugees remained separate from the nearby sufferings of the wounded. Some, however, were witness to a tragic misfortune. Dr Pilz had tried to undo a badly soaked-through dressing in the loin area of a wounded man, thus causing the wound to begin to bleed strongly. An attempt to clamp the leg artery failed. Dr Pilz tried to compress the artery and had the patient carried to the operating theatre. On the stairs the doctor had to crouch below the stretcher. He stumbled, his hand slipped and Dr Pilz heard the blood running out into the bowl. By the time he struggled to his feet again, the patient had bled to death.

Several civilians had been standing in the passageway and silently watched the scene. But only one woman let out a small cry as she saw the man stumble and noticed the blood. The others were too concerned with their own predicament. They waited at the entrance to the dispensary for news of their relatives, who were treated by a children's doctor from Gerdauen and a civilian doctor from Elbing. These two doctors were fighting a losing battle, like Dr Pilz. A whole row of elderly people were lying on sacks of straw, undernourished and exhausted, on the verge of death. In a little cabin nearby, which formerly had contained ultra-violet lamps and other similar apparatus, lay six children with diphtheria and scarlet fever. Only the captain and the medical staff knew of this hazard. Although resources were scanty, it had been possible to isolate these cases.

On this trip there were over 100 deaths among the wounded and civilians. They were put in paper sacks and laid on the boat deck under a tarpaulin. The paymaster wrote out the death certificates and packed the dead persons' valuables and identity cards in brown envelopes that were handed over to the Red Cross later if there were no relatives on board.

After a 20-hour journey the ship dropped anchor in the Sassnitz roads. The refugees pressed up on deck and wondered at the picture they saw before them. Half a dozen escort ships and individual ships of all types and sizes occupied the bight. Near them lay the big 22,117-ton *Hamburg*, sister ship to the *Deutschland*. In the background loomed the picturesque white cliffs of Rügen Island. There was no one to be seen on the decks of the *Hamburg*, for she had already been unloaded. But no lighter or ferry was approaching the *Deutschland*, for Sassnitz was overfull.

In the afternoon several hundred women with children were able to leave the ship. There were still no trains available for the others. Until late in the evening and into the night they stood in the gangways, pressed close to the bulkheads of the exits, ready to be the first out in any event. At about 2200 hours the refugees morosely settled down to sleep. The stink coming along the passageways from the dirty toilets was almost unbearable.

Bruno Damerau wandered around. He discovered an unusual restlessness among the crew. They were hurrying along the passages, bulkheads were closed, he heard subdued orders, and then he saw the first sailors wearing lifejackets. He asked several of them in vain what was happening. Some of the sailors' darlings, refugee girls that had sought accommodation with the crew, were also wearing lifejackets. Damerau hurried back to his family. None of the crew were to be seen below decks.

It was 2230 hours. On land the air raid sirens were howling. The ships' officers gave the order over the loudspeakers for everyone to remain in their place and to keep the gangways free. At 2300 hours the sound of aircraft was clearly audible. Pathfinders dropped parachute flares, in whose bluish-white light the black ghostly silhouettes of the many ships stood out.

The aircraft were from the 5th Allied Bomber Group. 150 Lancaster bombers were directed at the harbour and its installations, and 41 Lancasters attacked the ships lying in the roads. Seven Mosquitos provided fighter cover. Almost 500 tons of bombs were dropped on the harbour, station and town during the one-hour attack, more than 170 tons of bombs being dropped by the British aircraft on the ships lying in the roads, including 4.8 tons of incendiaries and 19 air mines. At the same time other aircraft were sowing the waters around Sassnitz with mines. The strong German anti-aircraft defences had no success. The anti-aircraft gunship *Sofia* and the wounded transport *Robert Möhring* went up in flames at the pier. 350 wounded were killed on the *Robert Möhring*.

Ten Lancasters concentrated on the *Deutschland* and the *Hamburg*. In deadly fear the refugees huddled in their places on the *Deutschland*. The bulkheads and the decks around them shook under the firing of the ship's anti-aircraft guns, firing from all 28 barrels, although the 20cm guns had little chance of hitting their high-flying targets. They could clearly hear the dull rumbling of exploding bombs getting nearer. The ship swayed under the blast of a near hit. Captain Feindt had ordered all men on deck and only allocated a few officers to the civilians. But the civilians seemed numbed with fear, only some children crying out with fear. The adults waited for the big blow that would be their end.

Dr Pilz stood in the entrance to the big A and B Deck dining saloons where the wounded were densely laid out so that he could see them, and waited for what was to happen. He could see flashes of explosions through the portholes. Then there was a frightful bang nearby – a direct hit on the destroyer *Z28*, one of the two that had escorted them here.

The crew of the *Deutschland* lowered several boats into the water and fished for the destroyer's survivors swimming in the oil. One after another was brought up on deck, where Dr Pilz and his assistants cleared the corrosive oil from their eyes and noses with soap and water. Meanwhile the enemy aircraft had flown off. The *Deutschland* was untouched, but Sassnitz was in flames.

For three days the Tapiauers and thousands of others had to stay on the ship. Only 58 pregnant women and several emergency cases were taken ashore in a lifeboat. Drinking water had almost run out and had to be rationed.

The day after the bomb attack the *Hamburg* hoisted anchor and passed under the stern of the *Deutschland*. Many of the refugees stood curiously on deck in the sunshine watching the manoeuvre. Suddenly a fountain of water rose from under the *Hamburg*. The bow of the vast ship rose and then slowly sank away. The explosion was so strong that the stern of the *Deutschland* shuddered. The *Hamburg* had run on to one of the many mines dropped during the night before. The refugees thought they were under another air attack and went below in panic, seeking shelter, falling head over heels down the steep stairs. Fortunately there were only a few minor injuries. The *Hamburg* sank within an hour, her crew escaping unscathed to the *Deutschland*.

Two days later Captain Feindt was able to land the first 1,600 refugees and 80 of the dead. Next day there were 1,800 refugees, then 1,400, then the wounded. There were some unpleasant scenes among the refugees, none of whom wanted to remain on board the ship. Bruno Damerau and his group managed it on the third day with the help of a friendly seaman to whom he had passed a packet of tobacco.

Sassnitz railway station had been bombed out. Wagons had been thrown about, tracks ripped up and a heavy, bitter smell of burning filled the air.

A long train had been prepared for the refugees on an emergency platform. An hour later they were on their way to Stralsund.

Captain Feindt and the *Deutschland* lay in the Sassnitz Roads another five full days after discharging the ship's passengers until the mines had been cleared. Then it steamed off towards Gotenhafen with the same crew, doctors and medical orderlies. On the way they heard that the Russians already had the town and harbour under artillery fire, and were urged to make haste.

Chapter 15

Danzig cut off

The Russian steamroller had gone past the edge of the Tucheler Heath and rolled on towards the Oder and Berlin. In the little county town of Tuchel they had thought themselves safe behind the Vistula defences. The barracks were occupied by Waffen-SS troops. The men of the Volkssturm exercised loyally and bravely, while the town and country policemen made their patrols. Now and again Soviet aircraft flew over the town; there were air alerts, but no bombs were dropped.

Much nearer than the Russians were the bands of Polish partisans. As signs of German defeat began to appear, the partisans began operating in the former Polish Corridor. In the last months of the war incidences of attacks on remote German farms increased. The partisans mainly robbed food, slaughtered pigs and forced the farmers to kneel down in front of pictures of Hitler before they began beating them. Later they even dared go into the villages, seizing the village savings bank and setting buildings on fire. An SS reprisal action, in which there were some heavy and often costly fights in the woods between SS units and the Poles, was unsuccessful. Even German deserters fought alongside the Poles. They had German nationalization papers, like about 80 per cent of the indigenous Poles, these papers having been forged in London.

Whenever aircraft noises were heard at night, Town Inspector Werner Fritsche climbed on to the roof of the town hall to observe the flashing light signals coming from the surrounding woods, by which the partisans signalled the dropping zones to the British pilots. They were supplied by air from England with wireless sets, weapons and ammunition.

In the last days of January the first withdrawing German units reached the town, at first in individual groups then in uninterrupted sequence. For Town Inspector Fritsche these long lines going through the dirty snow had an unreal appearance: German soldiers in retreat! They came separated from their units, unshaven and without weapons. There was some looting in the town until the SS and military police erected barriers and directed the fleeing soldiers to collecting points.

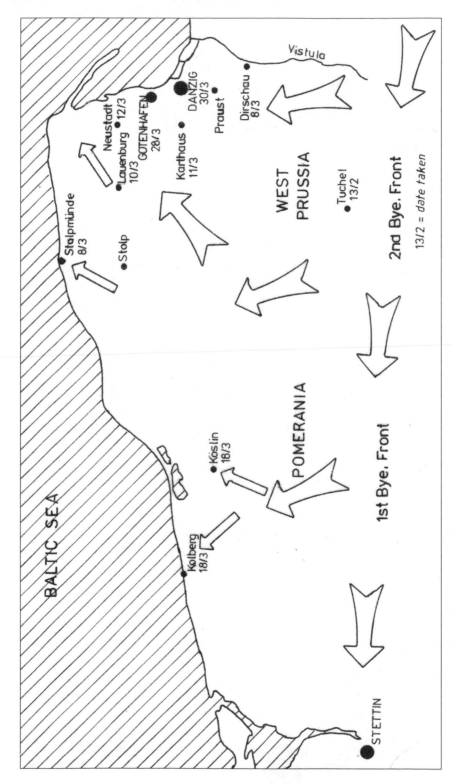

Map 4. *The Soviet invasion of West Prussia and Pomerania*

On the 9th February the thunder of the guns came from a south-easterly direction. There was heavy fighting near Schwetz, but the Gau headquarters in Danzig would still not permit the official evacuation of the town. The town administration issued a summons to all Polish girls and women for them to appear before the town hall and be set to digging trenches. Tuchel was to be prepared for all-round defence. That afternoon a single Soviet aircraft attacked the town with bombs and machine guns. Next day the commander of the 4th Panzer Division, General Betzel, had the town cleared of civilians, on the grounds of military security, it was said. In reality the Russians were less than 20 kilometres southeast of the town and were quickly drawing nearer. Counterattacks by German tanks could only slow down this advance, not stop it. Instead of driving a wedge into the enemy's flanks, they had to pull back to meet the Russian tanks now attacking northwards. As they could not get through to the west by rail, Tuchel's inhabitants and the county southwest of Danzig fled with the trek drivers to the Hansa city.

The Soviets were preparing to cut off Eastern Pomerania and West Prussia as they had done East Prussia. Infantry and armoured units of the 1st Byelorussian Front were switched from the Oder to the north and got stuck into heavy fighting towards Kolberg and the Baltic. At the same time the armies on the left flank of the 2nd Byelorussian Front marched north to Köslin, splitting up the German troops. The main forces of this front – the 65th and 49th Armies and the 5th Tank Army – swung on Danzig in a wide arc from the northeast.

The Soviets reached the Pomeranian Baltic coast during the first days of March. Köslin fell on the 5th March, but surrounded Kolberg held out for another two weeks. The Soviets thrust into the middle of the fleeing treks. Ponderously those cut off wandered back east towards the Bight of Danzig. Refugee and hospital trains were left lying on the railway tracks. Treks that found themselves between the Soviet thrusts could go neither forward nor back and had to wait to be overrun by the Russians.

Day by day they drew the cauldron tighter together on the west side of the Bight of Danzig and the towns of Gotenhafen, Zoppot and Danzig. Marshal Rokossovski wanted to expedite the taking of Danzig so as to release troops for the decisive battle for Berlin. In no way would he let his forces become tied up in front of Danzig as had happened with the 3rd Byelorussian Front in East Prussia. On the German side they had only an unclear idea of the Russians' current fighting strength, for there was no longer any reconnaissance of the enemy, and hardly any prisoners were being taken. Whole Russian armies seemed to have fallen from the heavens. On the other side, however, the German leadership knew that the very hard-fought positional defence by the German formations had weakened the

Soviets. 'We received no reinforcements,' said Army General I. Batov, commander of the 65th Army. 'Our divisions had at most only 40 per cent of their establishment. We had to comb the rear areas.' Political instructors went to the field hospitals and talked the lightly injured into returning to the front. They reduced the number of runners and took every man from the supply units they could catch. The Russians made good progress. Colonel-General Weiss had no choice but to bring back the remains of the German 2nd Army into the Danzig area, incurring the loss of many heavy weapons, tanks and assault guns because of lack of fuel, which had to be blown up. Meanwhile the field fortifications on the outer defence ring were being prepared under great pressure.

Teacher Lippke was also involved in the digging of fortifications with his spade after his flight had been interrupted by the Volkssturm round-up. At first Lippke's company lay in Gross Gabeln. They set off at 0500 hours and dug out metre after metre of trenches until at 1800 hours they returned soaked through and frozen. This went on for quite a while, but one day in March a group of tanks appeared. Soldiers with Lippke took these for returning German tanks – until firing broke out. The old men were happy to have dug their trenches and could vanish in them. The Russians were long gone when finally the overrun German units appeared that had been forming the front line until then.

From then on the war for the Volkssturm too was one of retreat. Hardly had they dug a few spadefuls when someone shouted: 'Clear the position immediately! We have the enemy in sight!' The men shouldered their spades and headed back the way they had come. They marched straight to Danzig and started digging again. Three lay dead from artillery fire. Lippke had had enough. After a long walk he reached the entrance to the village of Gute Herberge. Along the village street stood a long row of mighty linden trees. Lippke sought cover from low-flying aircraft behind a tree trunk. As he emerged, a shell exploded close to him and he suffered a severe blow to his left leg and fell over.

Fortunately there was a medical post in the nearest building. The teacher was given first aid, an emergency bandage and an injection. The leg was completely shattered up to the knee. One hour later he was lying on an operating table in the Viktoria School field hospital, and the leg was amputated 15 centimetres above the knee. When he regained consciousness he saw that his clothing was neatly bundled alongside him. Only lacking were the trousers in which he had stuck his wallet with 360 Reichsmarks.

While the teacher mourned the loss of his money, thousands were running and driving for their lives into the area west of Danzig. Irma Neuber was with the trek from the Mehlenden Manor, Gerdauen County, that had come right across East Prussia, over the lagoon and past Danzig, and had reached Neustadt in West Prussia, about 45 kilometres northwest of Danzig. The little town offered a peaceful picture, even if many soldiers filled it: women shopping, children playing, and at a few stands farmers selling potatoes and eggs. In Nanitz, two kilometres beyond Neustadt, the trek eventually stopped for a rest.

Overnight the peaceful picture was transformed. From the west, without pause, refugees and troops flooded into the town. From the soldiers the Mehlenders discovered that the Russians had broken through, blocking the route to the west. So there was nothing else for them to do but pack up and go back the way they had come.

With difficulty they formed up with the columns pushing towards the coast. Beyond Neustadt there was hardly any progress. Soldiers forced them on to a narrow chaussee on which they drove three abreast, then on tracks across the fields. Many people came running out of Neustadt and overtook the slowly moving wagons on foot: women with children in their arms, old people with hardly any baggage, young people coming across the fields on their bicycles. A group of female concentration camp prisoners appeared on the roadside. Some swung themselves on to the wagons but were unable to hold on for long and vanished again. In Rameln on the Oxhöfter Kämper the trek came under artillery fire. Soldiers advised them to drive on to Gotenhafen, where the cauldron would definitely hold. They only made slow progress in the hilly country. Again and again they had to unharness the horses and give the wagons a push themselves. Towards evening they reached a large forest in which several naval artillery batteries had deployed and were firing shot after shot to the west. The horses from the wagons pranced nervously and the Neubers' wagon tipped over, breaking the right rear wheel. SS men helped them to push the wagon to one side. They took a wheel from an abandoned field kitchen and fastened it provisionally to their axle. But it took half the night before they were ready to move off.

At dawn they approached the outer suburbs of Gotenhafen. The city lay as if dead. The streets showed signs of low-flying attacks with dead horses and torn-up wagons. But the Neubers had no eyes for this. Their emergency wheel wobbled and they reckoned it would fall off at any moment. They gave up their plan of driving through to Danzig. Just before Zoppot the Mehlenders turned away from the column and sought shelter in an empty private house on a side street in Steinfliess. First of all they asked the local Party leader for horse fodder. 'Shoot the nags and break up the wagons, then you won't need any more fodder!' was his reply. They had more success with the district farmers' leader. In exchange for fodder they were to put their wagons at the disposal of the town. Under the thunder of the artillery,

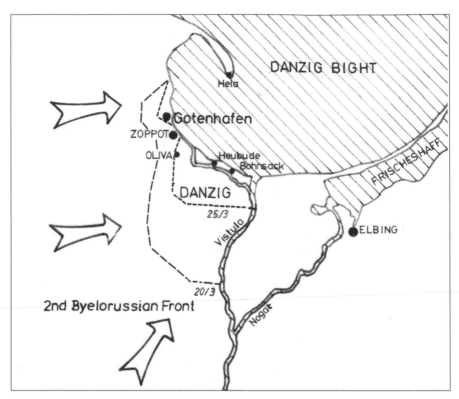

Map 5. The envelopment of Danzig

the refugees recovered potatoes and turnips from clamps in the fields far from Danzig. Irma Neuber obtained work in the farmers' union shops, and all received food tickets. It seemed as if the Mehlenders had at last found rest, that they could recover their strength undisturbed and await their return home.

But the Soviets had already closed up to within ten kilometres of the city in places. On the heights before the coast German naval anti-aircraft, tank and infantry units sought to stop the Russian advance with all their might. Naval units engaged in the battle from out at sea. The warships *Prinz Eugen*, *Schlesien* and *Leipzig* fired in one day over 700 280cm and 230cm shells from their guns and several hundred shots from their 105cm guns. A single anti-aircraft artillery regiment fired 245,000 128 and 105cm shells against this part of the hotly fought front.

One of these shells landed as a direct hit on the observation post of the Soviet 37th Guards Division and killed the divisional commander General S.U. Rachimov, the political officer Colonel A.A. Smirnov and a whole row of other officers.

The German units compressed into an ever-narrower space engaged the Russians weakened by their too-rapid advance in bitter individual fighting. In the command post of the 340th Regiment of the 46th Luga Rifle Division they suddenly found themselves facing five attacking German tanks and a company of infantry. Their three guns opened fire, setting one tank alight and immobilising another, but the remaining three tanks of the 4th Panzer Division made short work of the three Soviet guns, and the infantry were about to clear the command post when several *Stalin* tanks appeared at the last moment, forcing a retreat. There was no longer any doubt who would win this battle.

On the German side it was now only a matter of survival. The soldiers knew that with every day and every hour they held on, so many more wounded, women and children could be taken to safety. Still in Danzig in January, as in Königsberg, Pillau and Marienburg, it seemed that the war would go on for years.

In January the official Alix Forstreuter went daily to her workplace at the County Forestry Office in Oliva. Most of the civil servants had been drafted into the Wehrmacht or the Volkssturm, but the female staff continued the work. The only matter of concern was that Polish partisans were chasing the forestry people. Some had vanished and others had been found dead.

Alix Forstreuter was happy to comply with the appeal to train in First Aid and as a German Red Cross assistant sister. For the whole war she had two or three times a week been on duty at the railway station. In the waiting room she had prepared a vast cauldron of pea soup for the soldiers, or dragged metal milk churns of ersatz coffee out on the platform to fill the water bottles on the trains.

At the end of January 1945 there were ever more troop and wounded transports, and finally a refugee train, running one after the other. The assistants no longer served pea soup and ersatz coffee. The town filled with refugees and camps were set up everywhere for which assistance was needed. So in February Alix Forstreuter came to the 'Sonne' hotel and dancehall in Oliva, about ten minutes' walk from her apartment, to assist with the refugees.

Oliva is a spa between Danzig and the sea-bathing resort of Zoppot and is more aligned with the wooded hinterland than the sea. Close to the hills of the Oliva Forest were a spa centre and a whole row of hotels. The 'Sonne' was not one of the best, but it was roomy. About 500 refugees had found room there. Straw had been strewn in all the rooms, the few beds being used for the sick. The majority had come over the lagoon ice on foot and there were none that were quite healthy.

Among the young women and children frostbite and intestinal infections were the most frequent. The toilets were dirty and as time passed a penetrating stench filled the building that could not be dispelled even by forced air. A fight arose between the janitor and the assistants about who was responsible for disposing of the filth in corners and jam jars. Many of the really old people had lost the last of their physical and mental strength in the strain of their flight. They were so dirty that the assistants spent the whole of their time washing those who needed it.

Alix Forstreuter once came across an 80-year-old praying on his bed: 'Please God, let me die.' Another had a severe head wound, the smell coming from it being almost unbearable. He had no clothing for changing and no one could bear being near him. Alix Forstreuter left no stone unturned to at least get him into a hospital. After many telephone calls and much begging she finally softened a sister in a Danzig hospital. 'OK, send me the old stinker!' Four Hitler Youths loaded the old man on a stretcher and carried him through the snow to Danzig. They slipped several times, letting the old man drop. One and a half hours later they reached their destination. Shortly afterwards the hospital sister rang the refugee camp. 'Can you tell us his name? He had no documents with him and has already died in the bath.' But nobody knew him and no documents or pieces of baggage were found in the camp. Pneumonia and frostbite were the main causes of death. There were so many frostbite cases that the assistants needed frost salve by the pound. If they were not already experienced, the refugees had no idea how they had become frostbitten. The East Prussians were used to the cold and upon the first signs of frostbite gave the usual massage with snow to help. But in the flight from East Prussia they were exposed to frost far longer than they were accustomed to. Most of them had no idea of the danger to them from it. And the winter of 1944/45 was a wet winter with excessive snow, compounded by the dampness of the lagoon ice. Damp cold brings on freezing considerably quicker than dry cold. Many, particularly the old and the poor, were not clothed warmly enough. They had set off in thin coats, ordinary shoes, short jackets and often without gloves. The stress of the journey, the sleepless nights, the fear and the often very sparse meals on the way had made them ill. Many sought consolation in schnaps, also in the hope of pepping up their circulation. Although there was a momentary feeling of warmth, the alcohol caused vascular constriction and quickly deprived the body of warmth. Deadly frostbite set in, the body poisoning itself with dead tissue. Many lying dead by the roadside had died in this way.

Many ignored the damage until they stopped somewhere and the pain set in. Alix Forstreuter tirelessly smeared frozen toes and fingertips and bandaged them. Dr Schneider, a long-pensioned doctor from the health office, came several times a week, saw to the severely ill and gave tetanus injections. Many had open wounds, especially the women plagued with varicose veins that had lived in dirt for weeks.

Despite all the difficulties the atmosphere in the 'Sonne' Hotel in the Oliva camp was not bad. The Party leader from Oliva supplied the various camps with barley, noodles, peas, sugar and ersatz coffee. With a re-emerging zest for life, the atmosphere improved. The BDM girls and Hitler Youth boys helping in the camp animated their elderly comrades among the refugees with evening singsongs and dancing, and there was a puppet theatre for the children.

Meanwhile the ring of Soviets around the Danzig-Gotenhafen area drew tighter. By mid-March nowhere were they more than 20 kilometres distant from Danzig and were pressing with strong formations north of the city towards the coast, while their air force increasingly attacked the city and the ships lying in the harbour with bombs and machine guns.

On the 21st March the Gau headquarters in Danzig ordered the evacuation of Zoppot. Inhabitants and refugees made their way to Danzig. A Party official brought women and children to Seesteg, the once most-modern bathing resort in the pavilion at the head end of the 600-metre-long pier, the longest on the Baltic, which previously had been used for naval recruit training. Now cutters and boats of all kinds took the women and children in a shuttle service to Hela. The refugee camp at the 'Sonne' Hotel in Oliva was also evacuated. Alix Forstreuter helped to load the people on to carts. Much luggage and bedding remained behind. Young women set off with their children on their own initiative, many seeking a cellar to sit out the storm in. A Party functionary who had been looking after the welfare of the refugees brought the wagons to Neufahrwasser, and they were taken on the 1,087-ton steamer *Hoheweg* to the west. There had been yet another uproar during loading. Military police with drawn pistols stopped about 70 Hitler Youths from getting on the ship. They were to be trained in Emsland for a Hitler Youth division.

Alix Forstreuter had hardly got home when a woman living in a neigh-bouring house asked her to pack quickly. The woman had persuaded the driver of a jeep to take them to Neufähr or Bohnsack with him. Alix Forstreuter was still dithering when a man from the local Party organisation came by: 'Are there still civilians here? All immediately to the assembly point in Langfuhr Market. There is already fighting in Ludolphinenstrasse!'

None of the occupants – with the refugees accommodated, 17 in all – moved. But, when Alix Forstreuter saw her friend throwing a suitcase and a handbag into the jeep, she took her bag and ran out of the house. Going around rubble and past burning buildings, they reached the Green Gate

(Grüne Tor), which was blocked with the remains of vehicles after a direct shell hit. They had to drive to the Women's Gate (Frauen Tor) before they could leave the city towards Neufähr, where they hoped to get away on a customs boat.

Many had a far less clear idea of where they were fleeing to. On the morning of the 23rd March the Mehlender trek was one of the last to go through the almost empty streets of Zoppot southwards towards Danzig. Only a few soldiers with fatigued, pale faces were moving about. Beyond Zoppot the traffic became denser and in Oliva they were directed to Brösen on the coast, a small village at the level of Neufahrwasser. There they found accommodation in a barracks that the Wehrmacht had given up. They were pleased to be out of Danzig, where the first fires were glowing amid the clouds of dust from the artillery fire. Out at sea they could see the big ships. Seeing them, all the Mehlenders were united. They were never going on the water. They would rather drive on for a few weeks anywhere. And that they would soon have to seemed inevitable. That afternoon the last refugees from Zoppot came running along the beach, together with many wounded and retreating soldiers.

This route was roughly the same as that used by the young army doctor Peter Siegel. On the 23rd March he was still working in the dressing station at Dock IV on the mole in Gotenhafen. The low-flying aircraft disturbed him less because he was working in a walled hall and so was sheltered from splinters and machine-gun fire. But the thought of being cut off at this outer post, and the risk of becoming a prisoner of war, had given him no rest. After many telephone calls he discovered that his Neidenburger field hospital was now in Danzig-Langfuhr and requested to be transferred there. His movement orders arrived in the late afternoon and before nightfall Peter Siegel was on his way south from the main dressing station in Gotenhafen. He went on foot and was sure that he would find a vehicle soon to take him the 16 kilometres. But he did not get far. A barricade had been set up at the exit from Gotenhafen. Military police and tank soldiers had blocked the way with cars and trucks. In the barricade was also a trolleybus from Insterburg, one of those buses on which Peter Siegel had once used every day to go to school. There were four German tanks on the far side. They had run out of fuel but were firing round after round at the heights to the west, where the Russians were preparing a thrust on Danzig.

Peter Siegel had no alternative but to turn back. At the local command post he discovered that a fishing boat took the field post from Gotenhafen to Danzig every morning. Next morning he actually caught the boat, which took him without any others. Out at sea he became aware for the first time what ceaseless traffic there was in the Bight of Danzig. On his mole he had

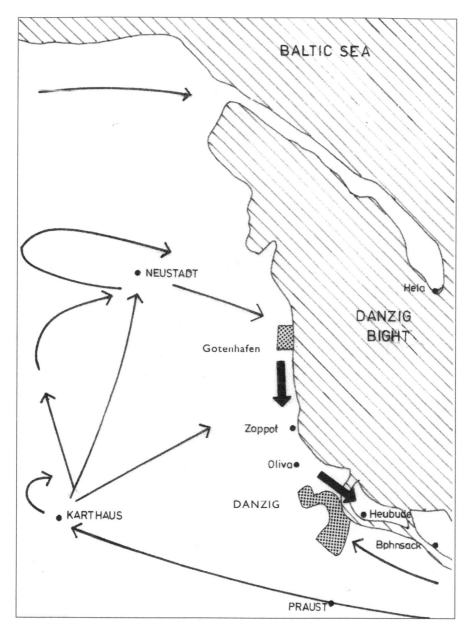

Map 6. Trapped refugee movements

never really been able to look out there, as he was mainly taken up with the ships carrying wounded. Here, out on the open sea, one could see the long rows of ships of all sizes. A series of explosions made him look around. On the beach – they were about halfway between Adlershorst and Zoppot –

fountains were rising as high as houses. The Russian batteries were firing at the coastal strip. Peter Siegel was no longer so certain whether it was clever to leave Gotenhafen. Half an hour later he climbed ashore at Danzig-Neufahrwasser and made his way through the waiting crowd to Langfuhr.

Despite the artillery fire there was still a crowd of several thousand refugees. The naval transport detachment of the Danzig naval command was directing all available ships to Gotenhafen and Danzig. On the 23rd March the 6,370-ton *Mittelmeer*, the 5,064-ton *Eberhard Essberger* and two other merchant ships left the Kaiser Harbour in Danzig at about 2200 hours with dimmed lights. They were carrying several thousand refugees, including Berta Rubenhauser with her mother and Trudl, who had come to Danzig from Pillau.

Next day several smaller units and the 5,791-ton *Urundi* left. The latter was carrying 3,500 refugees and 1,000 wounded, and set off again that evening. The lines of refugees in the harbour began to thin out. The low-flying attacks and the artillery fire had persuaded many to go on foot along the coast towards Neufähr and Bohnsack.

The way would have remained open for many if military bureaucracy and other administrative authorities were not bent on saving 'worthwhile goods' for the west instead of people. A large steamer was loaded to the gunnels in Gotenhafen with expensive artillery range-finding equipment, leaving room for only 76 refugees. In Neufahrwasser a 2,000-ton freighter was loaded with molasses that no one could use any more. And then on the 24th March the railway authorities in Danzig succeeded in getting a 40-ton machine aboard the old steamer *Samland*. The loading took hours and over 100 people had to relinquish their places.

On Palm Sunday, the 25th March, a tall, black cloud of smoke rose above Zoppot. The first Stalin-Organs were firing from Zigankenberg and Oliva into the town. The naval command offices in Danzig closed and the staff set off for Hela in two cutters. The 1,293-ton *Otterberg* and shortly afterwards the 6,000-ton freighter *Fangturm* approached the harbour entrance. A naval speedboat that was engaged in unmooring the guiding buoy sent both ships back. But no one warned the 9,555-ton *Ubena*. Together with the *Deutschland*, *Herkules*, *Licentia* and a row of other ships, she was there to remove refugees and wounded from Gotenhafen. Because of the strong artillery fire, the ships had moved off towards Hela during the day so as to steer for Gotenhafen again at night. Captain Lankau had no desire to have his ship shot up and went on to Neufahrwasser and went in despite there being no navigation lights. In turning in the not very wide Vistula, his stern ran firmly aground. They tacked about half the night and finally broke free under their own power. As day broke, the news had already spread among the remaining refugees that a large steamer was lying there, and the quay was again filled with a mute crowd. The crew hurried to get the people aboard up the gangways. Captain Lankau had cargo nets hanging over the side for the boys and girls and some men to climb up like cats. Artillery fire resumed in the middle of the loading, salvo after salvo. Fortunately most shells hit the opposite bank. Splinters penetrated the walls of the promenade decks without injuring anyone. Captain Lankau and his crew were on tenter-hooks. It had gradually dawned on them that they were latecomers and that the navy had moved their transport service to Danzig. After four hours every-one was on board at last and the *Ubena* could cast off. She steamed at full speed back to Gotenhafen, where she took on more refugees and wounded under cover of darkness.

Shortly after the *Ubena* had left, the two ammunition ships in Neufahr-wasser, *Bille* and *Weser*, blew up. After that no other ships left the harbour where the 30 remaining German submarines waited to be taken over by the Russians.

The Neidenburg field hospital moved out towards the Vistula mouth with 36 horse-drawn ambulances, and was caught in an air attack while passing through Breitegassestrasse. The horses went through but when they at last had the burning buildings of the Speicher Island behind they were down to only 16 wagons. Peter Siegel saw to the left, down a bit of the Mottlau River, the wooden part of the imposing crane tower in bright flames, and thick smoke poured from the window spaces of the baroque facades on the Langen Bridge. On the waters of the Mottlau a customs boat was heading towards the Vistula. The engine stuttered; it was not going to go far. The field hospital was carried along with the military units and refugees across the bridges of Heubude and over the Vistula crossing points to Steegen in the Elbing part of the Vistula flats.

Now there were almost no civilians, only soldiers on the streets in Danzig. On the 25th March the Soviets dropped leaflets over the city. Marshal Rokossovski demanded that the generals, officers and soldiers of the German 2nd Army accept unconditional surrender. Those who surrendered would be guaranteed their lives and allowed to retain their personal belongings.

The leaflets had no success. Waffen-SS men were fighting for Oliva and the heights in front of Danzig were defended by Volksgrenadier Divisions and units of the naval flak to the last round. The 4th Panzer Division had moved its headquarters to the Schichau shipyards, its commander, General Betzel, having fallen in the streets of Danzig. The Soviets could only advance a foot at a time. They reinforced their artillery engagement and the machines of the Red Air Force were constantly over the city.

Nevertheless, Alix Forstreuter had returned. The customs boat had already gone. Now she needed two boarding tickets and had been told that she could only get them in Danzig. Her route led straight into the temporary quarters of the county forestry department near the arsenal. In the main office she took a telephone under a table and tried to reach a higher office. It was useless, no one answered any more. But, undeterred, she kept on dialling and was finally uncertain whether she was dialling the right number as next to her stood her second cup of liquor. Someone had discovered a whole stock of it in the cellar and there was no one in the whole building that was still sober.

Shortly after, air raid wardens brought two women, apparently mother and daughter, into the building. Both of them were half unconscious, their hair and furs dripping wet. At the last moment the men had fished them out of the Mottlau, where they had tried to drown themselves from fear of the Russians.

While looking for hand towels and clothing for the two soaked-through women, Alix Forstreuter went upstairs. There she found three old men sitting in an empty room between a battery of bottles playing skat. The bursting of the shells did not trouble them in the least, and when the young woman asked one of them if they wanted to disappear, he did not deign to reply.

Alix Forstreuter found neither clothing nor hand towels, so she went on and passed a kitchen where a group of army medical orderlies were waiting for some commitment to action. They offered her a bottle of schnaps and asked her to sit with them, but she soon took flight as the soldiers had come straight from the 'refugees' glass house', a former BDM Home in which refugees had been accommodated. There explosive bombs and incendiaries had wreaked havoc, and the medical orderlies excelled in the description of cruel details, talking of heads ripped off and limbs stuck between the bars of beds, burnt and mutilated children, hysterically screaming mothers. Alix Forstreuter was angry and she left, making her way to her friends in the Neufähr customs building.

As in the county forestry department, in a whole number of offices the officials remaining behind were waiting for orders to evacuate. In the Oberfinanzpräsidium at the Horst-Hoffmann-Wall Governing Director Dr Kappes waited and tried to hold back the officials of the main customs office subordinate to him and other financial offices. He had already on Friday the 23rd March telephoned Government President Dr Huth requesting evacuation and travel orders. Dr Huth had demanded the request in writing, and duly received it during that lunchtime. That Friday evening came the information that the matter would be considered.

On Saturday no one answered the telephones in the Gauleiter's offices. That afternoon Dr Kappes sent Customs Secretary Kämmler over. He returned with the news that a crowd of people was waiting outside the building for departure permits but that there was no one in the building. No one was there also on Sunday the 25th March. Dr Kappes never received the permission.

Gauleiter Förster, Governing Director Huth and their close staffs had driven to the mouth of the Vistula on the Saturday morning to take the little steamer *Zoppot* to Hela in order to take the opportunity of going west from there.

The officials remaining behind did not know what to do. Without orders, they dare not do anything. Some reported to the Volkssturm, others sent at least their wives and children to Bohnsack. But the increasingly stronger artillery fire, the fires and the collapsing buildings made attempts to flee ever more difficult.

Map 7. Refugee routes through the centre of Danzig

On Monday the 26th March Dr Kappes tried to reach the main customs office to brief those of his officials still remaining. He only got as far as Breitstrasse, where fires and collapsed buildings as far as the Grünen Bridge blocked the way. He turned back and informed a colleague that the service was practically dissolved. The main tax office had taken a direct hit from a bomb.

In the building of the Oberfinanzpräsidium on the Horst-Hoffmann-Wall Customs Secretary Kämmler had meanwhile taken over the organisation. On the first floor a military police company and the secret field police had occupied several rooms. In addition the staff of an artillery regiment had moved in. There were further Wehrmacht staffs in the cellar and dozens of civilians, mostly civil servants with their wives and children. Among them was also the wife of the Customs Secretary, who had been completely paralysed by severe diphtheria.

On Tuesday the Russians reached the Olivaer Gate. Volksgrenadiers held them back with a plentiful supply of Panzerfausts but could not stop the Soviets breaking through and getting to the station along Schichaugasse lane. Volksgrenadiers and Waffen-SS opened fire towards the station from the windows of the Oberfinanzpräsidium. The Russians fired back with captured Panzerfausts. The building shook down to its foundations. Then the Germans cleared the field. The paralysed woman in the cellar who could only move her eyes waited for the Russians to take her. Then she heard an officer saying to her husband: 'We won't leave your wife in the dirt!' Then soldiers lifted the cripple and her 8-year-old son into a car. Other civilians scrambled on to the ammunition truck of a passing anti-tank detachment. They had hardly got past the Danziger Hof when they ran into a firefight. The Russians were pressing for the Mottlau bridges. From the Zigankenberg sounded loud loudspeakers as members of the National Committee for a Free Germany demanded their former comrades' surrender. After each of these demands they played gramophone records of Mozart's *Kleine Nachtmusik* and *In der Nacht ist der Mensch nicht gern alleine*.

On Monday evening the hospital quarter between the Fish Market and the old city moat was in bright flames. In the chancellor's house the sisters formed a bucket chain to the nearby little stream and tried to save what they could. But whenever they managed to subdue the flames at one point, the wind blew sparks from the blazing buildings in the north across to them. The garages and the inspector's house were burning sky high, but the occupants of the air raid shelter had got out at the last moment.

At dawn several daring ones attempted to leave through the burning city. Their bravery was lost in the low-flying attacks and artillery fire. The inspector knew that both his daughters drowned in the Vistula when the blast wave from a bomb threw them into the water.

The remaining Danzigers and refugees huddled in the cellars and waited tearfully for the end; they could not imagine it. They were pleased when any stranger, soldier or civilian, came in with the latest news, even when it increasingly seemed to mean disaster. In the Alstädter Graben the vicar of the evangelical church sat with his wife and 30 refugees in the cellar of the vicarage. Their neighbours and the other occupants of the buildings had long since gone off. Until a few days before there had still been burials. Often they had to finish the opening prayers behind the nearest gravestone when low-flying aircraft disturbed them. But then there were no more pall-bearers for the many more dead, so they gave up. The vicar's wife had taken a heavily pregnant Elbinger woman with three children from the street and brought her to the cellar. The others had arrived bit by bit. Among them was also an Austrian NCO with eight men who had first camped in the big room on the ground floor and given the civilians in the cellar a sense of security. Now machine-gun fire raged from the window openings on the ground floor. But on Palm Sunday the men too came down into the cellar. Outside German troops were heading towards Heubude and only a few civilians joined them.

Chapter 16

Chaos at the Mouth of the Vistula

Alix Forstreuter and her friend, who was holding her dog Bruno in her arms, crouched on the back of an army truck. The vehicle belonged to the 4th Panzer Division, which was withdrawing towards the Frisches Haff lagoon. They came safely out of burning Danzig but when they reached the Heubude bridge over the Dead Vistula it seemed that their wild flight had come to an end. Tanks, trucks, carts and pedestrians formed a complete tangle. Low-flying aircraft had reaped a rich harvest and were still trying to hit the bridge with repeated attacks. Right and left of the approach lay shot-up vehicles and carts. Alix Forstreuter saw the corpse of one driver slumped over the steering wheel of a burning ambulance. The ground had been torn away on one side of the bridge and sappers were busy reinforcing the wooden piles.

At every approach of the low-flying aircraft the soldiers threw themselves down where they stood, but the refugees ran around madly screaming, making matters worse. The truck carrying Alix Forstreuter and her friend took almost an hour to reach the bridge.

In Heubude the driver set both women down in the street as he had to report somewhere. They found another unit that was ready to move, waiting for orders to go to Pillau. An NCO allowed them to throw their sparse baggage on a truck. Until departure the two women sat down in the sunshine against the wall of a building in sight of their baggage and their escape vehicle. Alix Forstreuter had difficulty concentrating. The ample consumption of liquor had not suited her and her stomach was churning.

They kept looking up at the clear blue sky that lost itself in a layer of mist near the sea. They did not see the low-flying Russian aircraft coming until its machine-gun fire and the noise of its engine overshadowed the din coming from Danzig. They turned their heads and jumped up. Flak bellowed away and two bombs fell at some distance, and then the spook was gone. A soldier chased them from their sunny spot to which they had returned: 'Get out, quickly! He's coming back!'

They darted down the street to the nearest stone building. It was the post office and the little shop was jammed full of civilians. They had to use their elbows to get in. The pressure on Bruno was so great that he had run off into the bushes. This was only realised when the low-flying aircraft shot some wooden buildings into flames on its second attack, and then went off again.

They spent nearly an hour looking for the dog, who had found an alsatian at the other end of the village to prove what a rake he was, and he had to be reluctantly torn from his booty by the two complaining women. When they returned to the place where they had been sitting, the truck had already gone and their luggage lay on the street. While they discussed whether they should go back along the street or look for shelter in the Heubude woods, another low-flying aircraft attacked. They ran away from the houses and threw themselves down in an open field seconds too late. A shower of sand and lumps of earth caught them on one side as a bomb exploded. Both thought themselves badly hit and lay still. Then they carefully checked their legs and arms, touching themselves, and stood up trembling.

Alix Forstreuter had a sharp pain near her hip, apparently a bruise. She brushed the dirt off her coat and was about to move off when she saw blood running down her friend's calf over her ankle and into her shoe. A splinter had gone into the calf just below the knee, but she was not in pain. Bruno followed at some distance as they made their way to the Heubude dressing station, where both were given anti-tetanus injections, and her friend's wound was dressed.

It was already becoming dark as they sought shelter in a Wehrmacht bunker, where they at last were given some soup, sausage and bread. The dog was still with them but Alix Forstreuter had lost her handbag with her papers somewhere, presumably in the field.

Early that evening Irma Neuber had also come through Heubude with the Mehlenden trek. They had driven on in the stream of Wehrmacht vehicles without stopping, hoping to be able to pull off in the big wooded area between Heubude and Bohnsack and have a rest. They took it in turns sleeping in the wagons and it was only because of the horses that they had to stop. But whenever they found a place where they could stop with all the wagons they were chased off by soldiers. Everywhere Wehrmacht units had deployed between the trees with guns and vehicles standing around, and foxholes and trenches were being dug.

Halfway to Bohnsack they were at last able to drive off into a clearing. It was only the following morning that they realised that a herd of cows belonging to a supply unit was grazing there. There was enough milk for everyone and drinking water was obtainable from a beach hut further away, where some soldiers and their girlfriends had made themselves comfortable. The search for fodder for the horses was also successful. They obtained hay from the uniformed cowherds, and a Wehrmacht cook gave them a few buckets of potato peelings. Their only problem was that a sergeant insisted they camouflage their wagons with pine branches.

Driving further along this rough and overfilled road was not to be thought about. They had not come far through the woods, and hour after hour more refugees were coming from Heubude seeking shelter under the trees.

Next morning Irma Neuber made a reconnaissance with the Belgian to the beach, where a row of corpses lay neatly alongside each other. They did not find a way through the thousands of people: 'What do you want? You can't get through here!' was all that they heard. Desiré, the Belgian, suggested they should creep through the Russian lines and then drive back peacefully to Mehlenden. They had already gone halfway, but Irma Neuber had no desire to meet the Russians. She wandered about in the woods for a while before going back to the wagon a few minutes too soon. She had just arrived when bombers raced across the treetops. They had not yet got under cover when a bomb exploded close to a Mehlenden wagon, killing one and wounding five. A Polish forced labourer got a splinter in his stomach and Desiré was badly injured in the leg. Frightful screams came from quite close. The soldiers of the cattle detail had been digging a bunker when they took a direct hit with eight killed and several wounded. Medical orderlies treated the soldiers, but the refugees had to find their own doctor. Six of them carried the Pole in a woollen blanket to the nearby village of Krakau. Desiré followed behind on a horse led by Irma Neuber. The field hospital there, a large hut, was only a pile of smouldering planks and beams. A medical orderly took them to a small farm on the edge of the village where the wounded were accommodated in a barn. There were no longer any doctors but, despite the great crush, there were still injections and bandages. The Mehlenders left their five wounded in the care of the medical orderlies, but had to remove them next day as promised, even the no longer transportable Pole. The Russians were getting ever closer and were already as far as Heubude.

The little troop of Mehlenders left Krakau in the wrong direction. Instead of leaving the place to the northeast, they went south and within about ten minutes had reached the Dead Vistula. From the crest of the dyke they could see across the sluggishly flowing water and the opposite dyke far to the south. Long columns were moving eastwards along the marsh roads, cart after cart, no larger than ants. Disappointed, Irma Neuber turned away, her secret hopes to find a way out of their situation dashed.

In fact the Mehlenders were better off than the refugees on the other side, especially as these treks were showing the senselessness and aimlessness of their route. After ten weeks of fleeing, in which they had made an almost

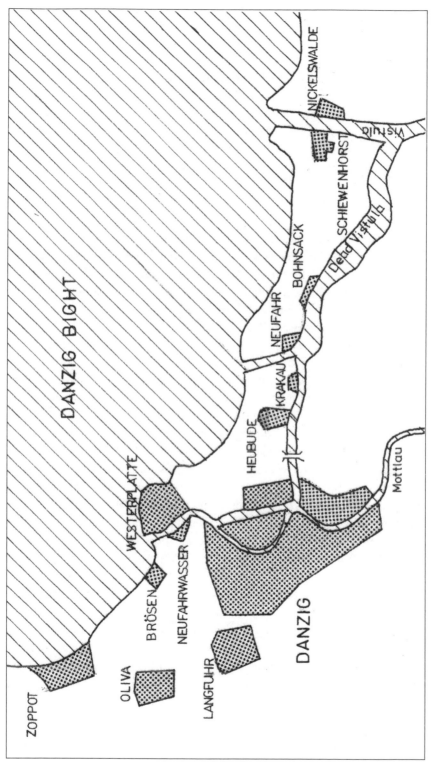

Map 8. The Vistula estuary

200-kilometre loop, they now found themselves only about 20 kilometres from their home village, Neuteichhinterfeld, in Gross Werder. Heinrich Ellers had set off with his family of five and the remaining villagers in an organised trek as early as the 24th January, when a reasonable District Leader in Tiegenort had given timely orders to evacuate. But after they had trekked through snow and ice for over 40 kilometres they were stopped in Prangenau and allocated private accommodation, remaining there until the middle of February.

Their departure from there coincided with the Soviet attack from the area of Tuchel towards Danzig. The Neuteichhinterfelders only got as far as Karthaus and then had to leave at speed to the northeast under air attack and wedged in between the Wehrmacht. They had a few days rest in Danzig-Zigankenberg, but on Palm Sunday the Russians were back again. The whole trek went through Danzig in a wild flight. For a bit they followed the same route as the Mehlenders, but before the Heubude bridge the Wehrmacht forced them to the southeast. They now drove south of the Dead Vistula right back to their original place. But shortly before they got there Heinrich Ellers and several other men were taken from their wagons and put in the Volkssturm to dig foxholes along the river. The trek was dispersed by the Wehrmacht near Herzberg, the women and children and old people being sent to Schiewenhorst 15 kilometres away in the direction of the Vistula cutting, from where there was an almost uninterrupted ferry service to Hela.

The Mehlenders were decisively nearer their goal at this point in time. From their wagons to the Hela ferries in Bohnsack was only three kilometres.

The anxiety of the refugees increased when the Wehrmacht started clearing the woods of civilians. 'Fighting is about to start here. Get out!' They had to leave everything behind and go on foot to Bohnsack. The Mehlenders packed the most important things on a horse and went under the cover of the trees to the Vistula ferry. However, the first jam occurred within only a few hundred metres.

Between abandoned trek wagons, hastily erected machine-gun nests and dismantled artillery pieces were infantry units wanting to get to the front. Irma Neuber used the opportunity to go back quickly and recover from the wagon some useful items that had been left behind, such as the file with her photos and the brown woollen jacket for cold evenings. She took a long time looking for the clearing, where the cows were still grazing, but the wagon had already been plundered and her things strewn over the ground. She could not see the file anywhere and the brown jacket was hanging between sheets and an empty strange suitcase in a blackberry bush. She did not want to take them. It was as if they did not belong to her any more. For the first time during the flight she had the feeling of having really lost something. She turned around and slowly went back.

After hours the ferry came into sight; it had already brought her once over the Vistula, but in the other direction. The Soviet aircraft were active again, but nobody sought cover from fear of missing the connection. By late afternoon they were in the queue. They were allowed on the ferry, crowded among the military traffic, but without the horses. That meant that their luggage, or what of it they had been able to rescue, they now had to carry themselves. Desiré too had to be carried between them. He was in considerable pain that he bravely tried to bite back. In Bohnsack they found shelter in a smokehouse and spent the night on sacks of salt. They had no idea how they should continue, apparently over the lagoon to Pillau, where ships were waiting.

Only a few paces away from the auxiliary field hospital that evening lay the schoolmaster Otto Lippke, the Danzig woman Alix Forstreuter and her friend with the dachshund Bruno. On Palm Sunday Otto Lippke was still in Danzig on the ground floor of an insurance building to which a large number of wounded had been brought, since there was nowhere else. Lippke heard some of them crying out in pain; others had been drugged and were in delirium. The medical orderly had constantly pressed him to take morphia tablets for his own wound and he detected not the least pain now, nor later. He only had one concern: would he get out of this damned city before the Russians came? Nobody seemed to be looking after the wounded, who had been attended to only once. There was nothing to eat or drink. Constantly new wounded were being taken past him into the building and if the Russians came he would be the first out. He was lying near the door.

Late afternoon two medical orderlies appeared and shouted: 'Let's go! Who shall we take?'

A couple of youngsters at the back, close to the door to the toilet, shouted loudest and were promptly carried out to the ambulance waiting outside. One after the other followed past Otto Lippke, who could not prevail over the loud disappointment and anger that broke out. He had to wait for the second load.

Enclosed in the grey-green boxed extension of the ambulance, Lippke no longer felt safe. The vehicle drove, stopped, drove, and by his reckoning they must soon be in Elbing, where the Russians were. Lippke did not know that they had driven to Neufahrwasser and only missed the *Ubena* by minutes. The driver had needed hours to get across the bridge to Heubude, but his cargo had not been unloaded and he had had to drive on further towards Bohnsack. On the way they ran into an air attack. In their dark boxes the wounded heard the exploding bombs and something hit the side of the vehicle. Two of them began shouting at the driver, but he had long since jumped out of the vehicle and taken cover. Upon his return he was greeted with a cannonade of complaints, which he shrugged aside. He brought Lippke and his suffering comrades to Bohnsack with the ferry and delivered them to the dressing station there. On leaving them he told them that he had had enough and they could go to hell. They had been on the way for 18 hours.

The old schoolmaster lay on a sand sack in the cellar with his stump lifted up. It was so unreal that he could not think clearly. Only the fact that he was again a little ahead of the Russians was somewhat firm. Even when he was told that a nearby barn had been burnt out that morning and a nursing sister and 80 wounded killed it made no impression on him. It was in that barn that Alix Forstreuter and her friend with Bruno had first rested, but shortly before the fire they had been thrown out because of overcrowding now that her friend's leg was all right. The wound was only a harmless flesh wound. They managed to get accepted by the auxiliary field hospital and now lay warm and safe on sacks of straw near the OP. Because of Bruno, Alix Forstreuter was drawn to the animal food kitchen of the farm, where the sweet smell of cooking turnips and potatoes fascinated the Dachshund, who did not want to leave and had to be chased round troughs, fodder cauldrons and buckets. She had found a children's station, whose nurse was delighted to have her additional assistance, and for two days she tended sick children, changed dressings and made leg compresses.

A military padre appeared several times and promised to see to her transport. Most of this was taken for idle promises and she made accordingly sneering remarks, but she had been mistaken. The padre had really arranged for two torpedo boats from the commander to take the field hospital's wounded on their next trip. It finally happened that the present occupants were saved, and that room was also made for hundreds of newly wounded lying about in private homes or in part in the open without any care.

On the third morning, a week since they had fled from Danzig, Alix Forstreuter and her friend climbed aboard a naval ferry with Bruno and a small group from the Mehlender trek that had found a place. Otto Lippke came on one of the two little grey-painted naval ships. He lay wrapped up in woollen blankets on the deck. It rained and spray came over him as the boat set off. Greedily the blankets absorbed the puddles that soon formed around him. He felt his nose slowly creep out of his clothing, which made him think of the Allenburger women who had complained: 'Oh God, if we had only stayed at home!' But he still had had his leg and his wife was apparently also still with him – or she was already dead. It was all pointless. One must only see to it that the little life left in one brought one through the next round. The journey over the Bight of Danzig lasted four hours. Once they were unloaded, the boats turned back, passing only eight sea miles past the Russian-occupied towns of Gotenhafen and Danzig.

A vast cloud of smoke stood over Danzig. The city had been in Soviet hands since the 30th March. The victors celebrated their success for two days then thrust out towards the Vistula estuary. They contented themselves with the taking of Heubude and Krakau, and got as far as the breach of the Vistula and thus rendered ferry traffic from Neufàhr impossible. Then Marshal Rokossovski pulled back his main forces to reinforce his attack over the Oder towards Berlin. The people in the Vistula estuary had a break of a good five weeks. So Heinrich Ellers, who was still digging foxholes, thus had a chance.

Chapter 17

From Hela to the West

Anni Grigo, an employee of the West Prussian Energy Administration, was one of the last to leave Danzig by ship. She had to choose between an open coal barge and a sailing fishing boat lying between Neufahrwasser and Neufähr. She was scared of the high sides to the coal holds and thus opted for the fishing boat. The boat had danced crazily over the rough sea and everyone, with few exceptions, became seasick.

Three hours later they ran into the fishing harbour at Hela. The roads were full of ships, and on the left towards the mainland were two large battleships firing at the heights beyond Oxhöft. There were masses of people in the little harbour, being kept from the pier by marines. At the pier were lighters and landing craft to take out women, children and old folk to the big ships in the roads.

In the naval harbour next to the fishing harbour there was nothing for the refugees. There were still naval units there, including the 9th Security Division, whose headquarters were on the moored ship *Rugard* busily organising the security boats for the escorts. That day the *Rugard* had had a visitor. Gauleiter Koch had left Neutief when he saw that the Heiligenberg cauldron was finished. Koch was not the man to simply hide himself like his colleague Forster; he always had to play the first violin. Whereas Forster had secretly established himself in a former Polish headquarters train located on the tracks of the narrow-gauge railway between Heisternest and Hela and disappeared into the nearest bunker 'in order to acquaint himself with the situation' whenever Soviet aircraft appeared, and was otherwise without a job, Koch had arrived by Fieseler *Storch* and immediately gone to see the commander of the Security Division, Commander Adalbert von Blanc, on the *Rugard* in order to inform Führer Headquarters of his change of location.

Shortly afterwards the *Rugard* signalled the *Potsdam* lying in the roads to send an officer to the *Rugard*. A young lieutenant of the reserve and staff administrative officer came in accordance with the demand. Koch led the discussion. In his opinion the *Potsdam* did not have sufficient provisions for the many wounded and refugees on board and he wanted to organise this as quickly as possible. The lieutenant contradicted him: the *Potsdam* had sufficient supplies for eight to ten days in its stores. Koch said that he was pleased and in the same moment found another point of debate: lack of personnel. It ended with the lieutenant, escorted by two marines, having to go among the refugees to find two hundred women and girls to look after the wounded on the big 17,528-ton steamer. He had doubts, but later it turned out that they could not have done better, as the women showed themselves to be a mixture of angels and hard workers looking after the wounded day after day and night after night.

Anni Grigo had the *Potsdam* in her sights, as she thought that the biggest ships were the safest. When she at last pushed herself to the front on the pier a submarine lay below her against the quay. Before she knew what was happening she was on board with 20 others and the boat steered for the *Potsdam*. Anni Grigo sat on a box of provisions, from which a sailor took a handful of biscuits for her. The side of the *Potsdam* seemed unendingly high, but several gangways had been lowered and the lighters fastened to them. The refugees on the submarine were pulled up four at a time in a net by a crane.

That evening at about 1930 hours the *Potsdam* weighed anchor. It was her fifth journey and the third time that she would be running to Copenhagen. Captain Schill and his crew had already had several eventful trips. They had been running shortly behind the *Wilhelm Gustloff* on the 30th January and quickly turned about when the disaster became known to them. Before they resumed their journey, the doctor reported scarlet fever and measles among the children. Later he believed several soldiers were showing signs of typhus. On one of their journeys the boilers failed and the big ship drifted into a minefield.

Anni Grigo had imagined her sea journey differently. The ship was indescribably filthy and people were lying next to each other on the decks on flattened straw. There was only thin soup to eat, although it was known that the crew had plenty of food, as did refugees who could pay. For the latter there were even cabins. But this was nothing in comparison to what awaited them on disembarkation in Copenhagen. Many of them would be living in Danish camps for years as prisoners of war.

The *Potsdam*'s place in the Hela roads had been taken by the *Urundi* and the *Herkules*. The *Urundi* was a former banana steamer of 5,791 tons, equipped as a troop transport for 1,000 men and accommodation for 105 flak gunners. Now on each journey she carried 4,000 to 4,500 refugees and wounded. The 2,369-ton *Herkules* had worked for the Sassnitz Naval Artillery School, being equipped for 400 men, and now carried 2,000 to 2,500 people to safety.

Irma Neuber and her small group, who had turned down a journey by ship so determinedly a few days earlier, approached the *Urundi* in a landing craft. She was so exhausted that she was no longer being seasick. As the boat came alongside, a wooden platform was lowered from above to its deck. Several sailors who had come down on it had first to secure the fragile thing to the landing craft before a dozen people could sit on it. Then it went up, the platform swinging dangerously from the crane, then swung over the hatch and set them down in one of the five lower holds.

Irma Neuber simply shut her eyes and waited until a sailor pulled her up with his hand after they had been set down.

There was an agonising lack of space on the ship and again the lack of toilet facilities made conditions much worse. The 55-man crew and the 105 flak gunners did without some of their rations so that the refugees,

Map 9. Hela – the last harbour in East Prussia

especially the small children, at least had something to eat. The *Urundi* carried no supplies. The children were astonishingly well behaved. It was the adults, whose nerves were at breaking point from hunger, who gave rise to some unpleasant scenes. One man was nearly lynched because of a hidden sausage. They were three days at sea and then lay another whole day in the Copenhagen roads. Only the next morning was the ship towed into the harbour, but no one was allowed off. Close to the *Urundi* lay the cruiser *Nürnberg* at anchor. Captain Wiencken had the First Officer, Lieutenant Commander von Müller, report to him. He requested the use of his telephone, which von Müller allowed after some hesitation. Captain Wiencken called several Party and Naval offices that he knew, described the serious situation on his ship and urgently begged for supplies. He was put off with promises that he knew would not be fulfilled. Lieutenant Commander von Müller, who was standing silently next to him and had heard everything, decided to accompany the captain and see for himself that the people on the ship were suffering from hunger. Von Müller was horrified by what he saw.

One hour later sailors from the *Nürnberg* brought large cauldrons of milk soup to the *Urundi* and hardly were the first ones empty when the next ones arrived. Hours later – the refugees were long since hungry again – cold and warm food was brought from a Wehrmacht kitchen in the town. The sailors of the *Nürnberg* did not want to be left out and that afternoon laid on a concert together with a collection that was shared out between the mothers with children. The *Urundi* had left Hela in the same convoy as the *Herkules*. Behind them was the cruiser *Leipzig*, which had hardly any fuel left and also had engine damage. At only six knots it remained well behind the convoy.

For the *Herkules* this was its fifth of nine trips with refugees and wounded. As the last ship in the convoy, submarines and aircraft made its life hard. Most of the day the crew were at action stations and the flak detachment had its hands full fending off the constantly returning Soviet aircraft.

Alix Forstreuter had found a place for herself and her friend on the between-deck behind the bridge. Bruno was so intimidated that he dare not emerge from his woollen half-blanket. The wounded were constantly calling for the medical orderly, but the latter was mainly occupied with the severely wounded and had little time to meet special requests. Alix saw no option but to give a hand to one or another. Soon men were calling out for the 'Miss'. With a churning stomach and weak knees, the Danzig girl brought them water and emptied the jam jars that she had acquired from the galley, laid a hand here and there on fevered foreheads and calmed them.

The stink of excreta, urine and sweat was terrible. Several times she had to go up on deck to take some air, and each time going down below again was harder. She obtained sleeping tablets for her friend, took Bruno under her arm and headed for the galley, for he had not eaten properly for two days.

Chief Cook Schierholz, a great animal lover, placed Bruno on a bench behind his work table and put a piece of wood with some horsemeat under his nose. The cook was so pleased with the dog that, out of gratitude, he also gave Alix a dish of goulash, which she devoured hungrily. While doing so, she observed the cook stirring an egg into a consumé.

'You don't live badly here then, with eggs,' she remarked. 'This is for our patient, who has to regain her strength,' said Schierholz earnestly. Alix then discovered that the patient was a 3-year-old girl called Roswitha, who was being looked after in the engineers' quarters. She had had a high fever for weeks that was at last beginning to subside.

Alix offered to take the soup to the cabin and so found out the story from Frau Voss and her daughter, whom she met there. Frau Voss was a war widow from Rosenberg. She had ventured to flee with her little daughter by train from Rosenberg on the 18th January. It was the last train and they had got no further than Marienburg. They had then continued on foot, by army truck and with treks, first to Karthaus, then to Stolp, back to Lauenberg, and finally entered Gotenhafen on the 28th February. There the little one had become seriously ill, apparently with pneumonia, and spent a month in a large warehouse at the harbour. On the 25th March Frau Voss gambled everything on the one card. She and the feverish child stood on the pier and waited for two whole days until the commander of a minesweeper took pity on them and took them out to the *Herkules* in the Gotenhafen roads.

She did not know whether she would stay on the overcrowded ship with her child, but the engineer Huckfeld found the distraught woman and offered her his bunk for the sick child, and looked after the little one like a father. The child gradually regained her strength in the quiet and warm bunk.

There was a farewell when the *Herkules* tied up in Swinemünde. Since they could not look after him, the girls left the dachshund Bruno in the care of the cook. When the cook wrote an account of his experiences years later, Bruno was still sitting beside him. He had made another four trips on the *Herkules* and had then remained with his new master.

Frau Voss and her daughter travelled on with the ship to Copenhagen. Two months later she became engaged to Huckfeld and they married the following year. On Saturday the 31st March the *Pretoria* lay with her meaningless white strip and Red Cross on the funnel again in the Hela roads with the *Deutschland* anchored nearby.

All day long ferries brought refugees on board. Towards 1830 hours the ships came under fire from Russian artillery near Oxhöft. Together with the *Pretoria*, the *Deutschland* moved a sea mile to the east, but hardly had they reached their new place when they were attacked from the air. They were able to deter the aircraft with their ship's flak, and it was soon so dark that the Russian aircraft could only be seen as shadows.

Ferry traffic from the harbour operated at night. From the land came boats of all kinds laden with soldiers and only a few refugees. These were the last Naval and Waffen-SS units to leave the last bridgeheads on the western side of the Bight of Danzig after some hefty fighting from the Oxhöft Kämpe. Up to the 4th April some 30,000 to 40,000 troops were evacuated under heavy Soviet artillery fire. The Soviets later claimed to have taken about 90,000 prisoners here.

Several boats from the Oxhöft Kämpe lay alongside the *Deutschland* and the *Pretoria* to unload. Among the last on them was a 50-year-old senior corporal from the naval flak, for whom the uniform was little more than fancy dress, as he had no idea about the flak or the navy; only his severe wound was real. He was Bruno Schuch, the head of the town's educational and cultural office, as well as the Elbing School of Physical Training. His wife and son had left Elbing on the 22nd January and had gone to Stolp, which was the designated reception place for Elbingers. After the Russian tanks had broken into Elbing Bruno Schuch set off on foot for Danzig and then followed his family to Stolp. Instead of what he expected, the Volkssturm were waiting for him, and he was sent back to Gotenhafen, where he was shortly sent to the naval flak. The last eight days he had spent in the auxiliary field hospital at the Hexengrund quarantine station. Perhaps he would never have got away if the 4th SS–Police Grenadier Division and the 7th Panzer Division had not chosen the Hexengrund as a loading ramp for their evacuation. So Bruno Schuch was quickly brought with the other wounded to the *Pretoria* to make room for the soldiers. On the *Pretoria* that day also lay the lame wife of the Danzig customs inspector Kämmerer.

Following this nightly interval the two big ships took on board refugees and wounded again. Despite the fine weather there was no sign of Soviet aircraft. This respite, however, was the only blessing this Easter Sunday. The Alleburger teacher Lippke was not fully conscious that day. Lippke was half dead from fear as the rocking lighter laid alongside the *Deutschland*. Sailors strapped him to a stretcher and hauled him up. For a long instant Lippke thought that he saw the swinging lighter going under and he imagined that a sailor patted him on the brow and said: 'Another lucky one, father!' But the lighter kept bobbing up and down so that it kept hitting the hull. One by one all the wounded came on board.

Lippke lay next to a Volkssturm man from Sinkehnen, near Tapiau. He was called Bojartel and was just as confused as the teacher from Allenburg.

They could not explain how all these things could have happened and what would happen to them now. In any case they were not hungry. Nevertheless they were annoyed that several of the lightly wounded sergeants had sausage and schnaps and gave it to others.

Lippke's neighbour on the other side could not be spoken to. Every few hours a sister stuck a pill between the man's lips. That evening she also came to Lippke, but he turned her away at first. He had never taken a sleeping tablet in his life, being always able to sleep when he was tired. Only when Bojartel took a pill – because he could not talk about home all night, as he said – the teacher also took one. Waking next morning, he was dizzy and his skull buzzed. The badly wounded man's space next to him was empty. Bojartel said that he had been taken away in the night because he had died. 'Don't take any more tablets!' Lippke warned the man from Sinkehnen: 'They want to poison us all as we are in the way.'

It was astonishing that there were still medicines available with so many wounded concentrated in so little space and the interrupted supply lines, but large quantities of supplies had been brought to Hela from Danzig. It was a different case with the doctors, especially on those ships not equipped as wounded transports or as hospital ships, where there was virtually no medical care. Even the *Deutschland* had lost its three doctors at Copenhagen, where they were urgently required on shore. When the *Deutschland* returned empty to Hela, Dr Pilz was the only doctor on board. His hopes of reinforcement at Hela were met in an unexpected manner, when the staff of a captured Russian field hospital – several doctors and nursing sisters – came across the promenade deck towards Dr Pilz under escort.

The Russians wanted to help and the doctor handed over the patients on A and B Decks to them. He himself went back to tend the wounded and sick refugees on the stuffy C Deck. Dr Pilz hardly noticed the time passing at his work. The *Deutschland* was about half way when an excited medical orderly called him to A Deck. There the Russians were tirelessly operating and tending to the wounded. They were doing this at a bewildering speed and often without anaesthetics. The orderly reported something less uplifting, however. Apparently, either from fear of an epidemic or simply because they were so used to it, the Russians made short work of the dead and simply threw them overboard at night without keeping their personal particulars and date of death. Ten soldiers had already vanished this way. Following an angry scene with the highest-ranking Russian, Dr Pilz took over the recording of deaths and the captain let the bodies be laid out on the forecastle. As previously, he declined to conduct sea burials, in contrast to a whole lot of other captains who stuck to the regulations and had the dead passengers sewn up in sailcloth and consigned them to the deep with weights. Later the sailcloth ran out and the corpses were sewn up in a cloth or dropped overboard uncovered.

The *Deutschland* anchored in the Drogden Roads off Copenhagen with 134 corpses on board. Eighty of them were placed on a launch and taken ashore. The refugees and the wounded took to the in-shore ships *Nürnberg* and *Der Deutsche*, but neither ship would take the remaining 54 corpses. Captain Feindt waited two days to dispose of this macabre freight. Finally he radioed a guard boat lying nearby, from which came a prompt reply: 'We are coming, but it will cost you a little something.' They agreed on four bottles of schnaps and the *Deutschland* was rid of the corpses. Next day, the 9th April, the *Deutschland* set course for Hela once more.

Meanwhile the situation at Hela had changed very much to the disadvantage of shipping. The Soviets had already occupied all the airfields in East and West Prussia with the sole exception of that at Neutief on the Frischen Spit. From these quickly restored airfields the Soviet air fleets were engaging the German bridgeheads. One of their main targets was the collection of ships in the Hela roads.

On the 8th and 9th April Soviet bombers sank off Hela the 10,850-ton *Franken*, the 1,335-ton *Hans-Albrecht-Wedel* and the 5,446-ton *Albert Jensen*, as well as several smaller vessels. The *Deutschland* had hardly reached the Hela roads when she had to defend herself against the first air attack. Nevertheless the loading continued and during the day a further 8,000 refugees and wounded were embarked. The Soviets attacked twice more from the air but were beaten off each time. The small delivery boats worked flat out and by the evening of that day the ship was able to sail away with only a few small scratches.

On the night of the 11th April a grain barge also chugged between the Vistula mouth and Hela. On the narrow deck and in the holds stood people so closely pressed together that only a few could sit. They formed a black mass with only the moonlight lightening their faces. Among them was Heinrich Ellers, who had found his wife and son again meanwhile. The barge made little progress, running hour after hour with those standing on deck anxiously watching the silvery surface of the water, waiting for a submarine to appear. But nothing happened, although 24 hours previously one of the many tragedies of these days had occurred in this area. The little steamer *Neuwerk*, with a 13-man crew, 854 wounded, 60 railway employees, seven medical orderlies and about 100 refugees, was on its way from Pillau to Hela. About 300 metres off was an escorting naval vessel. Between midnight and 0400 hours the bridge watch lost sight of the escort. The *Neuwerk* changed course and headed for Gotenhafen instead of Hela without realising it. Shortly after 0400 hours the First Officer saw two fast boats that he assumed to be German. After a series of light signals that the *Neuwerk* did not reply to, shots were fired across the steamer's bows. The end came quickly. Heavy fire rained on the deck and bridge. The captain was wounded and the helmsman fell. The First Officer brought the ship round to a northerly course, but at about 0420 hours the *Neuwerk* was hit amidships by a torpedo. The ship rolled and broke apart. A German S-boat saved eight crew members.

Years later a Polish recovery vessel brought up the stern of the *Neuwerk*, which lay on the sea floor about two sea miles from Gotenhafen. The Poles found 540 corpses in the obviously overloaded ship. In a four-man cabin they found 15 corpses, mainly soldiers. There were also female corpses and some babies. Many of the dead were wrapped in blankets, from which it was assumed that the ship had sunk while they were asleep. They were buried in three mass graves in the Gydnia-Witomin town cemetery.

The torpedoing of the *Neuwerk* went unnoticed by the ferries operating between Schiewenhorst and Hela. They were heading into quite another catastrophe.

It was a bright morning when the grain barge with Heinrich Ellers on board arrived at Hela. A naval boat directed the barge to the 7,862-ton *Moltkefels*, which had arrived under Captain Voss at about 0500 hours. Three hours later it took on the refugees. At 1105 hours the work was interrupted by an air alert. Two enemy machines came in from the east and dropped several bombs and fired at the ships without causing any damage. Captain Voss ordered the loading to continue. This was done with haste as at any moment they could be attacked again, and the *Moltkefels* had considerably fewer guns on board than the *Deutschland*. In uninterrupted succession small boats and ferries brought their human freight alongside. Loading stopped at about 1400 hours when the *Moltkefels* came under fire from Hexengrund on the Oxhöfter Kämpfe. Captain Voss had the anchor hauled up and moved the ship slowly up and down at a considerable distance from the shore. At 1430 hours boarding was complete. On board were about 2,700 refugees, 1,000 wounded and 300 soldiers as well as the crew. The Ellers were in a big hold astern and waiting anxiously with the many others to finally sail. However, the *Moltkefels* remained in the roads as she had to wait for an escort.

At about 1600 hours alarms sounded through the ship. Heinrich Ellers heard the flak crews running to their guns. 35 Soviet machines dived on the *Moltkefels* and the 1,069-ton steamer *Posen* lying nearby. The Soviet pilots managed to silence the *Moltkefels*' flak in their first two attacks. Ellers heard the metallic explosions of the machine-gun bullets close above his head on the deck planks. Chalk white, the refugees cowered in the half darkness of the hold, some children crying. Then several heavy explosions shook the ship.

Radio Officer Heinz Balzer was about to leave the bridge by the after ladder, when he saw how the hatch of Hold 3, in which the wounded were accommodated, was curving upwards. The bomb exploding inside overcame the bang with which the hatch fell back again. Balzer went forward, passing the dead flak crew on the bridge deck. Thick smoke was rising from the gangway to the engine room and flames were spurting from several places on the foredeck. He could hear cries coming from the hatches, but the fire drove him to the stern, where panic had broken out among the passengers.

Members of the crew tried with the help of the crane of a small steamer lying alongside to reach the foredeck hold in which 300 severely wounded were shut. But the flames formed a thick wall, silencing the cries of those inside, and the little steamer had to lay off in order not to catch fire itself. On the return journey it was able to fish the survivors of the *Posen* out of the water, sisters and doctors, that had got out of the hell on the burning freighter. It sank shortly thereafter with 300 men.

The bows of the *Moltkefels* slowly dipped forwards. Captain Voss had two tugs secured to the stern to pull the ship to the beach and prevent it sinking. First Officer Hermann Ottjes and the radio officer meanwhile tried to calm down the refugees in the after part of the ship. Some had lost their heads and jumped overboard. Hermann Ottjes had the exits blocked to bring the confusion under control.

A 13-year-old girl was standing on one of the companionways with her mother. Below decks she had seen how people had vanished screaming in a wall of fire, and in fleeing up the steep iron ladders she too had been touched by the flames. Her mother had been badly burnt on her back and head, her hair comb having gone up in flames. The girl, who had been ahead of her, had burns on her legs from this. A sailor cleared the way for them through the people recklessly pushing to the railings. The girl bravely climbed down the boarding net and let herself drop the last metres into the arms of a sailor when told to. Her mother was carried by two medical orderlies down a gangway to the waiting lighter.

A whole fleet of small boats had come alongside the stern. The people went down on ropes, rope ladders and netting, many being careless and tearing their hands on the sharp ropes. Others had to be helped down step by step. Heinrich Ellers saw to it that his family got away from the ship and then helped for hours bringing down wounded. In so doing a sharp-edged bit of iron fell on his head and wounded him considerably, but he only realised this much later.

Meanwhile the whole of the foredeck was in flames, and thick smoke was emerging from midships, where at about 1800 hours there were several strong explosions. The petrol tanks of several trucks parked below decks blew up. Shortly before Heinrich Ellers left the ship, he was witness to an unusual scene. A young naval lieutenant ran with a drawn pistol behind two crew members and drove them to another group of sailors that were standing idle on the deck. Ellers saw how one of them took a machine pistol from one of the flak positions and the weapon only vanished when Hermann Ottjes appeared. But the sailors that were fully exhausted from their rescue work had still to move 200 boxes of flak ammunition to the guard boats lying alongside at the lieutenant's insistence.

At about 1900 hours the last man left the ship. The *Moltkefels* continued burning well into the next day until she lay burnt-out on her side on the shallow sands. 400 people had died.

Heinrich Ellers had his head dressed by a medical orderly in a shipyard shed in the naval harbour of Hela. His only concern was that nobody would recognise him with this thick head bandage. He looked for his wife for a long time in the throng of civilians and soldiers and finally gave up. Then he met the wife of his friend Alfred Jantzen, whom he had met on the *Moltkefels* and himself had lowered from the wreck. Frau Jantzen was so pleased with the good news that she gave Heinrich Ellers generously from her supplies. He was only not to touch the big piece of ham that was there until they had met her husband again so that they could share it with him.

Next day Ellers left Hela on the training ship *Regulus*. On board were many of those saved from the *Moltkefels*. The ship was so overloaded that after two days a large number of the refugees had to be transferred to the *Walter Rau*, which was sailing on the same course. Heinrich Ellers also went. The first person he knew that he met on the big ship was Alfred Jantzen. The ham was quickly divided. The remainder of the journey they spent their time playing skat and destroying lice, as the *Walter Rau* was swarming with vermin, like almost all the other ships. The people went ashore at Eckernförde. Ellers found his family in Flensburg weeks later through the Red Cross tracing service.

One of the ships that had assisted in saving the survivors was the small steamer *Kurisches Haff*. During the past weeks Captain Sudemeyer had brought thousands from Bohnsack at the Vistula mouth to Hela, and then acted as a ferry from Hela harbour to the roads. Just a week after the *Moltkefels* catastrophe, he had taken 600 women and children from the fishing harbour to the *Goya*, which was anchored far out in the roads. This 5,200-ton ship was overloaded with refugees and wounded. The *Kurisches Haff* had just laid alongside when the nearby lying *Pretoria* was attacked by Soviet aircraft and badly damaged. One bomb fell into the sea just a few metres from the stern of the *Kurisches Haff*; the ship rose up with the force of the explosion and fell back into the resulting hole. The lines broke, the gangway fell from the upper deck on the railing, people that had been standing in the bows were knocked overboard and about 40 were badly injured from joists and objects flying around. The crew refastened the lines to the *Goya* and brought the uninjured and injured aboard the ship with its bizarre camouflage. It would be of no use to the refugees, for when the *Goya* hoisted anchor on the evening of the 16th April she was already sailing into disaster.

Chapter 18

The Fall of Königsberg

In the last days of March of this murderous spring the Soviets also broke the resistance of the German 4th Army in the Heiligenbeil cauldron. For ten whole weeks the German troops had bitterly resisted their overwhelming might in a struggle that had been hopeless from the very beginning. In the second half of February and the first half of March the Russians had merely reduced their pressure as a result of a change in command and regrouping of their forces. General Tschernaikovski, the commander of the 3rd Byelorussian Front, had been killed on the 16th February in front of Mehlsack and Marshal Vassilevski had taken over command.

During this pause thousands of refugees had managed to cross the frozen lagoon. Gradually this stream had come to an end. The last wagons drove over the breaking ice on the 4th March. Afterwards individual groups were brought to Rosenberg and smuggled across in the engineers' landing craft. The Braunsberger Gendarmerie Lieutenant Otto Loppnow kept this communications route open with his men. Only when the refugee movement had completely dried up, and the patrols found no one that still wanted to flee or could, did Loppnow pack his rucksack and obligatory briefcase.

On the 15th March the Soviets began their decisive attack. On the 17th April they took Brandenburg on the lagoon north of Heiligenbeil, cutting off the 4th Army from Königsberg. On the 20th March Braunsberg on the southern side of the cauldron that Loppnow had left with his men only the day before also fell. A Wehrmacht truck took them to Rosenberg, where the Gendarmerie major from Heiligenbeil with a number of gendarmes, members of the police and fire brigade were waiting for them near the mooring of a lagoon steamer. They were the last, if also uniformed, civilians to leave. That sounds simpler than it was, as at this point the Soviets were concentrating the whole of their firepower on the area Heiligenbeil-Rosenberg-Balga. Heiligenbeil, overfilled with wounded, was in flames. Those able to move, or even crawl, made their way to the landing stages where ferries and assault boats lay, despite the bombs, machine-gun and artillery fire. Larger vessels came at night, but boats longer than 50 metres were unable to manoeuvre in the small harbour.

As the policemen boarded the small steamer, Loppnow recognised it immediately: it was the *Möve*, which in peacetime had taken happy week-enders and holiday-makers between Elbing and the seaside resort of Kahlberg. On the 23rd January the ship had departed Elbing with about 800 refugees on board on the day that the Soviet tanks had shot their way through the completely surprised town. She had gone through to Danzig along an arm of the Vistula. From then she had provided a shuttle service between Fischerbaken and Danzig. On the 11th March she sailed to Pillau with troops. Then she was given the task of providing a shuttle service for wounded from Rosenberg. Aircraft and artillery made it difficult for her. The once smart white ship soon looked as if she was ready for the scrapheap. The railings were broken in several places, the quarterdeck was sunk in while the deck was bulging upwards over the engine room, one porthole was squeezed half out of its frame, the poles for the sun awnings bent or broken off, the stern light was missing, the big searchlight splintered, and overall were traces of shrapnel and machine-gun fire. Nevertheless the old steam kettle still went flat out and night after night conveyed wounded and refugees from Natangen and the banks of the sea canal to Pillau. By day Captain Arendt hid his ship under the trees along the banks of the sea canal and hung branches over the outward side. The crew were exhausted and Loppnow made a point of wishing them good day. Fascinated, he watched the fireworks on the coast around burning Heiligenbeil.

Heiligenbeil fell on the 26th March, Balga, the last strong point, on the 28th March. In the last two days German engineers under General Henke were able to convey the 4th Army's almost complete units to the Frische Spit. At the very last minute the rearguards at Balga were taken to safety. Many soldiers in panic had tried to cross the lagoon by their own means. They threw themselves into the water in inflatable dinghies and rowing boats, on beams and planks, canisters and anything that floated. Many were fished up by the lighters but still quite a few drowned.

An endless stream of refugees passed through the army camp on the opposite Spit, mainly people on foot from Danzig and the Danzig Flats, all hoping to get to a ship in Pillau. Once again the town of Pillau was completely full. During the second half of March all shipping had been redirected to Gotenhafen and Danzig, and many thousands had assembled in the little port once more. Lieutenant Loppnow was already afraid of being left stuck in this chaos, but the policemen were immediately put on a train standing by and taken to Königsberg into action. They were mainly elderly and very old men who that night were taken close to the Russian positions on the still open line to the besieged city.

On the same train were crowded many refugees returning disappointed to Königsberg. They had hoped to get away on a ship, but life in Königsberg between their own four walls seemed safer. In fact, the provincial capital was relatively quiet in March. The panic following the first encirclement had died down, factories were working, cinemas and shops were open and the newspaper appeared daily. To the policemen from Braunsberg and Heiligenbeil the hustle and bustle was almost peaceful, despite the air attacks and the artillery fire nearby. Divided up among the police stations, they immediately found themselves fully occupied, as many of the Königsberg policemen had left the city at the end of January and were now serving somewhere in the Samland.

Towards the end of March the Soviet artillery fire increased and air attacks on the city also resumed. The Soviets were preparing for the final assault. Once they had cleared the cauldron at Heiligenbeil they had over four armies at their disposal, including the battle-strong 11th Guards Army with altogether 60 rifle divisions and two armoured corps to bring Königsberg and the Samland into Russian hands within a few days.

In Soviet eyes, Königsberg represented everything Prussian, everything German. With almost 400,000 inhabitants at the beginning of the war, Kant's city with its famous university, its opera, and its theatres, was one of the largest centres of trade in east-west affairs, principally agricultural products, and long before the war had had its own airline to Moscow. Nevertheless, Königsberg was no 'Gateway to the East', as it had been founded as a fortress after the construction of the castle of the German Order in 1255. First seat of the Grand Master, then of the Duke of Prussia, it became the coronation city of the Prussian kings, and since 1843 it had been surrounded by a ring of forts. The Soviets had such a respect for these fortifications that they had exercised their storm troops on models of these forts already for weeks before launching their attack.

The beauty of the city lying between both lagoons and the Masurian Lakes had already suffered heavily the year before from Allied air attacks. Now the Soviet artillery and the Red Air Force were being sent in to reduce the city to rubble and ashes.

The defence of Königsberg under General of Infantry Otto Lasch consisted of four complete divisions and a colourful mixture of battle groups that included Volkssturm, Naval and Police units, Hitler Youth, Technical Emergency units and the fire brigade. They had hardly any ammunition and, apart from the ancient forts, there were no defensive installations. So once more the Volkssturm were set to digging. The Schwalbenberg Labour Battalion from Pillau was also there. The Volkssturm men were conveyed on a goods train and carts to Königsberg. The leg-amputee office stud Heinz

Kroll, who had already fled from Königsberg with his mother, bore his fate with composure. In view of his artificial limb held together with string, he had long since given up any idea of further flight. While his comrades were digging trenches and anti-tank ditches in Königsberg-Ponath, erecting barbed wire and anti-tank barriers, he maintained the lists of materials and personnel in his office. The latter were always complete, since the Braunsberger Police Lieutenant Loppnow's men were detailed to keep order behind the lines and saw to it that no one disappeared.

Heinz Kroll had occupied an abandoned private apartment in Spichersdorferstrasse that was still completely intact, even the bedding being fresh. Kroll had immediately felt himself well and at home. Now nothing was lacking in his good fortune other than his new artificial leg that he had ordered six months earlier from a workshop in the inner city, and it should be ready by now. So he set off under the cracking of artillery shells over the rubble and past the fires.

He went past the orthopaedic business twice, as the firm's sign had gone and there was only packing paper in the shop window. The workshop was empty. They had moved to some school or other, said a woman in the building. So day after day Kroll clattered along from school to school during his free time, hobbling on his old prostheses, the pain showing in his face. After four days he eventually found himself in a gymnasium in which stocks of leather, stamping machines and sacks of sawdust were stored. A thick layer of brick dust and dirt covered everything, as half the roof had been ripped off by an artillery hit. There was not a person to be seen. Kroll began to burrow and found what he was looking for. On a shelf lay about a dozen leg prostheses set out neatly next to each other and on one of them was a brown label with 'Heinz Kroll, Wehlau'. With his new leg tucked under his arm he happily made the long journey back to his quarters.

It seemed as if the Volkssturm did not really need him and his new leg, although the latter fitted well and gave no pressure. From about the 4th April onwards he lived in the cellar, as did all others not required outside.

The Russians shelled the inner city ceaselessly while the bombs from low-flying aircraft exploded among the rows of buildings.

Until that day the individual groups had been able to leave the city by train or on foot, or were taken by ship through the Sea Canal at night. Some transports were organised by the local Party office. On the 4th April the war widow Hildegard Grunewald with her two 5- and 6-year-old children was taken from her apartment by a Party man to join a refugee transport. To her question whether her friend living in the neighbourhood would also be on the transport, the Party member said: 'Only the most worthy families from each area are coming.' Together with her neighbour, who had six children with her, and some other families, they were taken by a horse and cart to the harbour, where the 473-ton *Ursula Heinemeier* was waiting and took them at nightfall under the thunder of the guns to Hela.

On the 7th April the news spread that the city was now completely surrounded. On the 8th April the Schwalbenberg Labour Battalion was issued with machine guns, carbines and Panzerfausts. Kroll also received a weapon. Punctually at 2100 hours a breakthrough via Ratshof towards Fischerhausen was to be effected to clear a road for the removal of the civilian population. This attack had been proposed to Gauleiter Koch by the Deputy Gauleiter Grossherr, as he could see that there was no longer any future in Königsberg. General Lasch had agreed to this proposal, as did General Müller, the former commander of the 4th Army and present commander of the armed forces in the Samland and Königsberg, who also wanted to get whole units to the west. General Müller allowed only the evacuation of the civilian population, for which the Volkssturm would provide flank protection, but Fortress Königsberg was to be defended to the last round.

The Soviets were now firing with every gun they had. They had been bringing in batteries for weeks and there was not a spot in the city that had escaped their attention. Soviet tanks and infantry knocked out position after position and took one fort after another.

While the troops and the Volkssturm were already ready by 2100 hours, the Party had summoned the population to the post office on Trommelplatz for 0030 hours. The confusion of orders and rumours resulted in many women and children already assembling on Trommelplatz at about 2100 hours and forming a procession with Volkssturm men forming up on either side. The civilians waited patiently for hours as the procession grew ever larger.

Towards midnight the German tanks, followed by Volksgrenadiers, set off westwards to Ratshof. They did not get far. The Soviets had recognised the move in time and opened fire. The first German tanks were stopped after a few hundred metres and fired off the last of their ammunition. The Volksgrenadiers bitterly fought their way forward. For the thousands still waiting to set off on the march from Trommelplatz, who could not distinguish between Russian and German fire, the sounds of the fighting were a hopeful signal. But then it broke over them. Salvoes from Stalin-Organs that had been deployed near Charlottenburg and on Littmannstrasse slammed into the crowd. Men, women and children ran about screaming, looking for cover. In no time the trenches on the Deutsch-Ordensring were overfilled. The Trommelplatz itself offered little cover. The people lay packed close together on the paving. Screams, calls for medical orderlies and the bursting of shells filled the air. The Steindamm nearby was in flames and illuminated the frightful scene.

The German attack had come to a standstill. General Sudau, commander of the 548th Division, fell. General Sperl, commander of the 61st Division, was badly wounded; Deputy Gauleiter Grossherr was killed. The fleeing German troops joined in the panic of the civilian population. Then it was possible to form a weak barrier and to prevent the Russians from pressing forward, but only for a few hours. There was no longer a front line by the morning of the 9th April, and the Soviets were in the city centre. That whole day individual German nests provided a bitter resistance. At about 1730 hours General Lasch offered to surrender to the Soviets.

In the surrender document the Soviets promised the conquered their lives, adequate rations and honourable treatment in captivity. They assured care for the wounded and the civilian population, and promised to release the prisoners home at the end of the war or to a land of their choice.

Involved were 30,000 to 35,000 soldiers, 15,000 foreign workers and more than 100,000 inhabitants and refugees from the province that yielded to the Soviets for better or for worse. With the exception of western prisoners of war and forced labourers, this was an unmitigated disaster for them. Officially the Soviet commander gave the Russian troops two days free to plunder – two days that became months in which arbitrary rape, robbery and murder were the order of the day. The defenceless population was exposed to everything. Many civilians went into captivity along with the soldiers. General Lasch was condemned to death by strangulation by Hitler in his absence and his family taken into custody.

Chapter 19

The Soviets occupy the Samland

With the fall of Königsberg, General Friedrich Wilhelm Müller as commander in chief of Army/Group *Nord* had fallen into disgrace and was recalled. In his place was appointed General of Tank Troops Dietrich von Saucken as commander of the *Armee Ostpreussen*, combining the remaining combat groups in the Samland, at the mouth of the Vistula and on Hela.

Dietrich von Saucken had been born in Fischhausen as the son of the then District President and went to school in Königsberg. He had started off from East Prussia as a cavalryman in the war against Poland. During the course of the Second World War he had become head of one of the best tank formations in the army. When the Vistula front collapsed at the beginning of February 1945, he had successfully fought his way back to the Oder with his armoured corps just ahead of the advancing Soviet troops and held out there in a defensive position against overwhelming superiority. He wore the Knights' Cross with swords and oak leaves. The commander of the new *Ostpreussen* Army Group had shortly before expressed his opinion of Hitler and the Party clearly.

On the 12th March Dietrich von Saucken was informed at a conference at the Reichs Chancellery that he was to take over the newly formed Army Group *Ostpreussen* on the 19th March. His visit created an impression of the determination and lack of concern of his kind of people that differed so much from the smarmy pomposity that Hitler, his surroundings and most Party people presented.

When von Saucken entered, Hitler was sitting at a map table flanked by Colonel-General Guderian, Bormann and an adjutant. With one hand resting on his cavalry sabre, his monocle fixed in his eye, he saluted with a slight bow instead of the Hitler salute obligatory since the 20th July 1944. This was virtually an act of rebellion as he had not left his weapon behind in the anteroom as was customary. Guderian, Bormann and the adjutant stared at von Saucken and waited for Hitler's explosion of rage. But nothing happened. Hitler ignored the general and curtly requested Guderian to start the briefing.

Von Saucken's behaviour was not without effect. After the briefing Hitler began a long speech that led to the division of the command responsibility.

The responsibility for the Danzig battle area was Gauleiter Förster's, with General von Saucken subservient to him except in completely military matters. Von Saucken very quietly but decisively placed his hand flatly on the map table and said: 'I do not think, Herr Hitler, I can place myself under the command of a Gauleiter!'

Hitler remained silent, sunk within himself, in front of his maps. Guderian and Bormann hastily spoke to von Saucken telling him to be reasonable – they knew that the general was playing with his life. But von Saucken only reiterated: 'I think not!' After long seconds Hitler broke the silence with a weak voice: 'All right, you command alone, Saucken.'

Von Saucken's love of his homeland, his geographical knowledge and his experience as a commander of troops, however, helped him little. His task was insoluble. He could not hold the last remains of East Prussia. His beaten divisions could only try to cover the removal of the last civilians as long as possible and accomplish their own retreat with minimum casualties.

In Samland, the next Soviet goal, there were only a few divisions opposing a crushing superiority. At the last minute these units could be reinforced with forces from the defeated 4th Army, including the *Grossdeutschland* Division and other troops from Pillau. But this small contingent possessed barely sufficient equipment and ammunition, the soldiers were exhausted and demoralised, and only moved mechanically into their new positions.

The post office driver Krause from Domnau had left Pillau in a northerly direction with his Volkssturm unit. He did this less unwillingly than most of the others. He still had only one aim: to return to his farm and family. At Fischhausen he had made about a half circle since leaving some two months before. From now on he had the feeling of really being on his way home.

Krause's battalion was a sad sight. Ahead of it drove an old army lieutenant in a car with a wood gas boiler which rose like a bathroom stove next to the front seat passenger and emitted a bitter white smoke. Behind followed a long train of trek wagons collected in Pillau on which the old men crouched indifferently. Only a few of them had unslung their carbines.

The deeper they went into the Samland, the fewer people they encountered. Scattered Wehrmacht units and individual refugee groups were heading for the coast. There were few civilians among the soldiers in the villages. Krause wondered that some were actually working in the fields, and thought of the work that awaited him at home. Everywhere they encountered military police controls looking for deserters. On the roadside they saw fresh graves and the wreckage from the first big refugee columns in January. Already for several days the weather had been rainy, so they were at least spared from low-flying aircraft.

The troops occupied quarters at the Neukuhren air base, the northernmost point of the Kursichen lagoon front. Action companies were established and equipped with a scanty assortment of old machine guns, captured weapons and Panzerfausts, and inserted in sections of the front line. Robert Krause was allocated a wagon and had to take rations, ammunition and building materials to the main front line only a few kilometres away, where engineers were still building bunkers and removing electric cables connected to the long-dead transformers.

Robert Krause combed around, mainly looking for animal fodder that he had to steal from the Wehrmacht. Sometimes he went with comrades into the nearby woods to cut dry grass for the animals. The Russian artillery shot harassing fire on Rauschen and the little fishing harbour of Neukuhren, in which there were still many people waiting for a minesweeper or a patrol boat to take them to Pillau.

Krause went several times to Rauschen, where a whole row of Party leaders had made their nest, engaged in busy organizational activity, in as much as they could do no better but seek shelter from the artillery fire. They could not slip away because they knew that Erich Koch was in Neutief and still wanted to know exactly who was doing what and demanding constant reports. So the civilian population was richly provided with horseflesh and barley from the NSV field kitchen. At the beginning of April there were even food ration cards once.

The remaining inhabitants and the refugees tried to lead a normal life. But, in view of the many soldiers, the machine-gun and gun positions in their gardens and the continuous thunder of the guns, this was difficult. The senior business teacher Käthe Pawel took refugees from Grosskuhren into her house and cooked for them. They were all waiting for the orders to evacuate. The business people had become generous. There were packets of Gustin in the shop and a whole leg of veal without ration coupons. The soldiers on the contrary were not so generous, although everywhere in the gardens there were slaughtered pigs and cattle hung head down from the trees by the cooks.

Once Käthe Pawel really had the feeling that something could go wrong. While drawing water from the nearby well, she saw sitting on the round benches under the lime trees several Russian forced labourers that appeared to be watching the hustle and bustle among the Germans with amused, malicious grins. A few days later, at the beginning of April, the Party ordered the civilians to find transport to the station with hand baggage.

Käthe Pawel had long since sewn together rucksacks for herself and a friend out of floor cloths, which together with small suitcases formed their baggage. As provisions they had packed 2 pounds of sugar, two jars of jam,

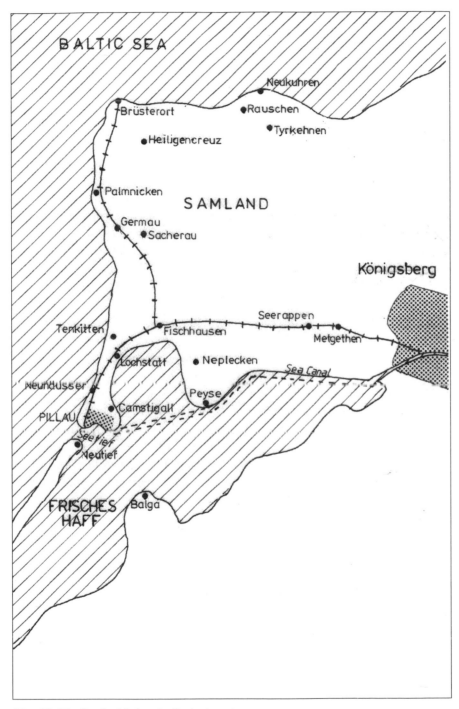

Map 10. The Samland before the Soviet invasion

200 grams of bread and two packets of Gustin. When they left Düne station in the morning they did not go as expected towards Pillau but only on the short stretch to Neukuhren.

They found accommodation for the night in a corridor of the Central Hotel and only the following evening were they able to get aboard a boat. Children were crying, and adults complaining about others flashing torches around 'attracting the Russian artillery to us'. Käthe Pawel opened a tin of sardines with her left hand that a soldier had pressed into her hand. The boat was an open cutter. In the hold sat and lay almost only women and children. Käthe Pawel and her friend sat on their suitcases on deck with other people and froze. A light rain slowly soaked them through. It took a full hour until the boat cast off. The water was almost up to their ankles. Below in the hold someone sang the song *Wer nur den lieben Gott lässt walten...* and all sang along with it as the boat slowly left their homeland.

In the early hours of the morning they found themselves off Brüsterort as a minesweeper crossed their path. The boat was on the way back from Libau and heading for Swinemünde, keeping close to the coast. Because of the rainy haze lying over the sea, visibility that morning was poor. The watch keepers paid no attention to the cutter following them. They were concerned with looking above to the pale blue sky between the dispersing clouds that announced better weather and the danger from aircraft with it.

'Masthead on the port bow,' said the helmsman in the boring tone of a tour guide, whose group can look out and see for themselves or not, as if he said: 'and to the left you can see the War Memorial.' The watch keeper looked through his binoculars. A ship's length ahead the masthead of a small vessel rose above the mist, apparently a fishing boat. Then he dropped his binoculars and looked at the helmsman as if he had seen a ghost. 'That can't be!' he muttered. Under the mast stood a cart with a horse harnessed to it. A Fata Morgana? Or were they so close to land and coming to a pier? Gradually the apparition became clearer. This horse and cart were standing on the deck of an unmoving fishing boat, bobbing in the light swell. Several muffled figures were standing on board and waving at them to approach. The minesweeper swung smoothly alongside.

'Hey, captain, can you give us a tow? We are stuck here!' called an old woman more commandingly than questioningly and swung a rope's end that would have sufficed at the most for a rowing boat. The young women and the children willingly let themselves be hoisted aboard the minesweeper, but the old woman would not move without her horse and cart. She had finally managed to get the cart into the fishing boat and now couldn't the captain do the same with his boat? With difficulty the sailors managed to bring the crying woman on board before they continued their journey. The boat passed Palmnicken and Neuhäuser and set course for the west.

The crew had the impression that they had rescued the last of the refugees from the peninsula, but on the 30 to 40 kilometre long strip of western Samland that was still in German hands there were several thousand that were in flight at the moment, and apparently as many that did not want to go any further or could not.

For the Fischhausener District Administrator von der Groeben, who in February had been practically the lord of this territory, it was not so much a matter of enabling as many people as possible to flee. The actual inhabitants of the district had for the most part already fled, but in their place were refugees from the eastern districts and Königsberg that were camping in the abandoned houses, barns, schools and in long columns along the blocked roads, and it was possible to provide some form of order for them.

No help came from the Party functionaries actually responsible. The alcohol flowed in streams in the Party offices. Gau Inspector Matthes, a cousin of Erich Koch, concentrated his whole attention on the construction of an air raid shelter in the garden of the District House in Fischhausen. From this secure position the 'leaders' would engage in the final battle. Among them the East Prussian women and their children sought shelter from the constant Russian air attacks in the overcrowded trenches and cellars.

The District Administrator did not concern himself with this danger. He rarely entered his office. He was mainly on the way organising food for the horses, carts for the field work or a doctor for the abandoned hospital. To counter the danger of an epidemic, he set up a corpse utilisation plant in Fischhausen that produced very useful soap and useless glue. The skins he sent to Pillau. Dressmakers and workshops were got going. Even the money business was resumed during these weeks. The industrious District Administrator had tracked down the remains of his County Savings Bank and brought it to Fischhausen, and reopened the branches in Rauschen and Palmnicken. Accounts were paid out and even credit given.

Von der Groeben made a tour of the Samland with the County Farm Leader from St Lorenz. In every place they sought suitable people who could function as mayors or farm leaders. Some especially trustworthy people were appointed commissars of large districts. The most pressing task von der Groeben saw was of herding together the available cattle and so securing supplies of food and fodder, the milking and conveyance of milk and getting the dairies to function again. A makeshift rationing system was introduced and the registering of refugees was begun. Everything was to be in order.

The District Administrator was himself surprised how quickly the refugees familiarised themselves. Those overseers appointed to the abandoned farmsteads got the interrupted threshing going again and prepared the spring crops. The former Chief Inspector Sathodoski of the Perkoppen Farm in Sellwehten, County Labiau, on the 17th March took over the Sacherau Farm that had lost its owner and worked it with the people of his trek and his family until the 13th April before continuing his flight. For four weeks he had supplied milk and butter for the Wehrmacht and civilians over a wide area.

Not all the lords of the manor had left their properties. Max Schneege, who after his adventures with the Volkssturm between Wehlau and Königsberg, had returned on the tracks of the Samland Railway to his Tyrkehnen farm near Rauschen, had long since resumed work with his people. On the 4th April he had brought seeds and grain in several carts from Königsberg and started with the spring sowing. Only a few days later constant low-flying aircraft attacks made all activity in the fields impossible.

Max Schneege did not want to risk flight with his family and his people. The dreadful scenes of the first refugee columns in January were still in his mind. The conduct of the German armed forces strengthened him in his decision not to leave his property. While the officers in the last days indulged in drinking bouts, the soldiers plundered abandoned houses. The mayor of Tyrkehnen had driven to Neukuhren with his family to get away by ship. Two days they waited in vain and then returned disappointed. Meanwhile their apartment, cupboards and containers had been emptied and everything that was not nailed down had been stolen. Part of their property was found among the German soldiers stationed in Tyrkehnen, who would take what these people had left behind before the Russians came. The morale of the troops was often so bad that the Frenchmen working for Max Schneege were appalled. At the beginning of April officers of Artillery Regiment 1/551 cleared a building of civilians and had soldiers set it up for a dance. They then celebrated all night long, some doubtful ladies being brought in on Wehrmacht vehicles.

This behaviour found even less understanding as the liquidation of concentration camp inmates in Samland was spoken about. The prisoners had belonged to a transport of several thousand Jews coming from the Baltic and were being driven on foot towards Elbing. As the route was blocked by the fighting, the guards led this vast column into the Samland, where they joined the general streams of refugees. In this way many of the prisoners lost their lives from hunger, weakness and mishandling, or were shot and left lying unburied on the roadside. According to an account by von der Gröben, the remainder were shot by some foreign auxiliaries of the Wehrmacht or driven into the sea.

Max Schneege had obtained an impression from eyewitnesses that the prisoners had come to Palmnicken, where manor farm director Feierabend had received the victims and accommodated some of them in a workshop and supplied them with food and straw to lie on. This act of humanity was taken amiss by the Nazis. He was immediately put into the Volkssturm and sent to the front in the area of Kummehnen.

Paul Koch, the police lieutenant from Königsberg Süd-Nord police station, had come to Palmnicken from Königsberg and took charge of the police stations along the west coast of the Samland. He was informed by the population that an SS commando had driven about 5,000 Jews into a shaft of the Bernstein Works and had then filled in the shaft from above. A great number had tried to escape across the beach and into the water but had been shot or drowned. Koch was not convinced that the shaft at the Bernstein Works had really been filled in. In the subsequent period the police buried over 200 corpses on the beach, most of which were reburied in the refugee cemetery at Sorgenau. Like Schneege, many civilians feared that the Soviets would wreak revenge on the population.

The Soviets lost no time now in breaking through the last German front, which extended from the Baltic coast by Neukuhren in the north right across Samland to the Frische Lagoon near Gross Holstein at the Sea Canal. After the fall of Königsberg, it took Marshal Vassilevski four days to regroup his troops and mass them for an attack.

On the 11th April the Soviet army leader had leaflets dropped over the German positions in the Samland:

> Half of Germany is in the hands of the Russian and Allied troops. Once the strongest fortress in Germany, Königsberg, fell in three days. The commander of the fortress, General of Infantry Otto Lasch, accepted the conditions of surrender I offered him and surrendered with the majority of his garrison. Altogether there were 92,000 German soldiers, 1,819 officers and four generals captured. German soldiers and officers that remain in the Samland! Now, after the fall of Königsberg, your situation is completely hopeless. Nobody will give you any help, 450 kilometres separate you from the front lines that run near Stettin. The sea routes to the west have been cut by Soviet submarines. You are in the deep hinterland of the Russian troops. Your situation is hopeless.

The pamphlet did not achieve its objective. The German soldiers in Samland had long since fought not for victory but for their lives and for the many wounded and refugees still waiting for the transport to carry them away from Samland, at Pillau, at the mouth of the Vistula and on Hela.

After two Russian air fleets had bombed the hinterland and massed Russian artillery with overwhelming firepower had crumbled the German positions, on the 13th April the enemy armoured and infantry divisions rolled over the German defence lines. Much to the surprise of the Soviets, strong nests of resistance formed and brought the attack to a standstill, but by the following day the German front had collapsed.

On the 14th April District Administrator von der Gröben drove in his duty vehicle from Fischhausen to Rauschen. He had to make his way through fleeing German units. Again and again aircraft fire forced him to take cover. At noon he reached the little town, which lay in beautiful sunshine in an unnatural holiday peace. The Party official responsible for refugees had left with the Wehrmacht in civilian clothes. Mayor Norgal, like the majority of people remaining in Rauschen, was determined to await the worst on the spot. From von der Gröben's point of view apathy reigned, when one thought that many had already fled two or three times, or had even been rolled over once by the Russians.

And again it was the younger people that did not want to leave the old and the sick in the lurch.

While, with the help of von der Gröben, a train with the hospital patients was setting off towards Warnicken, this being the last train to leave Rauschen at about midday, many people were sitting in the sunshine in front of their doors waiting for whatever was going to happen. The District Administrator left the town at 1315 hours. There was nothing more for him to do there.

Robert Krause, the post office driver from Domnau, was also in Rauschen that day and waiting. The Russians arrived in the town at about 1400 hours. The first combat teams behaved decently. The rapes occurred that evening, but mainly the Russians were only searching the buildings for German soldiers, for whom they had the greatest respect. Next day Krause saw children already playing in the streets. One of them drew his attention and nervously led him into the garden of a villa to a summerhouse. There Krause found a man covered in blood kneeling on a pile of straw. A dead woman lay in one corner. He had cut her throat and then tried to do it to himself. Apparently the cut was not deep enough for a quick death and he had only been bleeding slowly. He had asked the children to bring him some water, but they had run away frightened. Krause brought some water. The man whispered that he was a Party member and that he and his wife had not wanted to fall into the hands of the Russians. Krause left him to his fate. Two days later he set off for home. On the way a Russian major who spoke German took him along in his vehicle. Krause told him about the barrel of rum that he had hidden. But when they came into Domnau other Russians had already dug the rum out of the dung heap and also found the butter in the garden. Krause's wife and son had vanished. He would never see them again or discover what had happened to them.

The determined resistance of individual units was only able to delay the Soviet breakthrough into the Samland in places. They immediately went straight through Rauschen and approached Tyrkehnen in the early afternoon of the 14th April. Max Schneege had determined that the order 'Save yourself if you can!' would be given, but the order did not arrive. Instead a small troop of Russian soldiers appeared in front of the manor with a German-speaking officer. At first nothing happened to Schneege and his people. He could remain as the manager. A large number of German prisoners of war were allotted to him as a labour force. All praised him as he successfully made their fate bearable under the Russians.

On the 15th April the Russians were already nearing the west coast of the Samland. The area of Palmnicken lay under heavy fire. Flight was only possible along the beach path out of view of the Russians under the cliffs. Chief Inspector Sathodski and part of his trek left the Sacherau Manor in good time and reached Pillau on the 17th April. A number of his people had remained behind in Nöttnicken, as the local Party leader had said: 'Nöttnicken is the safest place in the whole of the Samland and will not be evacuated for a long time.' They believed this only too readily and thus fell into the hands of the Soviets.

On the afternoon of the 15th April the policeman from Heiligencreutz reported to his lieutenant in Palmnicken: 'The Russians have broken through to the coast!' Lieutnant Koch dutifully reported this to his superior in Pillau, an Austrian lieutenant colonel, in the hope that he would get the order to pull out. But the Austrian did not feel competent, although his superior, an East Prussian police colonel, had left for the Reich from Brüsterort airport the day before. After a few anxious moments the Austrian gave the last Königsberger police commando his agreement to leave. Lieutenant Koch and his men went on foot.

Von der Gröben also left burning Fischhausen on the morning of the 16th April under the fire of the Russian artillery. With some of his officials, he made his way on foot to Pillau, as with a jeep he would not have got far in the turmoil of Wehrmacht vehicles and fleeing soldiers. A few hours later the Russians took the town and struck out towards Neuhäuser. Near Tenkitten the 21st Infantry and the *Grossdeutschland* Infantry Divisions had formed a strong defensive belt between the narrow isthmus and Fischhausen water meadows.

Chapter 20

The End of Pillau

In beautiful late afternoon sunshine on the 10th April, escorted by several guard vessels, the 2,369-ton *Herkules*, the 1,923-ton *Santander*, the 2,575-ton *Adele Traber* and the 1,127-ton *Nautik* came from Hela through the Seetief. They had to travel slowly to avoid endangering with their bow waves the countless landing craft and barges carrying their human freight. (The ferry traffic from Pillau to Neutief was running constantly and often low-flying Russian aircraft tried to shoot them up.) Captain Klein on the *Herkules* at the rear searched the skies with his binoculars. It would be a wonder if the Russian aircraft did not appear soon.

The ships had reached the Pillau roads when the convoy was flown over at a great height by twelve Soviet bombers. Automatically the flak gunners on the ships aimed their gun barrels at the machines flying over. They knew that the Soviets would turn around and attack out of the sun. It was only a few minutes before the Soviets were back again, lower this time and almost invisible in the glaring sun. The ships turned hard to port at full power as the flak opened fire with all barrels. The bombs fell near the ships. Escorting fighters raked the *Herkules* with their weapons. Hardly was that over when the ship came under artillery fire from the opposite side of the lagoon and to add to this the bosun reported a leak in Number 4 Hold.

Instead of running into the harbour, the *Herkules* turned about and moved a bit seawards. As a result of the breach the ship had a depth astern of about eight metres, too much for the shallow Pillau harbour. At nightfall a recovery vessel pumped out the water and towed the steamer into the harbour, where that same night the stern was provisionally strengthened.

The situation in Pillau had become more critical during the past weeks. With the last big surge of refugees from Königsberg and the Samland, more soldiers, staffs, supply columns and wounded had come into the town. From the lagoon the newly regrouped remains of the 4th Army had come over to reinforce the Samland, fresh troops had come from Hela to protect Pillau and from the Samland came the pitiful remains of defeated units, stragglers or simply deserters.

As few ships had come into Pillau harbour during the second half of March, the pier was packed with people waiting there to be taken on by one of the few ammunition ships or wounded transports. Lieutenant Commander Schön, who was responsible for maintaining order in the harbour with his company of marines, could only concentrate on the security of the harbour installations. The rest was chaotic. Schön saw how babies were thrown from the decks of the loaded ships back into the crowds ashore to enable relations – sisters, aunts, mothers-in-law – to get aboard. Some soldiers who had tried to smuggle themselves aboard in female clothing were arrested and promptly shot. At first deserters had only been hanged from lampposts as a deterrent, but that had borne little fruit. In order to get through the harbour security, soldiers snatched children from their mothers and told the sentries that they wanted to take their families aboard. And people were being pushed into the water, especially when artillery fire caused panic to break out. Only very few could be fished out again. At such moments soldiers were able to swing their way aboard over the railings and hide themselves until they were out at sea. The crews and captains closed their eyes to these things.

The military police ashore had finally lost control. Some of them had vanished on the ships. Once, when a freighter tied up in Stralsund, three sergeants had reported to the captain and announced themselves as military policemen. They said that they had searched the ship thoroughly during the voyage and found no deserters, so everything was in order. The captain knew that there were at least 20 soldiers hiding in the bows and that the whole thing was a ruse. He had to hold himself back from having the three of them beaten off the ship. So he asked the 'gentlemen' to forget the matter.

Once Danzig and Gotenhafen had fallen and the last troops had been evacuated from the Oxhöfter Kämpe, there were more ships available again for Pillau. But now at the beginning of April it was also precarious in the little harbour town on the Seetief. The Russian batteries that had been brought forward to Balga on the banks of the lagoon had fired on Pillau. Their artillery observers were directing their fire from a captive balloon that glistened undisturbed over the old Ordensburg. At the same time the red air fleets released from the Samland and Königsberg attacked the town and the shipping.

The ships that had arrived with the *Herkules* began loading during the night. The badly wounded were carried over from the tall bunker at the Seedienst Station and the other field hospitals. A batch of refugees was let aboard from time to time, but by daybreak the ships were only half full. The Russian artillery resumed firing and the captains had no choice but to lie and wait until nightfall.

The aiming of the Soviet guns was not very accurate at this distance. Although they fired all day long, they only succeeded in setting on fire a barge with several hundred tons of rough fodder. The smoke cloud rising from the fire together with the strong flak defences made it impossible for the Soviet bombers to hit the ships during their five attacks that day. Loading continued sporadically throughout the day. When the four ships slipped out of the harbour at nightfall, they had 2,350 wounded, 6,500 refugees and 400 soldiers on board.

But thousands were still waiting for a ship in Pillau, and again the captains and crews of cargo vessels risked everything to help these people. On the 12th April the 1,923-ton *Weserstein* was sunk in Pillau harbour in an air attack close to the spot where the 3,717-ton *Meteor* had been hit several times by artillery fire and forced aground. 60 of the wounded died on the *Weserstein*. The 5,869-ton steamer *Wiegand* took a direct hit from a bomb on the forecastle. It was a dud, but because of its position it could not be disarmed. So the captain set sail with 2,800 refugees and the bomb, arriving safely in Rendsburg.

On Friday the 13th April the *Mars* was the last big ship to arrive at Pillau. She had to endure five air attacks before she could take aboard the 2,000 wounded and refugees from the pier. During the night she slipped out of the harbour without an escort and headed on the northerly route directly to Copenhagen.

Next day the little hospital ship *Adler* dared the witches' cauldron at Pillau. Despite heavy artillery fire and air attacks she got away unscathed with several hundred wounded and a small number of refugees. After that only the ferries and engineers' landing craft remained to take the last civilians, wounded and troops across the lagoon or direct to Hela. In the final phase all available naval ferries joined in so that on one night 19,200 troops were evacuated from Pillau.

But the apparently safe way across the lagoon did not lessen the risk. Many who reached Hela this way were taken aboard the *Goya* on the 15th and 16th April. At about 1900 hours on the 16th April the 5,230-ton wounded transport *Goya*, badly damaged from previous bomb attacks, left the Hela roads. With over 6,000 refugees and soldiers on board, she travelled in company with the smaller transports *Kronenfels* and *Aegir*, escorted by the minelayers *M256* and *M328*.

At nightfall the ships formed line abreast and travelled 400 metres apart. The *Goya* took the position furthest out to sea. On the ship the tension, the fear of air attacks, eased off among the refugees. But the groans of the wounded and the fear of mines and submarines were omnipresent. The people crouched down in their places.

The crying of babies and the whimpering of the small children cut through the darkness. In the animal-like confinement life continued in dull blows, quicker and thicker than before: the half-suppressed groaning of a sick person or someone giving birth, the wheezing of a couple – bodies that accident had pressed together and would shortly be free of each other again. At the same time someone quenched their thirst, a purse vanished from a handbag, a loaf from a rucksack. And somewhere a mother or a husband said in a quiet voice something calming, consoling.

The air below deck was unbreathable, but no one dared go above, where soldiers guarded the companionways. Military apparatus and kit was packed below the shot-up upperworks, between which sat several hundred soldiers and civilians trying to keep each other warm. The men on the bridge also froze in the icy night air blowing though the broken windows. The illuminated compass glimmered weakly but everything else lay in complete darkness on the grey-blue background of the sea at night. At 2203 hours the lookout reported a shadow to starboard and at the same time the *M328* fired an illuminating shell and tracer bullets raced over the glistening water. The shadow vanished. Apparently it was a submerged submarine.

Towards 2230 hours the *Kronenfels* slowed down and stopped with engine problems. The other ships turned to and waited while the crew of the *Kronenfels* tried to repair the damage with the tools they had on board. The two security boats circled the ship ceaselessly to prevent a possible submarine attack. After an hour the damage was repaired and the convoy resumed its course at a speed of 11 knots.

Captain Rabeck, the shipping officer on a divisional staff, walked to and fro on the deck of the *Goya*. His division had been wiped out in the Danzig area. The staff were supposed to go ashore at Swinemünde and be reformed. Captain Rabeck was still hoping for a countermanding order that would allow him to remain on board until Copenhagen, as he would apparently fall straight into the arms of the Russians at Swinemünde. Morosely he strode between the packages and tested the lashings to see if anyone had done anything to the valuable contents. Since the front had collapsed in January, stealing had become a mania, everyone taking what came into their hands. Even a holder of the Knights' Cross had been caught and shot for stealing from a comrade.

Leaning against a box he saw a young married couple that he had fallen out with during the loading. He became angry as he recalled the scene. It was shortly before the *Goya* cast off. In the lighter alongside his hold stood a group of five persons. The young couple were with their young son and two old persons, apparently the husband's parents. On this spot there was only room for two persons. The old ones were standing next on the gangway and about to climb up. But the young man held them back. Loudly and clearly he told them that they were no longer of any use and that they, the young ones, had more right to continue living. The young woman holding the child by the hand also spoke to the two older ones. They only stood there saying nothing until finally the young man forced them back into the lighter and climbed aboard with his wife and child. The old couple had to go back to Hela. If there had been more time they perhaps would have found a place for the old couple, but the *Goya* hoisted anchor and steamed off.

Slowly Captain Rabeck went over to the lee side in order to light himself a cigarette out of the wind. Still 15 minutes to midnight, then another officer would relieve him. Captain Rabeck never finished his cigarette as two mighty explosions shattered the ship, which immediately began to roll over. Baggage and people slid across the deck as it began to sink by the stern. From somewhere out of the darkness came the cry: 'Save yourselves if you can!'

People ran screaming and jumping overboard. The tumult of panic rose from the ship's interior. People forced themselves up on the gangways, many vanishing with a desperate cry as the people following them pulled them back. Shots were fired. It was the same frightful picture as had already occurred on the *Wilhelm Gustloff* and the *General von Steuben*. Captain Rabeck, who was wearing a lifejacket, wanted to jump overboard, but calmed himself. Others would jump on him and force him under water. He hurried to the bridge over the ever-steeper sinking deck to reach the highest point. Half-way he was caught by a wave racing forward over the already submerged poop. He was torn up high and caught in the vortex of the sinking ship and then shot up again to the surface by an air bubble, being thrown against an empty float. The captain pulled himself up. At the same moment a house-high streak of flame rose from the water and a series of explosions could be heard – apparently as the boilers exploded.

The surface was strewn with ship's debris and corpses. In between were despairing swimmers and people grabbing at each other. Women's voices cried out for help, men shouted curses, gave orders, called for comrades, a shot was fired. The captain pulled out his pistol and dropped it in the water so as not to be tempted. Other swimmers had discovered his float and hung onto it, making it tilt. Then a silent bitter fight developed for the hand ropes. With kicks, fists and battens the strong ones enforced their rights. Murder, deathblows, self defence: anything was fine if ten centimetres of rope meant survival. Those hit went under or saved themselves on a piece of wreckage. The water was ice cold. Many were thinly clad, as it had been warm below in the ship.

With every passing minute the number of swimmers grew less. Soon those hanging on to the float stopped fighting for their place. The icy fingers grasping the rope indicated how the cold was weakening their bodies. They could hardly hold themselves up, snorting ever more often, as they realised that they were sinking centimetre by centimetre. At the last minute the *M328* fished them out of the water. Half unconscious, they were hauled on deck. In their ears they could hear the cries of swimmers who thought that the crew had not noticed them and would move on. The *M328* rescued 100 people from the water. Among them were four refugees, two men and two women; all the others were soldiers. About 6,000 went down with the *Goya* or drowned before they could be hauled out of the water.

The *Kronenfels* and the *Aegir* steamed on to get away from the dangerous area of the submarines, the *Goya* having been hit by two torpedoes amidships and at the stern. They later took over those saved by the naval vessels.

The news of the sinking of the *Goya* did not reach Pillau. There were only a few small vessels in the rear harbour at this time. Among them was the little steamer *Erna* of 757 tons built in 1904. The *Erna* had set off on Easter Sunday with a load of briquettes for the field kitchens. Because of the artillery fire nobody wanted to unload her as there was no more use for her cargo. For over two weeks she was given up to the Soviet air and artillery attacks. The bridge and the ship's side were sieved through from machine guns and splinters. The steam steering system had been hit, so that Captain Gütshow was obliged to use manual steering. On the 15th April he at last got rid of his coal and moved to the sea service quay on the 16th April as the last refugee ship. Within a few hours the ship had filled with over 1,000 people, including a number of soldiers who had swung themselves aboard avoiding the gangplank. At about 2100 hours Captain Gütshow cast off. The pier was empty and he believed that he had taken the last civilians from Pillau.

Captain Gütshow could not know that there were still hundreds of civilians in Pillau, mainly officials and Volkssturm men who dared not leave. There were still Party staff, organisers and district leaders at their posts and keeping those around them in fear and horror with orders to hold out and dark threats.

Town clerk Hugo Kaftan felt like one of their victims. He had set up his quarters in the police prison in the town hall and in the last days had brought along the civic register, the tracing file and the office equipment together with the typewriter. Mayor Scholz had vanished. Allegedly he had left the town on a naval ship. District Leader Grau had had his call-up into the Volkssturm sent to him on the 15th April. Meanwhile a warrant for his arrest had been issued to bring him to trial. What angered Kaftan most about the whole thing was that not he but Müller, a Party official, had been entrusted with the business. The chaos around him at this time had reduced his status. In his records there was thus no mention of the explosion that had shattered Pillau Harbour II and contrasted in strength and effect with the explosions of Russian shells and bombs. Close to the spot where the fodder from the *Adele Traber* had gone up in flames, a Russian shell had sent stacked German artillery ammunition bursting into the air.

For about an hour the 88mm shells flew into the air and inflicted severe damage. Worst hit was the Pillau Water Traffic Office and some of its ships: the *Blink*, the *Samland* and the cruising steamer *E. Kummer*, and a motor vessel from Elbing. For days the officials of the Water Traffic Office and their staff had been waiting for the Party's permission to leave with their boats for the west. Dr Dzubba, who was still living in the pilot tower, had constantly refused.

The ammunition explosion appeared to bring all hopes to nothing. When Fritz Lange, sea-going captain and commander of the *Delphin*, which meanwhile lay aground at Neutief, looked out of the Building Office's bunker to see the damage, the *Blink* and the motor ship from Elbing had vanished from the sea surface. The engine of the *Blink* lay in the parking area of the Water Traffic Office. The *Samland*, which had laid further off, had got away with light damage. The steamer *E. Kummer* lay abeam the Russendamm opposite the Seedienst railway station, its funnel half torn off, its bridge and upperworks riddled, its anchor lost, the lifeboats battered in the davits and the engine room scuttle torn away. Later one saw that the deck of the *E. Kummer* was strewn with bits of explosives, including four unexploded shells that could go off at any time. Fritz Lange climbed up the mooring rope on deck and threw the scrap overboard. The last of the four shells exploded on the harbour bottom and sent up a vast fountain of water.

That was enough for the omnipotent Dr Dzubba, and he permitted the evacuation of the Water Traffic Office. The offices' labourers worked as if obsessed until the *Samland* and the *E. Kummer* were ready to sail again, which took seven hours. However, the engine of the *E. Kummer* would only go forwards. Then at about 2100 hours on the 17th April both ships left Pillau to the accompaniment of the Soviet disruptive fire with 300 people who, like thousands of other East Prussians, would never see their homeland again.

Next day another group of those left behind set off. Among them were the Pillau teacher Fritz Liebert and the Königsberg foreman David Balzer. Both were ordered by the Quartering Office to see to the loading of the refugees. Since the transfer of the last refugee columns to the lagoon, the Quartering Office had had nothing to do. Those responsible there had withdrawn to a cellar in the Customs Border Guards building in the Breitestrasse.

They wanted to wait there until ordered to march off, having themselves helped so many Party members to leave.

From his apartment in the Hans-Parlow-Strasse Fritz Liebert had brought a suitcase with two suits, an overcoat and underwear, as well as two leather briefcases and a rucksack, equipped for all occasions. He took the suitcase back when it became known that he would not be able to go to the Reich on a ship but would have to flee on foot via the lagoon.

On the evening of the 18th April they made their way to the Seetief and waited in the entrance to the pilot house in case a vessel should appear. Although their seven items were constantly in sight, one of them, Eugen Kieszewski, had a suitcase stolen in which, among other things, were a suit and a long-life sausage. Kieszewski went after the thief, who was wearing a uniform, but was unable to catch him.

They were lucky. Below their feet lay a small lagoon steamer that was completely empty. 'Are you from the Quartering Office?' called the boat-man, 'Come on, quickly! We are going on!' The six men threw their bags, rucksacks and suitcases over the railings and climbed unaided after them. The boatman and his assistant had meanwhile unfastened the lines. The boat puttered out into the night. A group of soldiers that had noticed them too late swore at them from the pier.

Liebert wondered why the boatmen would take no one else, but dared not say anything as he did not want them to turn back. In the town's silhouette there were still flashes of light between the fires; only towards the lagoon was it pitch dark.

To their surprise, they discovered that the boatmen were not turning to the south but were instead going alongside the mole out to the open sea. 'We are going to the west directly,' whispered one of them. 'Ask the skipper where he wants to go,' someone suggested. At this point the vessel turned hard to starboard around the lighthouse at the end of the mole and headed back to the peninsula. The town lay on their right, the light of the fires and the noise coming closer. The men ran forward to the wheelhouse, trying to force the boatman to change course. It then transpired that he had been tasked with picking up the inhabitants of the old folks' home in Bad Neuhäuser and that they were there to assist him.

The men looked anxiously at the near embankment, which lay in the shadow of burning Pillau. One could see no light from Neuhäuser where they were, only the outline of buildings as the boat swung in gently to the wall of the little promenade. Hesitantly the men climbed up the ladder, damp from the night air. Machine guns were tacking to the north and far-off flares stood for seconds over the woods. From one of the buildings two sisters with several people rushed towards them as suddenly over their heads came the sound of an aircraft engine. Someone called out: 'Lie down!' The sisters came on. 'We still have to get out those inside,' one of them shouted to Liebert, who was crouching behind a bollard, while the others lay flat on the ground. The noise of artillery fire coming from Pillau covered the aircraft's engine noise again. Liebert stood up and was immediately exposed in an impossibly bright blue light. The Soviet machine had dropped several flares that illuminated the northern part of Pillau almost like daylight. Liebert and the others ran into the shadow of the buildings, feeling their way in the darkness to the rooms of those old folk that could not walk. They took one after another from their beds and couches, and, aided by the care staff, carried them across to the boat, where they all found places in the passenger saloon. There were about 30 people. Hardly were they all aboard than the boatman took them in a wide curve out to sea and headed towards the lagoon.

So they reached the narrow spit of land near Kaddighaken. Because of its draught, the boat was unable to reach the landing platform that had been built for the lighters. The Quartering Office men helped the old folk ashore on running boards. Some fell into the shallow water, but were quickly helped out again. Others had to be carried, being unable to walk or stand, and some began complaining that they were being abandoned on the beach. But Kaddighaken was the end point of the track that ran about ten kilometres westwards over the dunes and was still being maintained by army engineers, and they conveyed the old people at least part of the way towards Narmeln.

The men from the former Quartering Office wrapped themselves in blankets and spent the rest of the night in holes on the beach. They were unable to sleep as German artillery fired at enemy positions over them from time to time. A light rain started to fall in the morning and persisted all day so that they were completely soaked through by evening.

On the 20th April, Hitler's birthday, Pillau underwent the worst air raid yet. Almost ceaselessly the explosions roared and one could not distinguish the difference between the effects of waves of bombers and artillery barrages. The Soviets were preparing for their decisive assault. The civilians and police officers in the cellars of the town hall thought that it would soon be over. Though Kaftan was still installed in the 'Heroes' Cellar' of the police lock up, which seemed to him to be the safest place, the police had set up their offices in the adjacent room of the former air raid shelter, from where they performed a sort of service. The duty officer directed the patrols that kept passing through the narrow passages in an endless coming and going.

On the evening of the 20th April the patrols were still searching remaining buildings, apartments and air raid shelters for civilians. They found several dozen and brought them back reluctantly to the 'Golden Anchor', from where they were taken in small groups to the Seetief ferry and across to the Frische Spit. Others made their own way there during the nightly pauses in the firing. There was a constant coming and going in the streets by the light of the burning buildings.

The policemen renewed the window coverings of their 'Heroes' Cellar' and added more sandbags. The water supply had long since given up and the toilets could no longer be used. Water had to be obtained from a pump in nearby Gouvernementstrasse. There had been no electric light for weeks.

It was comparatively quiet on Saturday the 21st April. The sky was clouded over, but it did not rain. Aircraft could not be heard. Hugo Kaftan used the opportunity to make a tour. There were bomb craters in front of the town hall and piles of rubble, a mass of wiring, ripped out window frames and doors, wrecked vehicles and dead horses. The big wooden notice-board, with its hundreds of scraps of paper, news and wanted notices, had vanished. All around the square were ruins. It was the same scene in Haffstrasse. A horse with a bleeding nose stood motionlessly in the middle of the street that was strewn with dirt, heaps of dung and rubble. The public toilets in Raulestrasse had collapsed and a frightful stench hung over everything. No one was tending the many fires.

Kaftan looked for offices in which he knew people, but everywhere he came across strange soldiers, the places swarming with staffs and headquarters that looked quite superfluous.

On Sunday the 22nd April the weather improved a bit and the evening artillery fire and air attacks resumed with the same, if not more, rage than the previous day. To the men in the town hall cellars it seemed as if their hiding place was one of the main targets. The walls shook and plaster was crumbling everywhere. 'The tower,' shouted one of the police officers. 'They are firing at the tower!'

Naturally the town hall tower stood several metres above the roofs, even if it was not quite as high as the pilot tower or the lighthouse. Gendarmerie Lieutenant Colonel Schindler sent the duty troop of air raid wardens to the roof with orders to saw it off.

After an hour the men returned with the job still not done. The bomb and artillery explosions were too dense, splinters and roof slates had flown about their ears, and when a shell hit the roof ridge they gave up. A little later the Russian flag was to fly over the tower.

On the night of the 20th/21st April the Soviets attacked the Tenkitten belt and the first Soviet tanks broke through the German lines during the night. Both the naval batteries at Lochstädt and Adalbertkreuz fired round after round at the advancing Soviets while the army units on both sides of the batteries withdrew. By about 0300 hours the Lochstädt Battery had fired its last shell. Meanwhile, the surrounded crew blew up their guns and made their way, led by their badly wounded commander, through the Russians into Lochstädt Castle, where they dug in and radioed a request for relief. As no one replied from the army side, the newly appointed naval commander, Captain Hellmuth Strobel, intervened. The Lochstädt Battery was to be brought out by sea in assault boats by an assault team together with some of General Henke's engineers. The rescuers received no replies to their signals and finally machine-gun fire forced them to turn back. The surrounded Adalbertkreuz Battery was also not communicating. No member of either of these batteries survived.

The German resistance forced the Soviets to resume their bombardment on Sunday the 22nd April. Now the last Party functionaries also gave up when the Deputy Reichs Defence Commissar under Dr Dzubba withdrew from the Pilot Tower and moved to Neutief. Chief of Staff Müller gave up his position but not before sharpening up the officials still remaining in the town and telling them that they would have to wait for further orders, and then had himself conveyed to the Spit.

On the evening of the 22nd April Hugo Kaftan stood in a niche at the entrance to the town hall watching the Soviet artillery hits. How could he get out of this chaos? The Russians seemed to be firing at everything and even the way to the harbour was in flames. Here and there the ghostly light from the fires lit up a troop of soldiers across the rubble–strewn square. He dared not join and accompany such a group, and he had orders to remain at his post.

Hugo Kaftan was moving along slowly when two uniformed figures suddenly appeared who had apparently been stalking alongside the buildings. His first thought was 'the first Russians!' But they were two military police-men. 'What are you doing here?' one asked as both came up to him. 'Civilians have nothing to look for here!' Hugo Kaftan told them who he was and that he was under orders. 'Get out, man, or we will arrest you!' shouted the military policeman louder as the artillery fire increased. The town clerk withdrew back into the town hall, where the policemen were already filling their rucksacks.

By the light of a candle stump Kaftan also packed a rucksack and two briefcases. He mainly stuffed files into the latter, including the population register. When he took up the rucksack, a completely unfamiliar travel item for him, he realised that he had packed it so badly and crookedly that he could not carry it on his back. A policeman helped him to unpack it. Then the column set off, but at the town hall door Kaftan had realised that he had taken too much and the rucksack was so heavy that he could hardly go a hundred metres. The policemen waited patiently as he removed boots, underwear and several files and put them neatly behind some steps.

The way to Seetief went quicker than Kaftan had expected. The shell bursts were not as close and he felt safer with the policemen. There were hundreds of soldiers pressing for the naval ferries and no military policemen to be seen. The Soviets were groping across the water with searchlights from Balga. Kaftan was swept aboard the ferry in the confusion. Ten minutes later he landed on the Spit at the flying boat base at Neutief. Kaftan had no time to concern himself with the picture of the burning town behind him that was mirrored on the water. They were driven on like a herd of cattle to make room for the soldiers following them. Only a good hour later beyond Kaddighaken were they able to take a short breather before the endless procession carried them further along the Spit.

But Hugo Kaftan was not the last civilian to leave Pillau. On the Monday morning Director Paul Kewitz and six Pillau officials sat in the waterworks at the inner harbour. The day before County Party Leader Grau had provided marching orders for part of the establishment. Now Kewitz and the others were waiting to be allowed to leave. Towards 1000 hours they still had no news so, despite the heavy artillery fire, Kewitz made his way into the town to get the order.

He encountered soldiers everywhere. The town school, into which the town utilities had moved, was empty. There was also no one in the town hall at Pillau I except for Police Captain Reps, who had remained as a rearguard and was already about to leave. Kewitz discovered from him that the civilians had all gone, but the director required his marching orders and made his way to the citadel. It took a long while as he constantly had to keep taking cover, make detours around rubble and fires, while at the same time not fall into the hands of the military police. He met no one he knew on the way, but in the citadel bunker among all the Wehrmacht staff was District Party Leader Grau. (He must have left Pillau during the course of the morning.)

Relieved, Kewitz requested marching orders for himself and his men; since the collapse of the electricity service, all the pumps had stopped functioning and they could only now wait for the artillery or bombs to smash them. District Party Director Grau had Kewitz understand that he should remain confidently at the waterworks. A decision could be made when things got so far.

Kewitz went back along the dangerous route to his people and told them the situation. It was quite clear that they would no longer get out. Except for a couple of tugs, the harbour was empty. Ships would certainly not be coming any more, while Russian air activity increased during the afternoon.

Farmer Neudieth had still a couple of pigs and the waterworks men needed the afternoon to slaughter one of them in order to live well again once more.

On Tuesday the 24th April the Soviets set all available bombers on Pillau. In strips of several hundred metres they covered the town area from east to west with bombs from a low level. There was hardly a stone left standing on another. There was no longer any German defence. At about 1600 hours bombs hit the waterworks sheds, then the works themselves and finally the transformer. The oil running out caught fire and forced the men to leave their shelter. They sought temporary cover between the pipes of the fore chamber of the water tank.

At about 2000 hours the shelling decreased. Kewitz and his men did not hesitate any longer. They packed bags of supplies on their bicycles and pushed them through the rubble to the Inner Harbour.

They had little hope of getting to the landing stage for the Seetief ferry. The night was lit with fires, parachute flares, tracer bullets and the Soviet searchlights. Amid the blasts of the artillery shells were now mixed dull explosions coming from the naval yards. Kewitz stood with beads of sweat on his forehead: 'They have started to blow up the harbour!' Kewitz threw his bicycle away and ran across to the pier. If perhaps they could find a rowing boat, they would possibly make it out of the inner harbour.

When he came to the red glistening water he could not believe his eyes. Two boats lay there with ticking engines apparently about to cast off. He called out loudly to the first one. It was the little oil tanker *Kolk* and behind it was the tug *Adler*. They climbed aboard the boats, which only had their crews and some members aboard. The ships slipped out of the harbour at half speed, but they had been noticed. From astern shells whistled over their heads, hitting the water at a distance. They could just make out the outlines of Russian tanks that had driven onto the beach near the harbour entrance. The *Kolk* set off at full speed, the *Adler* overtaking her, but both made it. At breakneck speed they wormed their way past the over-laden ferries in the Seetief and reached the open sea within ten minutes. It was 2300 hours as these last two ships left Pillau with the last fleeing civilians.

At the same time Lieutenant Commander Schön received the order from the harbour commander to clear the citadel of the remains of the fortress company, some 80 marines. They were to take a ship from the inner harbour. Schön received a radio message from the Camstigall Battery: 'Ammunition fired – guns destroyed – leaving.' Then the troop set off.

The Soviets were already inside the town. The Norderole Battery had to defend itself with close-order fighting, and the soldiers of the 83rd Infantry Division were still fighting. Their commander, Major General Wengler, had regarded the situation as hopeless and the engagement of his troops as senseless from the beginning, knowing this meant death. He was killed in the fighting for Pillau.

Lieutenant Commander Schön marched with his men without fighting to the Inner Harbour, but found no ship. They watched the landing stages from safe cover and waited. The artillery fire from the railway grounds behind them ceased. Machine-gun and rifle fire came nearer. The buildings on the Russendamm were burning sky high, as were the Sakuth dockyard and the harbour office. The first belts of machine-gun fire were already sweeping over the Inner Harbour from the Russendamm. At about 0400 hours the waiting men heard the sound of tank tracks from behind them. Lieutenant Commander Schön no longer had any option. He and his men had to break through to the ferries individually and in groups, jumping from cover to cover. Miraculously, they got through unscathed across the Holzwiese and the Hindenburg Bridge, through Königsbergstrasse to the 'Golden Anchor'. Only the inn's façade remained. In front of it lay the last naval ferry to leave Pillau. It was 0430 hours as it left the pier with about 800 men, including Lieutenant Commander Schön and his company, going slowly past the burning Kurfürsten Bastion to Neutief. Thousands of German soldiers were left behind on Pillau pier, some of whom tried to reach the Frische Spit by swimming.

The Russians occupied the harbour at 0500 hours in the morning and landed the same day from assault boats near Neutief airbase, where they established themselves. Next day the Soviets erected a pontoon bridge across the Seetief and sent some armoured units across. The German units continued to maintain a bitter resistance. General Henke, whose sappers had saved so many people, fell in the close-quarter fighting while defending his command post in Neutief.

Chapter 21

The End at the Vistula and Hela

The Spit offered at this time the same sad picture as in the previous months, but now the retreating soldiers were in the majority, sweeping along the last fleeing civilians with them. Elements of the VIth Army Corps laid a defensive belt right across the narrow tongue of land and so held the Russians back. Narmeln only fell on the 1st May. At this point there were no longer any civilians on the Spit, but the remains of their months-long flight lay beside the roadside: wagons, dead horses, broken-open baggage and the shallow, quickly dug graves of refugees who had died or been killed.

At the southern end of the Spit came the Vistula estuary, the river system of the Vistula delta and the Nougat River, one of the most fruitful areas of the east. Most inhabitants had already left on treks on the 24th January and individually driven wagons had got through to the west, having parted from the East Prussian treks moving towards Pomerania and the Danzig Heights. The remaining farmers had decided to wait, although they had all packed.

Farmer Max Dyck from Zeyersvorderkampen had already started loading his wagon on the 21st January, but when the evacuation order arrived on the 24th January he and his neighbours stayed on in the village. The roads were overfilled with treks, the temperature minus 20 degrees and the nearby thunder of the guns deterred them from leaving their warm farms.

Snowstorms swept over the estuary. In the frost-clear nights one could see fires over the dykes and ditches on the eastern and south-eastern horizon. On the 31st January a renewed evacuation order was issued, but again the Zeyersvorderkampeners remained at home, for how far could they drive their cattle through the deep snow? Only the women drove a few kilometres northwards away from the sounds of the fighting, which came across from Elbing even stronger there. However, the Soviets did not come. Instead German artillery entered the village. The cheese was taken from the cheese factory, and carts requisitioned for the wounded. At night the farmers had to run patrols, afraid that their cattle would be taken, and also because foreign workers were being driven into the area. The countryside is not easily surveyed because of the numerous dykes and ditches. One day the cattle were gone, confiscated by the Wehrmacht. The Zeyersvorderkampeners brought their wives back into the village and set off with five trek wagons for the west.

Snowstorms resumed in the middle of February. In the village, among other things, the German batteries pulled out after having attracted enemy fire on the place, but there was hardly any damage. The farmers slaughtered their pigs. On the 9th March they learned that Dirschau had fallen to the south. On the 15th March water gurgled everywhere. The German engineers had breached long stretches of the Vistula dykes and almost the whole area between Danzig and Elbing, with the exception of some patches of higher ground and the coastal strip, was flooded. The Wehrmacht had not warned anyone.

In Danzig-Gross Waldorf the extensive allotment gardens were under water. Farmer Paul Paetschke, director of the Under Dyke Association Gross und Klein Waldorf, was thunderstruck when the local Party leader came and categorically demanded the flooding of the allotment gardens. But the power for the bucket elevator in Klein Waldorf, which normally served to pump out the water, had long been interrupted. Paetschke only had a diesel engine at his disposal, but without any fuel. The cellar of the building had been occupied by the staff of an artillery regiment and Paetschke asked a captain for some diesel oil for his pump. The officer had almost accused the local Party leader of sabotage, but the pump remained still and the gardens wet.

Even if Paetschke had got his pump working, it would hardly have reduced the mass of water, which covered many square kilometres of fields and meadows at an average depth of one to one and a half metres. Only the railway line, some roads and places rose above the silver-grey to black surface.

Karl Schliep, the manager of the Dirschau Agricultural Association, had only got out of the town on the 8th March minutes before the Russians entered and just before the flooding. He was an auxiliary flak gunner and had had to see to the harnessing of the horses for pulling the 37mm guns at the last minute himself. Without firing a shot, the men withdrew to the north from village to village through the estuary. Actually they were supposed to provide low-level cover for an 88mm battery, but it had vanished two days previously, leaving the civilians alone with their guns.

On the southern edge of the coastal strip, a few kilometres distant from the sea, they occupied a position near the Vistula. Meanwhile the water between them and the Russians had diminished. They kept coming under artillery fire, but they themselves from their standpoint could see how the Soviets were working their way around the lagoon and concentrating on Danzig about 25 kilometres away. A little away from the Vistula they could see the ferry traffic from Nickelswalde. The men had no thought for their own flight. They had sent off their families on treks by train to safety, and they themselves waited only for the war to end.

A large barge was moored to the river bank in front of them. It was fully laden with supplies and the boatmen were waiting for a tug to take them off to the west. They would not hand over any of the cigarettes they were carrying. Even when two officers came and wanted to load their car from the barge, they remained firm. 'What do you want then, the war is as much as ended!' shouted one of them with a bright red face as if he had gone crazy. That was enemy propaganda, and they would have him shot. They only quietened down when the boatman assured them that they had no crane and without one they could not do anything. They left the car where it was and walked off towards Nickelswalde. Soon some Russian would drive it away.

Karl Schliep wondered how everything fell into the hands of the Russians. They had got the whole association warehouse in Dirschau with corn,

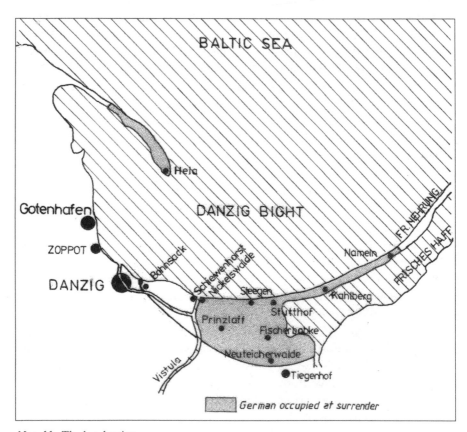

Map 11. The last bastion

potatoes, ham, seed and machinery. In the distillery at Preussich Stargard, about 20 kilometres south of Dirschau, were stored millions of litres of alcohol, which it was said would be turned into aircraft fuel. It had been debated for days whether the store should be set on fire or the spirit let flow into the little Ferse River. If one set it alight, it would result in damage to buildings, and if it was simply allowed to run out that would be the end of the rich fishing in the Ferse. Then on the 7th March the Russians were suddenly there and carried off the whole valuable lot. And soon the Home Flak-man Schliep was jammed behind his gun and helping to push it into the deep water of the Vistula. At least they would not get the gun.

Not far from Schliep Farmer Friedrich Steinhagen from Lupushorst was driving around in his cart. He too was not thinking of flight, but was only looking for a secure spot with his cart since the Soviets had taken Lupushorst. German units had thrown the Russians back out of the village and now dug in, but the situation could change at any moment. The Lupushorsters had gone to the 21 kilometre distant Neuteicherwalde woods from where they saw to their surprise that the small-gauge railway to Lupushorst was still running. The small goods trains, with Italian prisoners of war as workers, were carrying away corn, coal and pigs from the place. Steinhagen was able to go with them twice and retrieve something from his farm. Then the Russians brought the little railway with the black smoke and sparks flying under fire and drove off the brave railway men.

Steinhagen harnessed two carts and drove with his host, a Frenchman and three women on his own initiative to Lupushorst again. The German sentry at the village entry made difficulties and they first had to obtain a pass from the Wehrmacht staff accommodated in one of the farms. They had to hurry, as the German artillery was firing continually over their heads on a nearby wood from where the Soviets were returning fire. Hastily the little group filled one wagon with wood and coal, and the other with corn and fodder. In his stall, which the Russians had cleared out, Steinhagen found a brown riding mare. Apparently the Russians had abandoned her as she had been wounded in the withers. From a long journey through mud and water, the horse was encrusted with dirt up to its belly. Steinhagen fastened the mare to his cart and the column set off.

On the way Steinhagen got the idea of going to Veterinary Surgeon Herzberg in Tiegenhof to have the animal seen to. Thus they went unexpectedly between the German and Russian lines and were shot at. Nevertheless they managed to reach the water tower at Tiegenhof, where on the streets there was a frightful confusion of soldiers and Wehrmacht vehicles wherever one looked. The Lupushorsters stopped for the first time and began sharing out the sandwiches. In the middle of their meal, Soviet shells arrived.

The two farmers and their people had no time to jump down from the wagons. They sat on their seats as if turned to stone as the shells burst around them. Only then did they take cover, throwing themselves in the ditch or under the wagons. Only one of the women did not move. A splinter had come sideways through the wagon box and gone through her lower leg, where it stuck. She was crying gently and blood was dripping through the planking. The others pulled her quickly from the wagon and someone called for a medical orderly, but the firing continued for almost an hour and a half, and many dead and wounded lay in the streets. Once it quietened down, the woman was tended to. A Wehrmacht cart took her to the Tiegenhof community centre, from where she was taken in due course via Hela to Oldenburg.

The Lupushorsters had to change quarters twice more as the Soviets advanced. The stench in the estuary became unbearable as the days became warmer. There were putrefying cattle everywhere. Several horse-drawn army units had killed their horses and simply left them lying there, though most of the dead animals – cows and horses – were loose animals that had wandered there without their owners.

The Vistula estuary only suffered from air attacks during the last phase after the taking of Pillau. Low-flying aircraft disrupted the ferry traffic from Nickelswalde so much that the ferries could only operate at night. The last refugees from the Samland, Königsberg and Pillau waited wrapped in blankets and greatcoats for their turn. There were only a few women and children among them. They were mainly old Volkssturm men that the Wehrmacht had sent away.

For weeks the Hela peninsula had been a vast army encampment. Here the remains of defeated army and naval units and tens of thousands of refugees had assembled. The wounded, old and sick, as well as nursing mothers, were accommodated in the little village and were given priority in transportation from there, while the vast mass camped out for kilometres among the pine-covered dunes, passing their days in huts, tents, holes in the ground or out in the open, dozing in the warm sunshine and waiting. Some primitive firing positions and latrines had been dug. Children's and women's washing hung from lines between the trees.

To some extent they were safe from the Soviet artillery firing across from the Oxhöfter Kämpe and concentrating on the shipping in the little harbour and in the roads. Now and then the belts of machine-gun fire from aircraft attacking the ships fell on the campers and caused casualties. Those accommodated in the village suffered the most from these attacks, so that many left the buildings again to seek shelter among the dunes.

There were always more dead and wounded. The little Hela cemetery had long since been overfilled and so mass graves had been laid out behind the naval base. This came under the responsibility of Colonel Schöpffer, the defender of Elbing, who had finally landed up in Hela. He noticed a woman of about 30 who crouched day and night over a grave. Her two children had been killed by machine-gun fire and were buried there. The woman refused to leave to join a transport, and was left behind with many others.

During his walk around, the colonel ran into an hysterically crying woman coming out of a half-destroyed fisherman's cottage. 'Husband, husband! I want to go home!' Together with a medical orderly, he went in after her and brought her, a wildly gesticulating 40-year-old, to the nearby school, where a doctor gave her a shot of morphine. In the cottage Schöpffer found an elderly couple from Königsberg that had been rescued from the *Moltkefels* and at no price wanted to go on the water again. They told him that the woman had already been four weeks with the fighting troops in the Vistula estuary because she wanted to be near her husband. They had reached Hela together, but since then there had been no trace of her husband. Apparently he had left her so that she could follow by the next ship, or he had been killed in an air attack. Schöpffer had no time to deal with individual cases.

While the provisions for those accommodated in the village came from the field hospital or the Gau headquarters' large floating kitchen, all available cooking and washing vessels, even bathtubs, were being used to cook soup among the dunes. Colonel Schöpffer and his small staff were also responsible for the feeding of the soldiers and refugees and the preparations for embarkation. No one needed to suffer from hunger, even if supplies were scanty at times. The military and naval supply systems were able to provide deliveries from the Danzig Flats right up to April, when the remaining stocks were cleared, and cows and horses slaughtered day and night. The comparatively regular nourishment and rising daily temperatures also caused dysentery to diminish.

No one kept an exact tally of the transports, no one having either the time or the interest in the numbers of soldiers, wounded and refugees transported to keep a precise figure. Perhaps Schöpffer's estimation that with every convoy about 20,000 people left the peninsula was about right, but his note of the morning of the 15th April: 'Newly arrived 18,000 wounded, 33,000 refugees and 8,000 Volkssturm men', could hardly relate to the arrivals of just one night. The ferries and small craft could not have conveyed so many people in such a short time. Most figures for each day had only a symbolic value and account for the fact that on these two tiny areas of earth there were so many people all wanting to survive. In any case every night thousands of refugees and soldiers arrived from the Vistula estuary so that keeping figures for the benefit of the soldiers began to slip. Often the lighters went straight to the ships waiting in the roads, thus taking the places of those waiting on Hela. The nervousness among the soldiers and civilians in the dunes grew. The chances for individuals grew less also on other grounds, for fewer ships were anchoring in the roads. Already in March 14 ships had remained stuck in Swinemünde because the coal supply had been interrupted and the oil had run out. The Western Allies had occupied the Ruhr and reached the Elbe near Magdeburg on the 12th April.

In order to avoid stopping all the sea transport, most tugs stopped working. Thirty large ships were tied up in the Kaiser-Wilhelm-Canal. In the Lübeck Bight, the Flensburg Förde, the Eckenförde Bight and outside Copenhagen the big ships like the *Deutschland*, *Cap Arkona*, *Potsdam*, *Walter Rau*, *Monte Rose*, all ships well over 10,000 tons, were anchored and taking no further part in the evacuation.

On the 20th April the *Eberhard Essberger* anchored in the Hela roads. It was the fourteenth and last refugee evacuation for this ship, which up till then had conveyed over 66,000 people to the west. In a calm sea and light air activity, this time she took on 15 wounded, 4,500 soldiers and 200 refugees.

Meanwhile Hitler's birthday was being celebrated ashore. Vigorous speeches were delivered and from the bunkers and accommodation came the muffled chorus of 'Sieg Heils'. Gauleiter Forster assembled his functionaries and a small group of officers and spoke of the turning point, eternity and the great German people. Gauleiter Koch, who was still at Hela, did not make an appearance.

Koch had his quarters near the *Rugard*, the headquarters ship of the 9th Security Division. As he had no ship at his disposal, he was dependent upon the navy for his flight. Forster's ship for flight was the *Zoppot*, which lay ready to sail in the naval harbour. Both Gauleiters had gone to Hela, both would have long since fled had they not mistrusted one another, and now they both feared the man whose deputies they were.

Their fear was superfluous. By this time Hitler had long since lost interest in his 'beloved German people'. Indifferently he received congratulations from his entourage on the morning of the 20th April. He knew that he had not only lost the war, but also that his own end was near. The Russians were marching on Berlin; 193 divisions with 2.5 million soldiers, 41,600 guns, 6,250 tanks and 7,560 aircraft were in the course of enveloping the city. The Reich capital came under artillery fire for the first time on the 21st April. On the 23rd April the Soviets took Potsdam and Döberitz west of the city. Street fighting started up in Pankow, Köpenick and Tegel. On the 27th April Berlin was surrounded. The occupants of the bunker were still hoping for General Wenck's troops to engage. A breakout attempt using all reserves failed. On the 29th April General Weidling informed Hitler that he could only hold the city for one more day. At midnight on the 30th April Hitler took his own life.

On the 28th April Koch learnt that Berlin was finally surrounded and that Hitler would not leave his bunker. Out in the roads lay the submarine-hunters *1222* and *1225*, the minesweeper *441* and the minelayer *Lothringen*, which previously had taken thousands of refugees to the west. A launch brought Koch and nine men of his staff to the *Lothringen*, which this time had only 1,056 wounded, 123 soldiers and, apart from the Party functionaries, no civilians on board. On the two submarine-hunters were altogether 295 soldiers and 240 refugees. The little convoy left Hela on the 29th April and arrived at Flensburg next day. Koch immediately disappeared after his arrival. Forster followed on the *Zoppot* the same day, diverted to Bornholm and vanished from the picture for a long time.

Koch, who was later caught and sentenced to death in Warsaw, today sits in a Polish prison in Wartenburg, not far from Allenstein.

The flight of these two men, like so many responsible for this catastrophe, remained unknown to the refugees and the military. They were too busy with their own concerns. Colonel Schöpfer too had other worries. He had to allocate the ever-diminishing shipping space between soldiers, wounded and refugees. After the *Eberhard Essberger* left Hela on the 21st April he still had several thousand women and children to dispose of. In the roads lay a convoy with the ships *Adele Traber*, *Lappland* and *Santander*. Despite continual air attacks, the naval lighters went tirelessly to and fro loading the ships.

On one of the ferries was Junior Army Doctor Peter Siegel, who had been torn away from his honeymoon at Rauschen in January. After being stationed at Pillau and Gotenhafen, where he had taken his wife and parents to the *Lappland*, he had landed up via Danzig in a field hospital at Steegen in the Vistula estuary.

The ferry carrying Siegel and the other medical personnel passed close to the *Lappland* on the way to the *Santander*. Siegel recognised the ship again from its unusual superstructure. Seeing it again was like a sign from his wife, for whom he had waited so long in vain. That the *Lappland* had obviously survived the journey from Gotenhafen to the west meant that his family had also landed safely in the west.

The little *Santander* took 2,350 soldiers, 400 wounded and 150 refugees on board. The two bigger ships were almost exclusively laden with civilians.

Franz Appel, the captain of the *Lappland*, pressed them to hurry. It was his ship's fifth trip with refugees, and he knew that there would not be a sixth. Again the boarding nets were dropped over the sides. Wounded as well as frail elderly people and the sick were swung up on pallets. Those who could walk had to use gangways and the rope ladders or climb up the nets. Within a few hours there were 7,500 people on board. Many wanted to stay on deck for fear of submarines, and the crew, mainly Belgians and Croatians, had to drive the refugees below deck. Only the wounded and the sick were allowed to lie down among the upper works.

It was similar aboard the *Adele Traber*. She too was almost exclusively laden with refugees. Captain Walter Richters wondered at the quiet and discipline with which the women and old folk followed instructions. Most of them were so exhausted that they gave themselves up dumbly to their fate. Only the thought of not encountering the Russians at the last minute seemed to move them. After three hours there were 3,000 people on board.

The convoy of three ships set off on the 21st April, separating on the way. The *Adele Traber* ran to Swinemünde, from where the refugees went on by train. Instead of travelling back to Hela as the captain intended, they were ordered to Ostwine to load the machinery and equipment of the naval equipping and repair workshops and take them to the Flensburger Förde, where they were to be re-erected.

The *Santander* went to Sassnitz, where the soldiers disembarked. Then she lay for a whole week for lack of coal, and on the 30th April was ordered to Greifswald. As the ship was about to enter there, the captain saw Russian tanks firing at the pier and quickly turned around. He did not return to Hela again, but at the last minute took soldiers and refugees from the island of Rügen to Copenhagen.

The *Lappland* reached Copenhagen on the 23rd April, where she lay in the roads with 7,500 people on board for several days, as the camps in Denmark were overfilled and room had to be made for them first. When at last the *Lappland* could have turned back, her coal bunkers were empty.

Between the 23rd and 27th April only individual ships appeared at Hela. The *Wesenberg* brought soldiers of the Kurland Army from Libau and took refugees on board. The little steamer *Bischoff* took soldiers and wounded. A convoy appeared again on the 28th April that took on well over 10,000 people, mainly refugees.

Among the ships was the 9,555-ton *Ubena*, whose upperworks showed the traces of splinters and shell bursts that she had sustained in her last journey from Neufahrwasser four weeks earlier. The ships anchored out in the roads and had to defend themselves all day long from air attacks. From the top deck of the *Ubena* the flak officer directed the fire of his sixteen 20mm and 37mm guns. His task was made more difficult as the captain constantly had to change position to counter the sporadic Soviet artillery fire. Nevertheless, he was able to keep the Soviet low–flying aircraft at bay.

With nightfall the ships moved round the southern spit of Hela and anchored in front of the harbour entrance, where the first lighter was already waiting with its cargo. Captain Lankau let down the gangways and several members of the crew jumped into the lighter and ensured that the people embarked as quickly as possible. It did not go without some pushing and shoving and some of the refugees complained once they were safely below decks about the crew's lack of consideration. The lighter was cleared in record time.

Long before daybreak the *Ubena* lay on the seaward side of Hela again. It was late afternoon before she set off for the west in convoy with the *Nautik*, *Ganter* and *Westpreussen*, two minesweepers and a fast motorboat. Thick fog had formed and the ships had to orientate themselves on the stern light of the ship ahead in order not to lose their escorts and be forced aside. But the fog protected them. The ships ahead of them had been attacked several times by fast Soviet boats and a submarine that they had only avoided by taking a zigzag course.

Colonel Schöpffer did all he could to get these people to safety. The thought that he would not be able to feed them for much longer played a role. The Gauleiter's big cauldron still steamed with pea and barley soup. The cooks and their assistants were ten elderly Volkssturm men that had been hauled from their treks in January. Schöpffer had put them into army uniform and supported them. They worked from morning to night. The soup became thinner and thinner and the meat rarer.

Then several days passed without a ship appearing. On the 1st May the news that Hitler had 'fallen' in the final battle came like a bomb, but caused no emotion, neither sorrow nor relief over the death of that man who had influenced every individual over the past twelve years. It was in keeping with the hopelessness of their situation.

Hitler's successor, Grand Admiral Dönitz, issued a proclamation in which he said: 'My first task is to save the German people from destruction by the advancing Soviets.' Naval officers raised their glasses to him and drank to the Grand Admiral who would put things right.

Berlin was in Russian hands by the 2nd May. At the new headquarters in Plön the Grand Admiral concluded a conference with Keitel, Jodl, von Friedeburg, and Schwerin von Krosigk with the decision to conduct surrender negotiations with the west.

They knew nothing about this at Hela. The *Sachsenwald* arrived that day and took several thousand people on board, including about 3,000 soldiers. Now that apparently everything was coming to an end, there came a separation between the civilians and the soldiers. Only for the wounded were spaces found and hatches reserved. The others had to win a place on the lighters.

There was no shouting, just a dumb, bitter shuffling and pushing with which the stream of people spilled out over the dimly lit decks.

Everyone was nervous; Captain Teegan too. Towards 2200 hours he requested permission to cast off. His ship was full, but lighters were still coming. At this point the flak on land opened fire. Captain Teegan immediately had all lights extinguished, ordered 'Up anchor!' and 'Cast off!' He did not want to become involved in an air attack with a loaded ship. The ship slowly moved away from the lighters and set course for the open sea. From the only half-emptied ferries rose a frightful screaming and cursing. But the *Sachsenwald* did not turn back, and many families were torn apart for years by the captain's surely correct decision.

That morning of the 2nd May the 6,000-ton steamer *Fangturm* coming from Libau sailed past Hela on a westerly course well out to sea. On board were only 700 army officers, railway engineers and soldiers, as well as several high ranking naval officers. Her cargo consisted of army property, including 30 trucks in whose space room could have been found for 2,000 people. Another ship from Libau, the 1,923-ton *Hendrik Fisser*, reached Hela that night, although the Soviets, who had seen flak coming from the *Sachsenwald*, fired with their field artillery all night at the harbour entrance. The *Hendrik Fisser* already had a large number of wounded troops from a Waffen-SS unit aboard but took on hundreds of refugees and soldiers that night from the fishing harbour at Hela. Before daybreak she set off for Nyborg. Her coal bunkers were swelling and fires kept breaking out because instead of coal she had received briquettes that kept setting themselves alight.

The responsible officers of the naval headquarters and the 9th Security Division began to doubt that the evacuation could continue. They sent radio message after message to the OKW and OKM: 'Please send ships!' But meanwhile the navy had given up caution over the scarce fuel supplies. All available oil-burning vessels were tanked up and sent off to the east, even some submarines. The last coal was scraped together, although far from enough, in order to send the largest vessels. On the 3rd May, before the majority of the participating ships had left, Allied bomber squadrons conducted a major attack on the ships anchored in the Schleswig-Holstein bights. 23 ships were sunk and many badly damaged. Nevertheless, over a dozen steamers, including the *Hansa*, *Linz*, *Nautik*, *Paloma* and *Havel*, left the western Baltic for Hela. The *Havel* still had a load of artillery ammunition on board, the *Paloma* 600 tons of horse fodder. On the way they encountered a kilometre-long convoy of craft of all kinds: tugs, cranes, ferries, fishing boats, etc., either being towed or under their own steam, and all completely full of soldiers and refugees.

This last armada assembled in front of Hela on the 5th and 6th May and upon their appearance the troops camping in the dunes made their way to the harbour. Now, as the door was about to be closed, they wanted to be there.

To avoid chaos, General von Sauchen had a cordon established around the village. The divisional commanders set up orderly arrangements of their units and a traffic control.

This also meant that there was not much left for Colonel Schöpffer to do. He had his last dealings with refugees on the 6th May. In his office stood a young girl in nursing sister's uniform. In her arms she was holding a 9-month-old baby that a patrol had found in the village church cemetery a few days before. It had been wrapped in nappies and a blanket and was crying from hunger. The search for its mother had proved fruitless, so the sister had taken charge of the child although she already had a whole house full of old and sick people to look after. Now she wanted to be embarked with the child and was waiting for a chit that Colonel Schöpffer was completing stating that she was not the mother of the child.

Schöpffer took her and about 30 old and sick people, and the child, to where the *Paloma* was tied up in the naval harbour. They had already finished unloading, causing the crew to laugh scornfully and grumble as if they were responsible for that stupid load of fodder. Once the little group of civilians was aboard, about 1,600 soldiers stormed the ship.

Next day the colonel reported to General von Saucken that 355,624 refugees, soldiers and wounded had been despatched from Hela to the western harbours in April. During the first week of May there had been over a further 50,000. General von Saucken released Schöpffer to go west. He was able to take five men from his staff with him.

Colonel Schöpffer returned thoughtfully to his quarters and so came past the former Gauleiter's people's kitchen. The men were still cooking, now mainly for soldiers. One of them, a farmer from Lötzen County, went up to Schöpffer. He looked embarrassed and Schöpffer asked him why. Half embarrassedly and half angrily, the man said: 'We have been doing our duty here for weeks now and would very much like to get the War Service Medal.' One hour later the colonel brought the awards and gave them to the ten old men in their dirty uniforms, shaking their hands. He had sympathy for them because they were unable to grasp that there was no longer a Greater Germany.

There were also others unable to grasp the situation. In the early morning of the 6th May, a launch set off from the about 10,000-ton cadet training ship *Hansa-Ostmark* taking ashore 25 16-year-old cadets who had been assigned to action. An hour later they went along the dunes track towards Kussfeld, where a defensive belt and anti-tank ditch extended across the peninsula. Each cadet was pushing a bicycle with two hanging Panzerfausts. The refugees in the woods on the side of the track called out to them: 'Where are you going? The war is over! Complete nonsense! Turn around!' Soldiers also whispered to them to give up this nonsense and throw the stuff away. But they went on, led by an old sergeant. Somewhere on the narrow front they encountered Russian fire that they returned with their Panzerfausts. 22 of the boys were killed. Only three returned. The *Hansa-Ostmark* had meanwhile left with 12,000 people on board. The three remaining cadets got away at the last minute in a fast boat.

During the night of the 7th/8th May there were still ferries and landing craft coming to the Vistula estuary, although there were not enough ships for them to hand over their human freight to. Instead of landing the troops at Hela, they risked the way over the Baltic to the west. About ten of them joined up with the navigational training ship *Südpol*, which escorted them to Kiel. The others had to trust to their luck, as hardly any of the helmsmen had any idea about travelling at sea.

Colonel Schöpffer set out at lunchtime on the 8th May with his five soldiers to look for a ship. They found no room anywhere: all were over-loaded with troops and wanted to take no more aboard. Schöpffer was about to turn back and prepare himself for captivity like the others when he spotted the Seetief ferry from Pillau in the harbour. Only the crew were on board and about to lower the gangplank to take on soldiers. Schöpffer and his men were lucky. They ended up in the captain's little cabin.

The order to surrender was issued at noon on the 8th May. After midnight no German ship was allowed to leave harbour, all vessels at sea had to steer immediately for the nearest harbour in Allied hands. This had applied to the westerly harbours since 0800 hours on the 5th May, but the navy had circumvented this by ordering all vessels at sea, especially the fast torpedo boats and destroyers, to Hela. From 0000 hours on the 9th May there was no longer any possibility of evasion at Hela. Whatever set off from there risked being attacked by Soviet naval and air forces.

So all the vessels lying at Hela set sail for the west on the 8th May. Among them was the escorting ship *Rugard*, from which Commander von Blanc had for months directed the units of the 9th Security Division in the vast ferry service in the Bight of Danzig and the convoy protection for the transports. On the 9th May the *Rugard* was attacked by Russian torpedo boats west of Bornholm. After being fired at with torpedoes, she opened fire and forced the boats to turn away. About the same time the *Julius Rütgers* and the *Lieselotte Friedrich* were attacked by Soviet torpedo boats east of Bornholm. The *Lieselotte Friedrich* was sunk but the *Julius Rütgers* got away with slight damage.

Some 40,000 to 60,000 soldiers remained at Hela. The few refugees watched as on the morning of the 10th May the remains of the German armies marched off to captivity in a long column past their commander in chief. General von Saucken and eleven other generals joined them.

The same kind of show was played out in the Vistula estuary. Friedrich Steinhagen from Lupushorst went on foot with several other farmers on the 9th May from Prinzlaff to Nickelswalde. They wanted to get horses and carts that the army would be giving up at the last minute, as the soldiers did not want to shoot the horses.

Friedrich Steinhagen had sorted out for himself four fine horses, two carts and two cows. In the hope of finding food for the animals and their families, he had traded and spent the night in a barn in Nickelswalde. It was only when he wanted to harness up next morning that he saw the Russians. They were suddenly standing next to a pair of German officers with whom they were having a quite friendly conversation. Shortly afterwards the German soldiers surrendered.

As if lost, the farmer stood near the front of the dejected soldiers. They wore all possible kinds of uniform of all possible arms of the services, dirty and torn. Only the leather overcoats of the officers still showed the old smartness. A young major gave a speech. Steinhagen heard him say: 'With immediate effect the military salute will now be given with the right hand to the headdress.' Steinhagen could not understand why this still played a role. A cordon of Soviet soldiers deployed as the German soldiers threw their weapons in a heap. The Soviet held their assault rifles at the ready and made grim faces. Then the German column set off. Friedrich Steinhagen had the feeling that from now on he would see no more German soldiers and would be at the mercy of the enemy troops. A foretaste came as a Russian with an angry 'Davai! Davai!' drove off his two newly acquired wagons. It was the beginning of a long sorrowful journey that he and all remaining Germans would have to share.

Sources

Allgemeiner Schweizer Militärzeitschrift, No. 131, 1965

Bekker, Cajus, *Flucht übers Meer*, 1964

Berichte des Oberkommandos der Wehrmacht

Besymenski, Lew, *Der Tod des Adolf Hitler*, 1968

Boldt, Gerhard, *Die letzten Tage der Reichskanzlei*, 1947

Brustat-Naval, Fritz, *Unternehmen Rettung*, 1970

Bullock, Alan, *Hitler – a study in tyranny*, 1952

Carell, Paul, *Verbrannte Erde, Schlacht zwischen Wolga und Weichsel*, 1966

Danziger Haus- u. Heimatkalender, 1970

Der Grosse Vaterländische Krieg, Moscow, Vol 5

Dieckert u. Grossmann, *Der Kampf um Ostpreussen*, 1960

Digest des Ostens, No. 6, 1963

Dobson, Christopher, Miller, John, Payne, Ronald, *Die Versenkung der 'Wilhelm Gustloff'*, 1979

Domarus, Max, *Hitler, Reden und Proklamationen*, 1962–1963

Eckert, Gerhard, *Besuch in Polen*, 1974

Elbinger Hefte, No. 15, No. 24

Engel, Hans-Ulrich, *Ostpreussen, wie es war*, 1976

Faehrmann, Willi, *Das Jahr der Wölfe*, 1962

Fittkau, Gerhard, *Mein dreiunddreissigstes Jahr*, 1958

Fredmann, Ernst, *Sie kamen übers Meer*, 1971

Der Freiwillige, No. 10, 1964/11

George, Bernard, *Les Russes arrivent*, Paris, 1966

Gilbert, Felix, *Hitler directs his war*, 1950

Guderian, Heinz, *Erinnerungen eines Soldaten*, 1962

Helm, Rudolf, *Volkssturm Saga*, 1961

Holst, Niels von, *Danzig – ein Buch der Erinnerung*, 1949

Hubatsch, Walther, *Flüchtlingstransporte aus dem Osten über See*, 1962

Hubatsch, Walther, *Hitlers Weisung für die Kriegsführung 1939–1945*, 1962

Hümmelchen, Gerhard, *Chronik des Seekrieges 1939–45*, 1968

Just, Guenther, *Alfred Jodl – Soldat ohne Furcht*, 1971

Kabath, Rudolf, *Abwehrkämpfe am Nordflügel der Ostfront 1944–45*, 1963

Kadelbach, Gerd, *Die Stunde Null*, 1962
Klöss, Erhard, *Reden des Führers*, 1967
Koniev, Ivan S., *Das Jahr fünfund vierzig*, 1969
Kydd, Sam, *For you the war is over*, London, 1973
Lasch, Otto, *So fiel Königsberg, Kampf und Untergang*, 1958
Lorck, Carl von, *Ostpreussische Gutshäuser*, 1953
Mai, Joachim, *Vom Narew bis an die Elbe*, 1965
Merian-Danzig, No. 4/7
Mitteilungsblatt Waffenring deutscher Pioniere, 1963
Murijew, D, *Durchbruch der Schützenverbände durch eine vorbereitete Verteidigung*, 1959
Nehring, Walter, *Die Geschichte der deutschen Panzerwaffe*, 1969
Ostpreussen, No. 15/9, 1964
Schäuffler, Hans, *So lebten und starben sie*, 1968
Schäuffler, Hans, *Der Weg war weit*, 1973
Schoen, Heinz, *Der Untergang der "Wilhelm Gustloff"*, 1953
Schramm, Percy Ernst, *Kriegstagebuch OKW (Jan. 1944–22. Mai 1945)*, 1961
Schroeder, Juergen, *Zwischen Hela und Pillau*, 1956
Sobczak, Kazimierz, *Rocinik Elblaski II*, 1963
Soviet Military Review, 1969, Nos. 4 & 5, 1975
Der Spiegel, No. 4, 1966
Thorwald, Jürgen, *Ungeklärte Fälle*, 1950
Thorwald, Jürgen, *Es began an der Weichsel*, 1951
Thorwald, Jürgen, *Das Ende an der Elbe*, 1959
Tippelskirch, Kurt von, *Geschichte des Zweiten Weltkrieges*, 1956
Trevor-Roper, Hugh R., *The Last Days of Hitler*, 1947
Trevor-Roper, Hugh R., Grunfeld, Frederic V., *Die deutsche Tragödie*, 1975
Tschuikov, M, *Aus den Erinnerungen – In Dokumentation der Zeit*, 1965
War Monthly, London, No. 30, 1976
Warlimont, Walter, *Im Hauptquartier der deutschen Wehrmacht*, 1962
Wilckens, Hans Jürgen von, *Die grosse Not*, 1957
Wilmot, Chester, *The Struggle for Europe*, 1952
Zeitschrift für Militärgeschichte, 1965